THEATRE LIGHTING
FROM
A TO Z

THEATRE LIGHTING

from

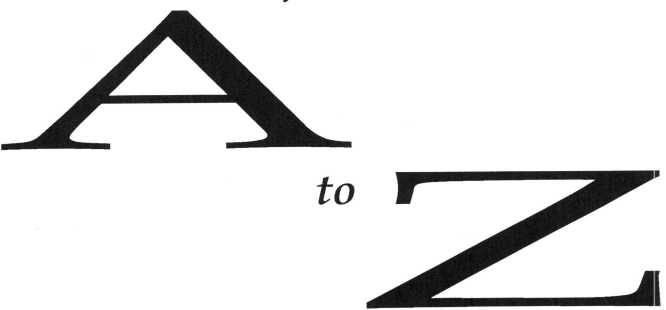

A *to* Z

Norman C. Boulanger
Warren C. Lounsbury

University of Washington Press *Seattle & London*

Printed in the United States of America

Library of Congress Cataloging-in-Publication Data

Boulanger, Norman C.
    Theatre lighting from A to Z / Norman C. Boulanger and Warren C. Lounsbury.
        p.   cm.
    Includes bibliographical references and index.
    ISBN 0-295-97214-9 (paper; alk. paper)
    1. Stage lighting--Encyclopedias. I. Lounsbury, Warren C. II. Title.
    PN2091.E4B59 1992
    792' .023'03--dc20   92-14620
                                                              CIP

An Apple Computer® Macintosh Plus and a Macintosh LC with La Cie 50MB Cirrus® hard disk were used in the preparation of this book. Text was written in Microsoft Word v3.02, and drawings were generated in Deneba® Canvas v2.01 and formatted in Aldus® Pagemaker v4.01. An Apple LaserWriter LS® was used for printing.

The paper used in this publication meets the minimum requirements of American National Standard for Information Sciences—Permanence of Paper for Printed Library Materials. ANSI Z39.48-1984.

To our most charming daughters:

Jennifer Lynn Boulanger

Kirstie Gay Boulanger

Judy Lounsbury Paschelke

Susan Lounsbury Nordstrom

Wendy Lounsbury O'Reilly

Preface

As an encyclopedia of lighting terms and practices, *Theatre Lighting from A to Z* must contain all of the lighting terms found in its companion book, *Theatre Backstage from A to Z*. If the reader experiences déjà vu, we request indulgence. Wherever appropriate, additions have been made to all repeated entries. We trust the many new definitions, explanations, and categories will make a significant contribution to the excitement and fascination of lighting stage shows.

This book covers all levels of theatre, from elementary-school performances to community and professional productions. The formula concept within will be denigrated by some, but we hope it will help those who need quick and easy solutions to their lighting requirements. We especially hope that this work will be useful in community theatre. Community theatre must be recognized as a high level of amateur recreational endeavor deserving of a high level of lighting. The various considerations, listings, and proposals need to be as inclusive as possible, but the readers must decide what is applicable for their situation.

We are indebted to many but especially to Helen Evans, Jacel Evans, Charles V. Jones, Gary Justesen, Lisa Taylor, Bob Bauer, Kevin Marks, Terry Sateren, Mike Boulanger, Michael Ramsaur, Pam Bruton, Ronnie Seyd, and Julidta Tarver.

THEATRE LIGHTING
FROM
A to Z

A

ABERRATIONS

Chromatic aberration. Colored rings, rainbows, or lens leaks produced by LENSES of unequal refractive powers. This phenomenon is found in PLANO-CONVEX SPOTLIGHTS (PCs) when their focus is sharpened to the smallest beam. It is rarely a problem with FRESNEL or ELLIPSOIDAL REFLECTOR SPOTLIGHTS because the FRESNEL LENS will diffuse aberrations and the light beam of the ellipsoidal is a fixed size, shaped by the shutters instead of the focus. *Solution*: (1) Make sure the lens is seated squarely against its retaining ring; it could be out of the OPTICAL AXIS. (2) If the size of the beam must remain small, enlarge the focus until the aberration disappears and then frame the light to the desired size with a top hat, funnel, or other LIGHT SPILL CONTROL device placed in front of the lens. (3) Mark the spotlight as one to be used with either open focus or diffused color media for COLOR WASH or for general coverage.

Spherical aberration. Failure of a lens or reflector to focus all rays of light from source to a given point. A common fault in inexpensive lenses, spherical aberration may cause stray beams of light to spill in a most objectionable manner. *Solution*: Check the alignment of filament, reflector, and lens. If alignment is not the problem, either the lens or the spotlight must be replaced. See ALIGNING INSTRUMENTS.

ABSORPTIVE. Dark, neutral colors are called absorptive colors because they reflect little or no light. In general, a pigment will reflect its own color and absorb all others. In multiple-scene plays or productions relying on a change of area lights for scene changes, reflected light becomes a great concern. The lighting designer should insist that PRODUC-TION CONFERENCES include discussions with the scene designer and costume designer concerning the use of darker colors for scenery and costumes that will absorb light rather than reflect it into areas that should appear dark during the scene and/or scene change.

AC. Abbreviation for ALTERNATING CURRENT.

ACCENT. To emphasize a particular action or character within a scene or play. The use of light is one of the most effective ways of accenting and it may be varied easily from subtle to blatant. Raising light intensity a point or two in the area to be accented will draw audience attention subconsciously, whereas blasting an actor with a followspot on a darkened stage will force audience attention immediately. Colored light may also be used to accomplish the same goal, with the more saturated colors attracting more attention. Generally speaking, subtle approaches are the most effective and most often used. See also FOCUS OF ATTENTION.

ACE. A professional colloquialism for a 1,000-watt spotlight.

ACHROMATIC. A lens is achromatic when it transmits light without separating it into its spectral colors. Since every color is a different WAVELENGTH OF VISIBLE LIGHT, it is impossible to make a single lens that will focus all colors at the same time. The blue fringe often seen around a beam of white light focused on a light-colored surface is caused by a lens designed for the red wavelength. The blue and yellow wavelengths thus remain out of focus. The eye easily identifies the blue fringe but ignores it more readily than it would accept a red fringe from a lens designed for a blue wavelength.

ACT CURTAIN. A curtain which begins and ends an act or scene.

ACTING AREA. Space on stage in which the action of a play takes place. The lighting designer draws a plan of the acting areas the director intends to use and then makes a scaled light plot of those areas and the equipment needed to cover that space. See AREAS; DESIGN FOR LIGHTING.

ADAPTOR (pigtail, jumper, patchcord, splitter [British usage])

Connector. Short lengths of electrical wire with appropriate plugs to join two devices equipped with connectors of different sizes or designs.

Lamp base. A screw-type plug used to change a mogul base receptacle to standard, or standard base to candelabra base, etc.

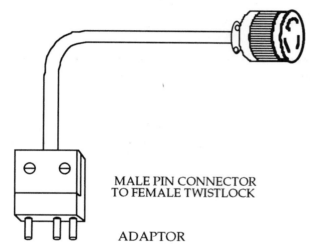

MALE PIN CONNECTOR
TO FEMALE TWISTLOCK

ADAPTOR

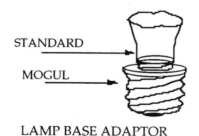

STANDARD

MOGUL

LAMP BASE ADAPTOR

ADC. See ANALOG-TO-DIGITAL CONVERTER.

ADDITIVE METHOD OF COLOR MIXTURE. See COLOR MIXING.

AKLO-GLASS FILTER. Tinted glass strips used in high-intensity projection equipment to filter out infrared rays, thus eliminating much of the heat, which otherwise destroys slides. Low demand and high cost have made these filters hard to find. See DICHROIC FILTER; PROJECTORS.

A-LADDER. A ladder shaped like the letter "A" with a straight, extendable ladder in the center (STICK), most useful for work on high light BORDERS. Available in heights ranging between 20' and 36'. Often mounted on dollies to facilitate moving. See also GENIE LIFT; TELESCOPTER.

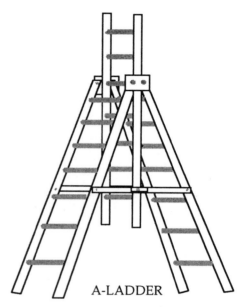

A-LADDER

ALIGNING INSTRUMENTS. Adjusting the reflector, lamp filament, and lens of a spotlight to a common focal axis. Alignment should be checked on all new instruments before putting into service and checked again after each change of lamp. Failure to do so can cause reduced intensity, uneven coverage, or, possibly, ABERRATIONS.

Ellipsoidal reflector spotlight alignment. Aligning the ELLIPSOIDAL REFLECTOR SPOTLIGHT generally involves moving the lamp instead of the reflector. In most cases the aligning adjustment is outside the instrument on the base of the socket and consists of one or more setscrews. The FRAMING SHUTTERS should be opened all the way, and as with the FRESNEL LIGHT, the beam is focused against a blank wall. (If possible, test the spotlight at low intensity so it will remain cool enough to handle.) If the field is uneven, adjust the lamp position by turning the setscrews until the beam coverage is as even as possible. Older ellipsoidal spotlights designed for "burn base-up" lamps have part of the reflector cut away to accommodate the lamp and, therefore, can never provide as even a field of light as the newer

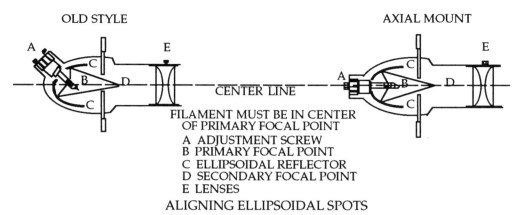

OLD STYLE   AXIAL MOUNT

CENTER LINE

FILAMENT MUST BE IN CENTER
OF PRIMARY FOCAL POINT
A ADJUSTMENT SCREW
B PRIMARY FOCAL POINT
C ELLIPSOIDAL REFLECTOR
D SECONDARY FOCAL POINT
E LENSES
ALIGNING ELLIPSOIDAL SPOTS

AXIAL MOUNT spotlight designed for TUNG-STEN-HALOGEN LAMPS. If there is a HOT SPOT when adjustment is finished, it should appear in the center of the beam. Some newer instruments have a JOYSTICK mounted to the lamp socket, which simplifies adjustment. Joysticks are usually unlocked by turning the handle counter-clockwise and then moving the stick until the filament is centered in the beam. Alignment should be checked and adjusted every time a lamp is changed, especially when changing wattage and/or lamp manufacturers. If the light is to be shuttered down to a PINSPOT, make sure the bright spot is in the center of the beam. This not only produces maximum intensity but saves the shutters from potential heat warp. Keep lenses and reflectors clean.

Fresnel spotlight alignment. Adjustments are usually made with setscrews controlling the exact positioning of the reflector. Aim the spot at a blank wall; if the reflector is not aligned with the filament and lens, two overlapping pools of light will be apparent, one originating from the lens and the other from the reflector. Adjust the reflector until both beams are covering the same area and then tighten the setscrews.

ALLIGATOR CLIP. One of several types of spring clips used for temporary electrical connections.

ALLIGATOR CLIPS

ALTERNATING CURRENT (abbr. AC). Current that reverses direction 120 times per second (60 complete cycles). DIRECT CURRENT (DC) flows in one direction only, from a negative to a positive potential. Any conductor offers resistance to the passage of current, resulting in a loss of voltage when electricity is carried any distance. For this reason, exceptionally high voltage is used to transport electricity, making the loss of a few volts per mile quite unimportant. TRANSFORMERS, such as those placed on telephone poles throughout residential areas, reduce this high voltage to 220 and 120 volts for home use. In order to prevent further "line loss" and to make certain each home receives the correct voltage, each transformer will serve only the homes within a few hundred feet. Since only AC voltage is easily increased or decreased with a transformer, AC is predominantly used in the United States, where generating facilities are commonly located many miles from the point of consumption. Because theatres originally used ARC LIGHTS and PROJECTORS that required direct current, they were among the last public buildings to convert from DC to AC. When in the late 1950s the touring production of *My Fair Lady* went on the road with autotransformer dimmers requiring alternating current, the popularity of that production forced major road show theatres in the country to convert to alternating current. Prior to that time many theatres east of the Mississippi River were wired for DC only. Resistance dimmers and incandescent lamps will operate on either AC or DC, and many kinds of motors, amplifiers, radios, etc., if so designated, can operate on either current. Transformers, autotransformers, and electronic dimmers require AC. See also ELECTRICITY.

ALZAK REFLECTOR, ANODIZED. Trade name of a highly efficient REFLECTOR, chemically coated with aluminum by a process patented and developed in the 1930s.

AMBER. A yellowish-orange hue considered a secondary color, used in color media for lights. See COLOR; COLOR MEDIA.

AMBIENT LIGHT. Stray light, either diffused or reflected into areas where it is not wanted. Highly polished or lacquered furniture, reflective hand props, mirrors, or even shiny floors will often reflect light in most disruptive ways. Frequently, it is a relatively small area that offends. *Solution:* Paint floors a darker color if possible, otherwise, cover with dark-colored floorcloths, carpets, or throw rugs; cover furniture with low-reflective tablecloths or runners; dull a shiny finish with Krylon dulling spray or jet spray Bon Ami and leave the finish whitened. Conversely, on stages requiring steep-angle lighting (**Arena stages** and **Thrust stages**; see STAGES) ambient light may be used to advantage to light faces with reflected light off a doily, tablecloth, white blotter, or other small, light surface, accomplishing the same purpose as footlights. Use sparingly to avoid unwanted coverage.

AMERICAN WIRE GAUGE (AWG). A standardized system of wire sizes and current capacities relative to the composition and amount of insulation surrounding the wire. See CABLE.

AMPERE (abbr. amp, A). A measure of current; rate of flow of ELECTRICITY. FUSES and BREAKERS, used in the CIRCUIT to protect equipment from overloads, are always rated in amps. DIMMER capacities may be rated in either watts (power) or amps (flow). Wattage ratings of lights are stamped on the bulbs. Since dimmers and fuses must never be loaded with higher wattage than rated, it is often necessary for the lighting designer and electrician to change ampere ratings to watts and vice versa. The "PIE" formula (power = intensity x electromotive force) or, expressed in different words, the "W. VA. (West Virginia)" formula (watts = volts x amps) may be used for this conversion. See ELECTRICITY.

AMPLEX. Obsolete. Trade name for reflector lamps (R lamps) available during the 1950s and 1960s with bulbs in nonfade colors. Similar colored lamps manufactured by other companies are still available. Plain R lamps cover wider areas at lower intensities than parabolic reflector lamps (PAR lamps) of the same wattage. See LAMPS.

AMPLEX

AMP TRAP. Silver-coated sand makes this a special fast-action FUSE designed to protect SILICON CONTROLLED RECTIFIER dimmer circuits. Amp traps should never be replaced with other types of fuses.

ANALOG-TO-DIGITAL CONVERTER (abbr. ADC). A device used in lighting computers to convert a direct current (DC) signal into digital information to be used by the computer. See also DIGITAL-TO-ANALOG CONNECTOR.

ANGLE OF ACCEPTANCE. The portion of source light that a spotlight or projector can accept. This angle is determined by drawing straight lines from the light source to the top and bottom of the lens opening and measuring the enclosed angle.

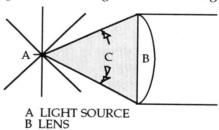

A LIGHT SOURCE
B LENS

C ANGLE OF ACCEPTANCE

ANGLE OF INCIDENCE. The angle formed between a surface and a ray of light striking that surface.

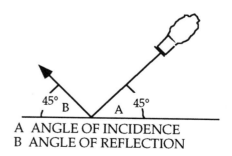

A ANGLE OF INCIDENCE
B ANGLE OF REFLECTION

ANGLE OF REFLECTION. The angle formed between a surface and a ray of light reflecting off that surface. The angle of reflection equals the angle of incidence.

ANGSTROM. A unit of length, most often used for wavelengths of light, equal to one ten-billionth of a meter. Named after the Swedish astronomer A. J. Ångström, 1814–74. See NANOMETER.

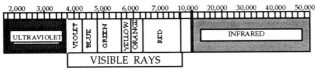

WAVELENGTH OF LIGHT
IN ANGSTROM UNITS

1 METER =	100	CENTIMETERS
	1,000	MILLIMETERS
	1,000,000	MICRONS
	1,000,000,000	MILLIMICRONS
	10,000,000,000	ANGSTROMS
1 INCH =	254,000,000	ANGSTROM UNITS

ANSI. Abbreviation for American National Standards Institute, an independent organization that establishes standards to promote consistency and interchangeability of the products of manufacturers. ANSI has assigned code letters to lamps used in lighting instruments. These code letters are arbitrarily chosen and assigned to describe the following characteristics of a lamp: wattage, voltage, size, life expectancy, base type, bulb shape, LUMENS, burning position, and color temperature. For example, irrespective of the manufacturer, any lamp bearing the designation BTL must be a 500-watt lamp designed for 120 volts, have a 500-hour life expectancy, have a medium prefocus base, be a T6 (tubular shape, 6/8" in diameter), produce 11,000 lumens, burn in any position, and burn at 3,050 KELVINS. ANSI was formerly the United States of America Standards Institute (USASI or ASI). See also INCANDESCENT LAMPS; TUNGSTEN-HALOGEN LAMPS.

ANTEPROSCENIUM. Areas in front (auditorium side) of the house. Stage lights from the front of the house (FOH) are sometimes referred to as anteproscenium lights. Anteproscenium lighting positions include BEAM POSITIONS, BOX BOOMS, CEILING SLOTS, and PORTALS. See also PROSCENIUM STAGE LIGHTING.

ANTICIPATE. It was once routine for the switchboard operator to anticipate cues by several words or even lines to compensate for delayed reactions of certain types of dimmers. Most modern control boards provide nearly instantaneous responses, but because filaments in large lamps are slow to reach incandescence and equally slow to cool, anticipating cues for certain occasions is still a necessary procedure.

APERTURE, SPOTLIGHT (gate). The opening inside an ellipsoidal spotlight through which both direct light and reflected light pass to the secondary focal point. Shutters, pattern slots, or an IRIS are located at this gate. See illustration under GOBO; see also ELLIPSOIDAL REFLECTOR SPOTLIGHT.

APPARITION. Supernatural appearance of something unreal or intangible. Apparitions are commonplace in plays of the Elizabethan period and may be shown or suggested in a number of ways, usually involving the electrician and lighting designer. Very realistic images can be projected by LASER HOLOGRAPHY on plastic film, but this process produces an image of limited size, is expensive, and requires technical knowledge beyond the means of most smaller theatre groups. Shadowlike images, pictures, or abstracts can be projected on the CYC (see PROJECTORS). Some realism can be attained by flying dimly lighted ghostlike cutouts on black wire. The effect may be enhanced by steep-angle lighting from above or below and through the use of bizarre colors. SCRIM placed between the effect and the audience may be used to diffuse the object and heighten the effect. If no equipment is available, the simplest solution is for the actor to pretend to see the apparition in the wings or at the rear of the auditorium. Producing an apparition should be thoroughly discussed and planned at the PRODUCTION CONFERENCE.

APRON. The part of the stage in front of the main curtain. The apron once constituted the greatest portion of the acting area. Its use was first abolished by the Haymarket Theatre in London in 1834. In many present-day proscenium stages, aprons are no more than a few feet in depth. However, since the 1950s, Elizabethan staging practices have experienced a renaissance in the form of the thrust stage, where the stage (or apron) extends into the auditorium with audience on three sides. The extended-apron stage is a shortened version of the thrust, usually about one-half to one-third the size, 9' to 12' in front of the proscenium. See also THRUST STAGE LIGHTING.

ARC. An electric spark jumping or sputtering between two hot contacts. Poor wiring connections and splicings sometimes arc and may result in serious fires. All wiring of a permanent nature should conform to safe wiring practices as set forth in the National Electrical Code (NEC).

Arcs occurring between pin connectors can be eliminated by spreading the split prongs of the male pin connector with a knife blade.

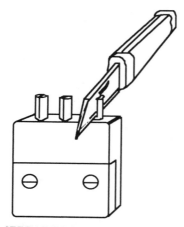

SPREADING CONTACTS
OF PIN CONNECTOR

ARC LIGHTS. Lighting instruments using the spark between two electrodes as the light source. Invented by the English chemist Sir Humphry Davy (1778–1829), the arc light was not used in the theatre until about the middle of the nineteenth century. During the last quarter of the nineteenth century, the carbon arc was used for special effects (backlighting sun or moon cutouts, lightning, projections, etc.). By the early 1880s, gas OLIVETTES were being converted to carbon arc lights, and by the beginning of the 1900s, LIMELIGHT housings were converted for the same purpose. As more concentrated and more efficient filaments were developed for incandescent lamps during the teens, the arc light became relegated to FOLLOW-SPOTS and PROJECTORS, where its performance was uncontested for the first half of the twentieth century. Design improvements in both follow-

spots and CARBONS (used to produce the arc) gave the carbon arc light a reprieve of another 20 to 30 years until the glass-enclosed ENCAPSULATED ARC and the HMI lamps reached the market. With the advent of these and other high-intensity lamps, carbon rods are on their way out of the picture altogether, and encapsulated arcs are assuming their places in high-intensity follow-spots and projectors.

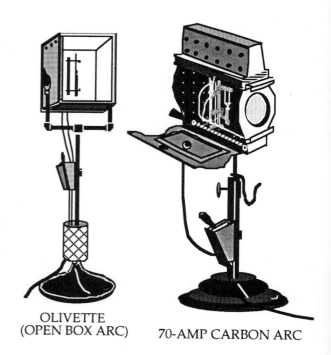

OLIVETTE
(OPEN BOX ARC)   70-AMP CARBON ARC

AREA LIGHTS. The specific instruments used to light designated acting areas. A number of different FORMULAS or styles of lighting may be used for this purpose but instruments chosen for the job are almost universally ELLIPSOIDAL REFLECTOR SPOTLIGHTS and FRESNEL LIGHTS. The ellipsoidal may be used in any or all positions but the fresnel light should be confined to areas upstage of the proscenium where diffused light from the fresnel lens cannot spill into the auditorium. With the advent of the variable-focus ZOOM ELLIPSE spotlight, fresnels are becoming less popular in new installations.

AREAS (stage locations). For convenience in directing, acting, lighting, and scene designing, stages are divided into 6, 9, or 15 areas depending on the size of the stage. Areas closest to the footlights are designated downstage, those closest to the

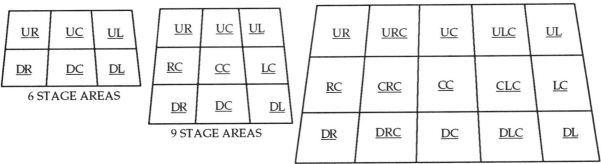

TRADITIONAL STAGE LAYOUTS FOR DIRECTORS AND SCENE DESIGNERS

backwall are upstage, and those in between are either center for the 9-area stage or downcenter and upcenter for the 15-area stage, as illustrated. Right and left directions refer to the performer's right and left when facing the audience. These designations are abbreviated for obvious reasons of simplification. Thus, DR is downright, UC is upcenter, UCR is upcenter right, etc.

Areas for directors and designers. Traditionally, stages are laid out and labeled as indicated above for the benefit of directors, actors, and designers. The terms "in one" and "in two" (see IN) are also applicable for entrance designations for both people and lights.

Areas for lighting layout (area separation [British usage]). The lighting designer often is better served by a layout of circles, partial circles, or simply numbers representing the diameters of the beams of lights. Designations in numbers are better adapted to light plots and dimmer assignments. It should be noted that in academic theatre lighting designers usually number, as shown in the illustration, from left to right, whereas professional designers number from right to left. The rationale for this is that the professional works with union electricians, whose point of view is looking out at the audience and working from left to right; hence the professional numbering appears backward on a drawing. For example, in the illustration of the 15-area stage, the number 5 would be the professional's number 1. See also DESIGN FOR LIGHTING; **Area lighting** under LIGHTING PRACTICE.

AREA SEPARATION. British usage for **Lighting layout** see under AREAS.

ARENA STAGE. A stage surrounded fully or partly by audience. See STAGES.

ARENA STAGE LIGHTING (theatre in the round). Arena stages include full round (audience on all four sides), three-quarter round (three-sided), T-shaped (three-sided), and the so-called football field theatres (long and narrow). Lighting arena stages (as well as the front areas of thrust stages) offers challenges in keeping light out of the audience's eyes. The methods for lighting the arena stage begin as described in the entries for DESIGN FOR LIGHTING, LIGHTING PRACTICE, and PROSCENIUM STAGE LIGHTING.

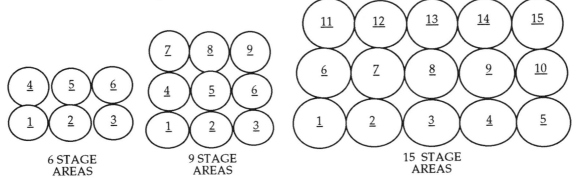

TRADITIONAL STAGE LAYOUT FOR LIGHTING DESIGNERS IN THE ACADEMIC THEATRE

Determine the number and the size of the areas to be lighted, including entrances, and lay them out in a floorplan. Using the BEAM ANGLE and FIELD ANGLE approach to BLENDING areas as detailed in PHOTOMETRIC CHARTS, determine the numbers and types of instruments to be used. Generally the mounting positions for instruments are formed by a grid of pipes hung from the ceiling on 4'–7' centers. Minimal lighting is possible from a four-pipe grid as shown in the illustration, but a more elaborate grid offers a much greater variety of lighting positions and a better choice of lighting angles. A few arena theatres have false ceilings built between the audience and the mounting positions, and lights are focused through slots cut in that ceiling. Aesthetically this technique may be more pleasing but it offers restrictions that severely limit mounting positions. Touring arena productions have sometimes resorted to mounting spotlights on pipe standards placed at the four corners of the stage. This is completely unsatisfactory and the standards should be replaced by a trussing system. See TRUSS.

Two basic FORMULAS are used for lighting an arena stage and they work equally well for all arena styles.

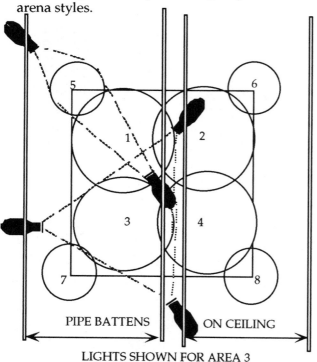

LIGHTS SHOWN FOR AREA 3
AND ENTRANCE 5 ONLY
MINIMUM LIGHTING PLAN
FOR AN ARENA AREA

120° lighting. Provides minimal coverage when equipment is in short supply. This formula uses three lights for each area, set 120° apart. The same color is used in each instrument to avoid distracting color changes on performers as they move around the stage. Washes of two or three colors are used for BLENDING, COLOR WASHES, and TONING LIGHTS and are mounted on inside and outside pipes and focused as DOWNLIGHTS. Usually with 120° lighting, all three lights covering an area are controlled by one dimmer, and all wash lights of the same color are on individual dimmers, allowing maximum variety in blending and toning within the confines of the method. *Advantages:* Uses very little equipment and provides basic control of areas and color with poor to fair blending potential. *Disadvantages:* With 120° between lights, it is difficult to blend lighting areas. In many situations this is not important. Suffice it to say this is not the system to use for HEAVY LIGHT SHOWS.

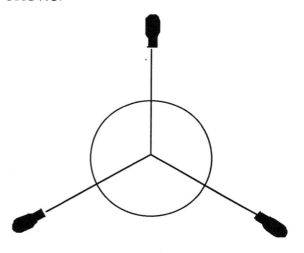

120° POSITIONING

90° lighting. This is the formula of choice if sufficient controls and spotlights are available. In this formula the instruments are placed 90° apart and, again, are GELLED the same pale color (if at all), and each area of four lights is controlled by the same dimmer. Color washes are used for blending and toning. Designers with no budgetary restrictions will find that DOUBLING, TRIPLING, or even quadrupling the number of instruments and dimmers for each area will give better coverage and much greater color flexibility. As money for equipment becomes available, the lighting designer should try for variations on these methods such as adding POOL lights, BACKLIGHTS, and doubling the formula. This will not only add interest but will make for better lighting. Greater flexibility can be added if each instrument has its own dimmer. *Advantages:* Reasonable color control, good area control, and good blending potential. *Disadvantages:* May require more instruments and controls than are available.

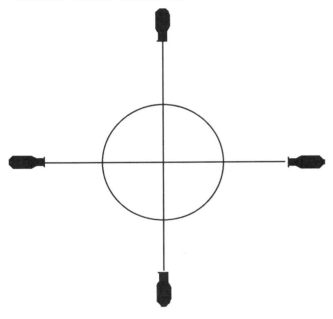

90° POSITIONING

Practice. Following these instructions, determine the THROW of the light from a scale drawing and choose the instruments accordingly. The HARD-EDGED, sharp beam of the ELLIPSOIDAL REFLECTOR SPOTLIGHT is favored for acting areas, and the SOFT-EDGED FRESNEL instrument (with BARNDOORS) for the blending, toning, and color washes. Fairly steep angles, usually around 50°–60°, are necessary to light actors in the outer fringes of the acting areas and to keep that light out of the eyes of the audience (a major problem). The floor may be used as an important part of arena lighting. Not only is it the main area available for scenic effects (GOBO projections may add considerably to the atmosphere), but it may also serve to absorb light for dramatic scenes requiring light pools, or it may be made to reflect

light for comedy scenes requiring brilliance. Over the years the importance of incorporating the arena stage floor into design and lighting has assumed its proper place and designers have learned to cope with the problems of handling the "sacred" carpeted or hardwood floor by superimposing floorcloths, Masonite, or plywood floors that may be painted to serve the show. Light-colored carpets or floorcloths will reflect the light, functioning almost as footlights and helping to compensate for the steep angle of area lights. The designer should be aware of the option of requesting props or costumes that may assist in one scene and be eliminated in others: a light-colored tablecloth, blotter, or runner on a desk; a throw rug, bedspread, scarf, or shawl. However, be careful not to overdo this effect; light also reflects into the auditorium, diluting the FOCUS OF ATTENTION. A flatter angle may be used for lights positioned over the audience and shining in to center stage. Ideally each entrance will use two ellipsoidals, one framed to shine in to the stage and the other framed to cover the exit or ramp without lighting the audience. If the arena theatre has a false ceiling, physical access to spotlights for focusing may not be too much of a problem. However,

45°ANGLE LIGHTING

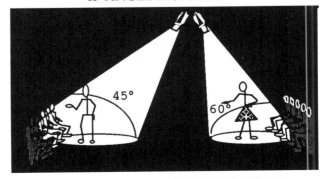

KEEPING LIGHT OUT OF THE AUDIENCE
ARENA LIGHTING PROBLEMS

with the false ceiling, visual access to the stage is usually impaired and in extreme cases, someone onstage must relay instructions to the person above, who is hanging and focusing blind. With the more conventional pipe grid, most hanging and focusing must be done from a ladder, which is often precariously straddling auditorium seats. Such challenges call for extreme care, extra hands to support the ladder, and careful planning so maximum advantage may be taken of each ladder positioning.

Color. Warm and cool color combinations sometimes used in proscenium lighting are not practicable on arena stages, where each area is lighted with three or four lights. Using warm and cool colors for modeling with any degree of subtlety or realism is accomplished by doubling the formula; then the actor is viewed and lighted from four sides by eight lights. With the single formula, it is generally advisable to use no color at all or, at most, a very light (TINT) color in each instrument and to rely on special color wash circuits to provide overall toning. Obviously, if more instruments and dimmers are used for each area, greater color control can be achieved. Minimum color control used in the wash lights will consist of one circuit of light blue and one of pink; but three circuits consisting of secondary colors or, preferably, dilute primaries are recommended. Permanent color lights (100-watt PAR 38 or 150-watt R 40 lamps) serve adequately for these circuits on smaller stages if top hats or some other LIGHT

SPILL CONTROL devices are attached to control diffused light. Color circuits are mounted on inside pipes and focused to blend in the center and cross to the far side of the stage.

Control. The elaborate control of lights necessary for proscenium stages is not always required for arena lighting, but the choice of plays that can be staged should not be limited because of inadequate light control. Separate dimming capabilities should be provided for the following: each acting area, each entrance and exit, all color washes, and all special lights. A minimal alternate plan calls for one or two high-capacity dimmers to handle all lights considered GENERAL LIGHTS in a production. Smaller dimmers could then be reserved for specials, color circuits, and specific areas requiring individual control. Since blackouts are used in place of a curtain, the control board <u>must</u> be equipped with a special blackout switch or heavy-duty master switches capable of withstanding continual operation with lights at full capacity.

ARIEL DAVIS. Owner-founder of the Ariel Davis Manufacturing Company of the 1940s through the mid-1960s. The company manufactured and distributed lighting instruments, dimmers, patch panels, and accessories. The dimmers were unique in that six slide contactors were used on one core, making a compact package that could be designed into a variety of consoles composed of any number of six-dimmer units. Davis dimmers and patch panels are still in use around the world. The company became Electro Control in the late 1960s and Strand-Electro Controls in the 1980s.

ARIELITE. Trade name for spotlights made in the 1950s and 1960s by the Ariel Davis Manufacturing Company. These spotlights used PAR lamps as their light source and were available in three forms: (1) with no lenses (a precursor of PARcans); (2) with step lenses and framing shutters to compete with ellipsoidal spots; and (3) with fresnel lenses to compete with FRESNEL LIGHTS. The unique fins forming part of the tubular housing helped cool the spotlights, replacing conventional venting holes.

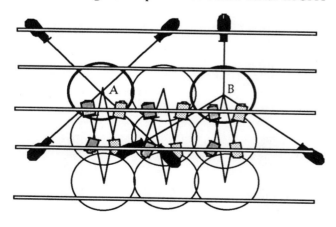

| | DILUTE BLUE WASH | A 90° AREA FORMULA |
| | DILUTE RED WASH | B 120° AREA FORMULA |

COLOR WASH PLACEMENT

ARIELITE
8" FRESNEL

ARM (side arm, hanger). A pipe used to support a spotlight, usually off to one side of a STANDARD.

FRESNELS ON SIDE ARMS
MOUNTED ON A BOOM

ASBESTOS CLOTH. A woven asbestos cloth border usually 24"–36" high by the length of the light PIPE on which it is hung. This cloth was used as a safety device, protecting hot lighting instruments from stage draperies hanging in the flies. No longer legally used in the United States because of health concerns, asbestos is being replaced by two fiberglass products under the brand names FIRECHIEF and ZETEX.

ATMOSPHERE. The atmosphere of a play pertains to the mood, as conceived by the author and expressed through staging, design, costumes, light, color, props, and sound effects. All efforts are combined to produce the desired atmosphere. Lighting, through its use of color and intensity, is often called upon to supply a great deal of this atmosphere.

AUDITORIUM (the house, out front, the audience). The part of the theatre devoted to the audience. Also referred to as FOH (front of the house).

AUDITORIUM LIGHTS. See HOUSE LIGHTS.

AUTOPAN. Spotlights or PARcans motorized to tilt or pan a stage area or auditorium. These units may be preset for automatic control or may be manually operated from a control board. Popular in rock, heavy metal, and rap shows, the autopan has relatively little place in theatrical lighting. Used mostly as a production gimmick. See PAN AND TILT.

AUTOTRANSFORMER. The autotransformer dimmer is based on the principle of changing light intensity by varying the voltage delivered to the instrument, in contrast to RESISTANCE DIMMER. Autotransformers consist of a soft iron core wrapped with copper wire to form a single coil. The size of the wire and the amount of core determine the capacity of the dimmer. A rotating or sliding arm containing a brush (usually carbon, graphite, or silver) makes contact either directly on the coil or with taps from the coil. The coil is placed in series with the input (line). The brush and one side of the line are placed in series with the output (load). Current required to operate the autotransformer is practically negligible, making it far more economical to use than the resistance dimmer. *Advantages:* Dims any size lamp up to dimmer capacity without a GHOST LOAD, offers smooth dimming with usually no more than a 1-volt variation between contact points, and is economical to operate. *Disadvantages:* Will not operate on direct current (no longer the problem it once was); some models are bulky and are not readily adaptable to compact GANGING. Autotransformers have been sold under a variety of trade names, including AUTRASTAT, DAVIS BOARD, LUXTROL,

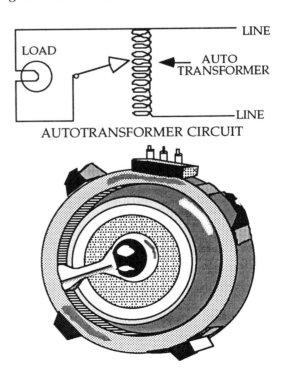

AUTOTRANSFORMER CIRCUIT

AUTOTRANSFORMER

POWERSTAT, RADIASTAT, and VARIAC. They have been popular from the late 1930s to the 1970s and are still in regular use. Newer installations usually use SILICON CONTROLLED RECTIFIERS. See also DIMMER.

AUTRASTAT. Obsolete. Trade name for an auto-transformer manufactured by WARD LEONARD COMPANY from the 1940s to the 1960s. This unit incorporated a rectangular-shaped core and a slider brush mechanism adapted to a handle control and mechanical master.

AUTRASTAT
(WARD LEONARD)

AUXILIARY BOARD. Any light control that is secondary or in addition to the main or primary lighting control board (SWITCHBOARD). In the days of PIANO BOARDS, an auxiliary board usually consisted of six or eight additional dimmers placed on top of the piano board and used to handle last-minute "add-ons" or special lights. The rationale was that piano boards consisted of a set number of dimmers, and renting or buying an additional board would be more expensive than acquiring the exact number of dimmers needed. AUTOTRANSFORMERS are sometimes used as auxiliary boards.

AVISTA. Changing scenery or scenes in view of the audience. Often this procedure has special lighting to accompany the move.

AXIAL MOUNT. A TUNGSTEN-HALOGEN (TH) lamp horizontally mounted in ellipsoidal reflector instruments. TH lamps burn in any position and therefore may be center-mounted (i.e., axially mounted) in the reflector, as opposed to older ellipsoidal reflectors designed for "burn base-up" lamps, requiring substantial portions of the reflector to be cut away to accommodate the lamp. See ELLIPSOIDAL REFLECTOR FLOODLIGHT; ELLIPSOIDAL REFLECTOR SPOTLIGHT.

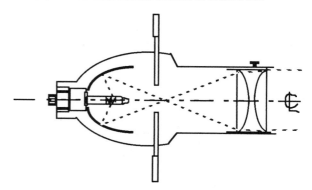

AXIAL-MOUNT LAMP

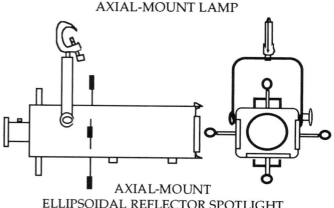

AXIAL-MOUNT
ELLIPSOIDAL REFLECTOR SPOTLIGHT
(ALTMAN)

B

BABY FRESNEL. High-wattage Colortran FRESNEL LIGHT designed for studio or film use. The 5,000-watt model has a 10" lens, and the 2,000-watt model has a 6" lens. Both instruments are less than 18" wide by 18" long, considerably smaller than older lights of comparable wattage, hence the name. These spotlights are designed for mogul bipost, tungsten-halogen lamps. See under LAMPS.

COLORTRAN 2,000-WATT
BABY FRESNEL

BABY LENS. Obsolete. Small, 7-volt spotlights attributed to Louis Hartmann and used as FOLLOWSPOTS in David Belasco's 1911 New York production of *The Return of Peter Grimm.* During this production, nearly a dozen "electricians" were placed on specially built platforms

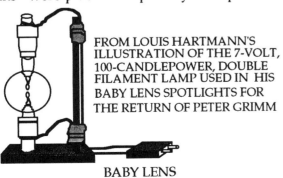

FROM LOUIS HARTMANN'S
ILLUSTRATION OF THE 7-VOLT,
100-CANDLEPOWER, DOUBLE
FILAMENT LAMP USED IN HIS
BABY LENS SPOTLIGHTS FOR
THE RETURN OF PETER GRIMM

BABY LENS

above and on the sides of the proscenium. Each was provided with a baby lens and assigned an actor to follow with his spotlight. These were among the first incandescent spotlights to be used in the United States.

BABY SPOT. Obsolete. A term given to Kliegl Bros. 250- or 400-watt PLANO-CONVEX (PC) SPOTLIGHTS. Prior to the late 1930s, baby spots were popular on small stages or for short throws of up to 15'. Their function was largely assumed by the improved small FRESNEL LIGHTS in the middle to late 1930s. The baby spot was more efficient than the average spotlight of its period, and catalogues boasted the interesting feature of providing a removable lens, "permitting it to be used as a floodlight." Baby spots were available as single instruments or in groups of six mounted in gyroscopic-type swivels in a CRADLE of six lights. With cast aluminum housings, these spotlights of the late 1920s and early 1930s were such durable lights that some are still in use today.

BABY SPOT

BACKDROP (drop). A screen, curtain, or painted cloth used as part of the scenery for a production. Prior to the use of realistic scenery (beginning in the second half of the nineteenth century) WING AND DROP sets were used exclusively for conventional scenery, and a standard set of backdrops would include a forest scene, garden scene, street scene, fancy interior, and a cottage interior. Today's backdrops are more likely to be draperies, sky cycloramas, or elaborate scenic drops prepared specifically for a certain production (opera and ballet productions especially make use of the last).

BACKING. A unit of scenery used to mask from the audience's eyes the backstage area through door and window openings of a set. A curtain, drapery, or cyclorama used behind openings of a set. An unlighted entrance or backing on a stage will draw unwarranted attention, and unless otherwise stated in the script, lighting should be provided for all entrances, windows, etc. See also **Backing lights** under LIGHTING PRACTICE.

BACKING LIGHT. Any instrument used to light a backing or to provide light through an opening from offstage. In the 1920s and early 1930s, small striplights were equipped with a hook on one end that could be placed over a toggle on a flat, thus providing the conventional unit for lighting backings. 10" SCOOPS were the light of choice at one time and in fact became so popular they earned the name WIZARDS. Spotlights, offering infinitely better control, have been the preferred source of light to use through door and window openings in more recent times. See also **Backing lights** under LIGHTING PRACTICE.

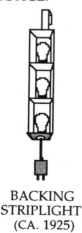

BACKING
STRIPLIGHT
(CA. 1925)

BACKLIGHTING. Illumination of actors from above and behind to provide a highlight or separation light from the background. Even with sufficient color contrast between costumes and scenery to keep the actors from blending into the background, a high-intensity DOWNLIGHT or backlight (different from a BACKING LIGHT) will

provide a clearer separation. Over many years, the practice of lighting from these positions has proved so useful that it has become an essential addition to most light plots (see DESIGN FOR LIGHTING). This is especially true for ballet, concert, dance theatre, and musicals, where it is becoming increasingly popular to use FOLLOWSPOTS for backlighting as well as frontlighting. However, either ELLIPSOIDAL REFLECTOR SPOTLIGHTS or FRESNEL LIGHTS are the more conventional choices for this job, and the colors may be either a combination of the chosen FORMULA colors, a TONING LIGHT color, or white light.

BACKLIGHTING

BACKUP. A protection copy of anything, for example, audiotape, computer cues, light plot. See COMPUTER LIGHT BOARD TERMINOLOGY.

BAFFLE, LIGHT. A metal shield built into lighting instruments to prevent the escape of light through ventilating holes or focusing slots.

BAKELITE. Trade name for a phenol-formaldehyde plastic that has been used extensively as an insulation material for electrical work because of its DIELECTRIC qualities. Control panels for switchboards and sound equipment are sometimes faced with Bakelite, a heat-resisting, thermosetting plastic, easily machined, drilled, and cut with a hacksaw or a skip-tooth bandsaw.

BALANCE LIGHT (verb). To adjust the intensity and color of light from one stage area to another. The problem is especially apparent in trying to balance light intensity between downstage areas

16

lighted from the BEAM (possibly a 40' THROW) and center stage areas lighted from the BORDER (possibly a 20' throw). Much of this light balance may be predetermined by the choice of instruments. If attention is paid to the distance of the throw, the diameter of the area to be covered, the size of the LAMPS, and their FOOTCANDLE output, instruments may be chosen to provide a reasonable balance of light from the outset (see PHOTOMETRIC CHARTS). Minor adjustments may be made by either dimming lights from the control board or through choices of color media. If balance is to be adjusted through dimming, the designer should be mindful of color changes resulting from lowering COLOR TEMPERATURES of lamps. In most cases this is not a real problem, but on occasion, costume colors or even complexions may change dramatically when lamp filaments turn from white to yellow as temperatures are lowered through dimming. See **Patch at level** under COMPUTER LIGHT BOARD TERMINOLOGY.

BALCONY LIGHTS (rail lights). Ellipsoidal spotlights, usually 750- to 2,000-watt capacity (depending on the THROW), mounted on a balcony rail or a HANGER in front of the rail. The balcony angle of 10°–20° is generally too flat to be used for AREA LIGHTS but this low angle may be put to advantage by using balcony lights as a COLOR WASH for the stage, thus providing uniform color for the APRON and downstage areas. This position often allows the use of fairly SATURATED COLORS, supplementing downstage area lighting from the BEAM, BOOTH, or COVE positions. See also PROSCENIUM STAGE LIGHTING.

BALLAST. In stage lighting, a ballast is usually a resistance of prescribed capacity wired in series with an arc light and used to control the flow of current through the carbon electrodes. Without the ballast, electrodes used in arc lights provide minimum resistance to the circuit, thus creating a virtual SHORT CIRCUIT. The ballast prevents this unrestricted flow of current that would otherwise certainly blow a fuse.

BALLET LIGHTING. Ballet is a graceful, precise, artistic dance using very formal and elaborate techniques. Often ballet tells a story. The function of ballet lighting should be to flow with the movement and style of the dance while coloring and heightening the story. As with a scripted play, the lights must enhance and complement the production rather then detract. Before approaching these problems, the lighting designer should become thoroughly familiar with the basics of lighting as discussed under LIGHTING PRACTICE as well as the procedures of DESIGN FOR LIGHTING.

Practice. Because of the fluid nature of ballet, area lighting is usually only a base on which to build the lighting design. Solo portions of the dance will often be staged in the downstage areas, referred to as "in one" or "in two" (see IN). The corps (the ensemble) for the most part will play "in three" and "in four." These separate locations should be bathed with an even light from the wing positions on each side of the stage. TONING LIGHTS, strong BACKLIGHTING, possibly POOLS, silhouettes, PROJECTED SCENERY, or SPECIAL EFFECTS may be added as determined by the theme of the ballet. SIDELIGHTING from the wings has always been a favored method of lighting dancers because ballet is color, form, composition, music, and motion all in one, and sidelighting enhances the dimensionality of the performer. If projections or the cyc will be used, sidelighting has the further advantage of not washing out the colors and projections, as will frontlights. Whether sidelighting is high (SLASHLIGHTING), medium, or low (SHIN BUSTERS), crosslighting is the most effective means of focusing attention on the legs and body. However, it must be remembered that vaulting leaps, high lifts, and complex foot movements are an essential part of dance programs and require crosslighting to be focused both higher and lower than would normally be the case for other forms of theatrical lighting. Do not allow the dancer to disappear in the dark at the very height of accomplishment. Dramatic shadows of a dancer projected on a CYC or SCREEN from spotlights placed in the footlight positions and varied by using saturated colors can be most effective. However, although the "bigger than life" shadows produced by this effect are fascinating, lighting must not overpower the dance for long periods. Scenery used for dance is of secondary importance and often consists of wings and drops, a few set pieces, and often projections. Pool lighting can be used for certain dramatic effects, but high-wattage backlighting is often a better and more efficient use of

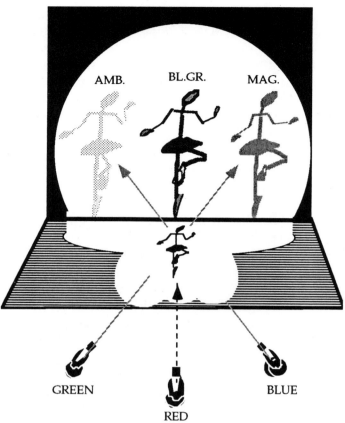

AMB.   BL.GR.   MAG.

GREEN   BLUE

RED

SHADOWS ARE SECONDARY COLORS BECAUSE EACH
ONE IS MISSING THE PRIMARY COLOR THAT CASTS IT
DANCE SHADOWS

equipment since it provides more positive separation from the background by highlighting the body, shoulders, and head. Sidelights hung on BOOMS, LADDERS, and TREES may be either beam projectors, fresnels, or ellipsoidals depending on the degree of blending the designer relies upon from diffusion. If sharply defined beams of light streaming across the stage are the desired effect, beam projectors or ellipsoidals should be the chosen instruments, whereas if a better blending of areas with a softer more diffused light is needed, fresnels will be the logical choice. In either case, in order to give an even coverage of light from one side of the stage to the other, short-, medium, and long-focus instruments will be needed and arranged as shown in the diagram under CROSSLIGHTING. Toning colors are often used to set the overall mood of the dance, either from BORDER LIGHTS, SIDELIGHTS, or COLOR WASHES, although if the color washes are used, they should be set at steeper angles than usual to

avoid spilling on the background. Fresnel lights are often the preferred spotlight choice for backlighting and should be of higher intensity (higher wattage) than frontlights or sidelights in order to provide an effective "punch" through the other lights. Backlighting may also be used to provide toning, in which case, even higher wattage lamps may be needed to compensate for lower light transmission through the more saturated colors. In ballet, followspots are often used for FOCUS OF ATTENTION on the principals to help separate them from the ensemble. In this capacity, followspots are best used from a steep angle to prevent background spill, and if they are kept in SOFT FOCUS, minimal attention will be drawn to the lights and maximum attention focused on the performer. If a projection cyc is used, the projector should be of sufficient size and intensity to fill the screen. If the background is to be sky, FLOODLIGHTS or CYC LIGHTS will be needed for the overhead position, and STRIPLIGHTS or FLOOR STRIPS (HORIZON LIGHTS) will be needed on the floor, preferably in three circuits each, providing maximum color variation for the background. If both fresnel spotlights and projections are to be used, be prepared to use LIGHT SPILL CONTROL devices to protect the cyc. *Caution:* A proper DANCE FLOOR, specially designed and constructed for resiliency, is sometimes finished in light, highly reflective colors that must be dealt with in lighting. It is possible to take advantage of this reflective surface to augment planned lighting, but the designer must be aware of the possibility of reflected light spilling onto the cyc or "bouncing" into unwanted areas. Focus adjustments or special light-absorbent materials may have to be used judiciously to compensate for such reflections. Portable dance floors are available for purchase or rental, and if either is contemplated, the lighting designer should be a member of the committee choosing the color.

Color. Since mood and atmosphere are so important, ballet is well served with saturated colors, but the light must be bright enough to see the dancers. Tints may be used to better show the technique of the dancers, with the more saturated colors in the background. To some extent the degree of saturation of colors chosen to light dance is determined by the equipment available. If equipment is available, DOUBLING the crosslights from the wing positions to provide warm and cool circuits in more saturated colors will offer greater variety and better color control. See COLOR SCHEMES.

Control. Maximum control is desirable with ballet lighting. In order to achieve effective lighting and maximum variety, separate color control of each side of the stage is essential. Because so much of the overall effect of lighting depends upon the board operator's precise execution and timing, it is important that the person calling cues be thoroughly familiar with the music and action as well as being sensitive to the choreographer's interpretation.

BALLYHOO (command verb). Using a FOLLOW-SPOT to sweep a production with figure eight patterns. This is a gimmick often used in ICE SHOW LIGHTING and for other extravaganzas for curtain calls.

BANGBOARDS. A strong stub wall about 3' high used to protect the audience from skaters in hockey and ice shows. In ICE SHOW LIGHTING the bangboards are usually hollow, with FLOOR STRIPS placed behind a translucent facing to provide a variety of colors to the ice.

BANK

Control boards. Many boards are arranged in tiers of dimmers or controllers known as banks. These are groupings of dimmers or controllers arranged for the convenience of the operator. Many electronic control boards are equipped with banks of scene presets consisting of duplicate dimmer controls that are set to predetermined readings prior to the scene and then activated by CROSS-FADING on cue from one set of dimmers to the other.

Lights. Several instruments (usually spotlights, PARcans, or BEAM PROJECTORS) hung together to provide a concentration of light. This grouping is intended to be used as a flood of light to bathe the stage. If a shadow-casting source of light simulating the sun is required, obviously that source must be a single high-intensity instrument. Multiple instruments cast multiple shadows, unlike the sun. Commercial units consisting of banks of lamps such as illustrated are available and highly efficient.

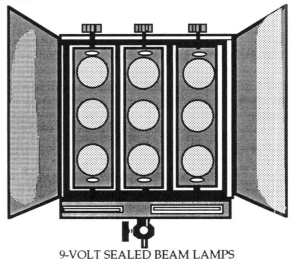

9-VOLT SEALED BEAM LAMPS
BANK OF LIGHTS

BARNDOOR. A mechanical device designed to slide into the color frame slot on the front of a lighting instrument and provide limited control of the light beam. Usually used with FRESNEL LIGHTS to help contain the normal diffusion from the fresnel lens. Commercially made metal shutters that shape the light pattern, with two flaps

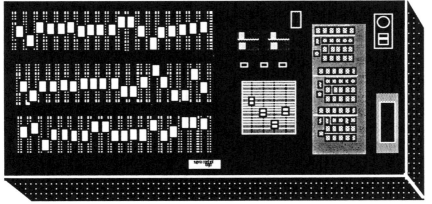

CONTROL BOARD WITH THREE BANKS

(two-way) or four flaps (four-way). One of the earliest of the commercial barndoors was manufactured and sold by the Pevear Color Specialty Company in the early 1930s. The Pevear PLANO-CONVEX SPOTLIGHTS were equipped with barndoors that could rotate, permitting the flaps to be aligned with the subject to be framed, a very useful feature prior to the ELLIPSOIDAL RE-FLECTOR SPOTLIGHT and internal SHUTTERS. See also LIGHT SPILL CONTROL.

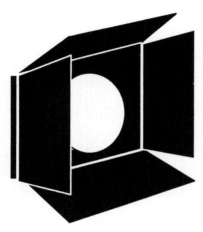

FOUR-WAY BARNDOOR

BASE

Boom. A heavy, cast-iron disk used as a footing for a pipe STANDARD (BOOM) to which lighting equipment may be attached. Available through theatrical supply houses or can be cast to order at foundries.

Lamp. Lamps used in lighting instruments include many different sizes and types of bases. Prior to the 1930s, theatre lighting equipment used lamps with screw bases. As better and more concentrated filaments were developed, the need for positive orientation of filament to reflector/lens became essential and the prefocus and bipost bases were introduced. In more recent years, with the introduction of the halogen and HMI lamps, double-ended bases have been added, providing positive, foolproof seatings relative to the OPTICAL AXIS. See under LAMPS.

BASE LIGHT. A television term meaning the minimum amount of light necessary for the camera to get a picture. The term designates the footcandles necessary for minimum illumination before KEY LIGHT and FILL LIGHT are added.

BATTEN, LIGHT. See LIGHT BATTEN.

BATTEN TAPE. A self-adhesive tape aligned with the centerline of each electric pipe showing the feet and inches left and right of center to help in the hanging of instruments. Specially made tapes for a ROAD SHOW will show precisely the location of each lighting instrument. See **Focus sheet** under DESIGN FOR LIGHTING.

BATTERY HOOKUP DIAGRAM. The responsibility of providing various sizes of batteries to power an increasing number of different devices in the theatre is logically being taken over by the electrician. Some of the battery-powered devices are communication phones between crew members, flashlights, radio-controlled operating equipment, and sound effects. The drawing shows an easy battery hookup with a bell and a buzzer, with pushbutton switches. See also BELL.

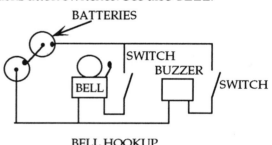

BELL HOOKUP
WITH BATTERIES

BATTERY OF LIGHTS. A BANK or many banks of spotlights, PARcans, or BPs placed in the wings or in the FRONT OF THE HOUSE to flood the stage with intense light. Often required for extravaganzas and outdoor staging, where batteries of lights on the stage have even been directed at the audience and used in place of an ACT CURTAIN. Some multilamp units formerly associated only with television or movies are gaining popularity onstage. See also BRUTE; BUNCH LIGHT.

BAY. Left and right stage openings usually between legs, wings, or other scenery and used primarily for CROSSLIGHTING and entrances. Sometimes called a lighting bay and often designated as in one, in two, etc., or by R1, R2, L1, L2. See also AREAS; BALLET LIGHTING; IN.

BEAM

Light. The cone of light from a reflector, lens, or spotlight.

Position. See BEAM POSITION.

BEAM ANGLE. A spotlight's cone of light in which intensity ranges from 50% of maximum to maximum. The cone of light ranging from 10% to 49% of maximum intensity is known as the FIELD ANGLE. In catalogues, these angles are expressed in degrees, stated as "a spotlight with a beam angle of 'X' degrees and a field angle of 'X' degrees." These angles become important when focusing spotlights on adjacent areas onstage. If the beam angles of each light touch, the field angles will overlap, producing a good blend of light between the two areas. Both angles are determined by light meter readings, and neither is apparent to the eye. A reasonable estimate can be made as to the overlap needed from the angle listings in catalogues (or from PHOTOMETRIC CHARTS). See BLENDING.

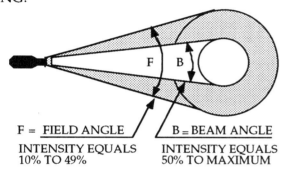

F = FIELD ANGLE   B = BEAM ANGLE
INTENSITY EQUALS   INTENSITY EQUALS
10% TO 49%   50% TO MAXIMUM

BEAM AND FIELD ANGLES

BEAM LIGHTS (cove lights, bridge lights, catwalk lights, ceiling slots). Ellipsoidal spotlights, usually 500- to 2,000-watt capacity (depending on THROW), located on a FALSE BEAM or equivalent position in the auditorium. The light angle to the stage should be between 39° and 45°. See also BEAM POSITION.

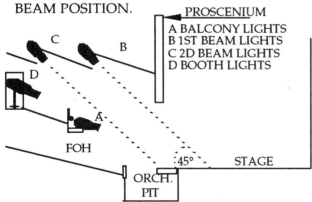

LIGHTING POSITIONS AND OPTIMUM ANGLE
FROM FRONT OF THE HOUSE (FOH)

BEAM LIGHTS

BEAM POSITION (beam port, ceiling slot). A slot or opening in the ceiling or a grid of pipes hung below the ceiling of the auditorium where spotlights may be mounted and focused to light the downstage acting areas. If beam lighting positions were not included in the original theatre design, pipes may be hung and safety pans or grills suspended below the spotlights for audience protection. Safety codes and safety inspectors must be consulted before making such installations. Consideration must also be given to those people involved in the hanging, focusing, and care of such units. Climbing ladders set between rows of seats on a sloped floor is hazardous work at best. The optimum lighting angles from beam to apron edge are between 39° and 45°. Instruments best suited for the beam position are ELLIPSOIDAL REFLECTOR SPOTLIGHTS with their built-in shutters. Ellipsoidals are used because of the HARD-EDGE light formed by their shutters, which cut unwanted light spill from the proscenium and frame the light to the exact area needed. See also ANTEPROSCENIUM.

BEAM PROJECTOR (BP). A type of floodlight with a parabolic REFLECTOR, producing an intense concentration of light. The use of the parabolic reflector and SPILL RINGS in theatre floodlights dates back to arc lights shortly after the beginning of the twentieth century. By the early 1940s, the 500-watt globular-shaped incandescent lamp was mounted behind a small spherical reflector that sent the rays back into the parabolic reflector, thus

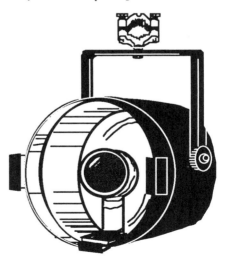

BEAM PROJECTOR

producing controlled reflected light. Other models used a lens in the center spill ring instead of the small reflector. In either case, the beam projector has been a durable piece of equipment that is still useful as a single source of high-intensity light, simulating sunlight or moonlight. Some focus is provided in most models but the beam projector is basically a narrow-beam instrument. BPs are sometimes mounted in BANKS to simulate intense **Motivational light** (see under LIGHTING PRACTICE).

BELL (sound effect). Various types of bells are used onstage: doorbells, buzzers, chimes, and telephone rings. It is useful to make self-contained units with at least one bell, one buzzer, and a door chime with either batteries or a transformer as a power supply. Batteries are used for portable units, enabling cues to be given from several locations on stage. Bell transformers, available in hardware stores, are more reliable and less expensive in the long run. Most door chimes and bells will operate on a 12- to 16-volt supply from either transformer or batteries. Many bells are designed for 6 to 16 volts. It is more than likely the electrician will be called upon to supply the "bell board" as well as the power to operate it. The series battery hookup illustrated provides a voltage equal to the sum total of all batteries included in the CIRCUIT. A telephone power supply can sometimes be begged or borrowed from a local phone company; these work well with a simple pushbutton switch for a phone onstage. See BATTERY HOOKUP DIAGRAM.

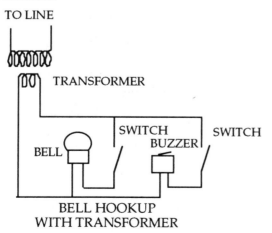

BELL HOOKUP
WITH TRANSFORMER

BISCUIT. A professional colloquialism for a self-contained speaker in an intercom system.

BLACK. The absence of light. A color or pigment that absorbs much light.

BLACK ALUMINUM FOIL. See WRAP.

BLACK LIGHT (UV). Ultraviolet light may be used to fluoresce a variety of available products, including paint, makeup, crayons, cloth, ribbons, fringes, and dyes. See ULTRAVIOLET LIGHT.

BLACKOUT (noun). Complete darkness on the stage used in place of a curtain and accomplished by pulling the main switch (or blackout switch [BO] on newer control boards) for a fast dim-out. The master dimmer is used for slower fade-outs. SPIKE MARKS of phosphorescent (glow) paint or tape will help actors and crew find their way in the dark.

BLACKOUT (command verb). The order to cut all light, used often by directors, designers, and stage managers. When cuing electricians, sound technicians, and other stage personnel, most stage managers use the more common cue "GO" as the preferred command. See also CUES.

BLACKOUT DROP. A dark-colored drape used behind SHOW CURTAINS and SCRIMS to prevent unwanted light from showing through to the audience.

BLEED. A term applied to light shining through a flat that is not completely opaque. *Solution:* (1) Adjust the light focus. (2) Shield the flat from the light. (3) Paint the back of the flat with a dark color, or hang a piece of black fabric on the back of the flat. Dark material or dark paint will prevent unwanted light bleeding through scenery from backing lights.

BLENDING

Light beams and areas. Overlapping FIELD ANGLES of area lights to ensure even coverage

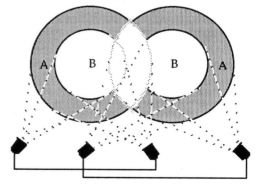

A FIELD ANGLE
B BEAM ANGLE
OVERLAPPED FIELD ANGLES
ENSURE SMOOTH BLENDING

from one area to another. See **Areas** under LIGHT-ING PRACTICE.

Entire stage. Using a wash of light over the stage in order to smooth the coverage and soften or fill any HOLES between areas. This kind of blending is best done with a wash from spotlights at a relatively low angle from the balcony or other FOH position. Often darker, more saturated, dilute primary colors are used.

CHECKING FOR BLENDING AT PROPER HEIGHT

BLINDER. Often a homemade LIGHT SPILL CONTROL device made of WRAP used to shape the spread of light from a spotlight. Sometimes a term used for a BARNDOOR.

BLIND RECORDING. See COMPUTER LIGHT BOARD TERMINOLOGY.

BLINKER. A signal light in series with a pushbutton or other switch, used to relay cues or to replace bells or buzzers on telephones backstage. Lamps in cue lights should be wired in pairs to safeguard against a missed cue if a single lamp burns out. See schematic under CUE LIGHTS.

BLOOM. Specular reflection from polished surfaces such as prop mirrors. *Solution:* (1) Spray with a commercial dulling spray such as Krylon, available in art stores. (2) Use Jet Spray Bon Ami, and rather than wipe off the whitish residue, let it dry.

BLOW

Breaker. A BREAKER in a circuit automatically clicks to "off" position when overloaded or short-circuited. Breakers may be reset.

Cues. To bungle a cue. "The distraction caused the electrician to 'blow' the cue."

Fuse. The alloy in a fuse melts and automatically opens the circuit when an overload or short circuit occurs. Fuses must be replaced.

Lamp. A burned-out lamp may be referred to as a blown lamp.

BLOWOUT. See BLOW.

BLUE. One of the primary colors in both pigment and light color charts. See COLOR.

BLUE-GREEN. Cyan. A secondary color in lighting. Complement of red. See COLOR MIXING.

BLUEPRINT. A white line print on a blue background made by placing a tracing on light-sensitized paper and exposing to strong light. A fast and inexpensive method of duplicating working drawings. The process is also used for black on white, brown on white, and blue on white backgrounds. Original drawings must be made on tracing paper. "Blueprint" has become a generic term for any of several methods of duplicating large drawings. See also DIAZO.

BOARD. A term used for the control board for either lights or sound. See CONTROL BOARDS AND CONSOLES. See also AUXILIARY BOARD; BOARD OPERATOR; ELECTRICIAN; LIGHTING CONTROL LOCATIONS.

BOOM. A light standard, usually includes a heavily weighted base and a pipe upright on which sidearms and lighting instruments are mounted. See also LIGHT MOUNTING DEVICES for other mechanical configurations that have similar usages.

LIGHT BOOM

BOOM BASE. See under BASE.

BOOMERANG

Color (box or magazine [British usage]). Any of several types of devices used to change colors in FOLLOWSPOTS. See also COLOR WHEEL; SCROLL COLOR CHANGERS.

Light tower. Usually a pipe tower on which lights are mounted. Most often used in the number 1 wing (teaser position). Sometimes the tower was on wheels and pivoted in and out of position, hence the name boomerang. See also GENIE LIFT; LIGHT MOUNTING DEVICES; TELESCOPTER.

Light standard. The standard pipe and base were mounted on a dolly pivoting in and out to replace the light tower, and the name boomerang was given only to be shortened to boom later. The weighted base and pipe upright became popular and were moved to any place in the theatre without the dolly underneath. See also BOX BOOM.

BOOTH, CONTROL (booth). A room located at the rear of the auditorium and equipped with lighting controls and often sound controls; in some cases also serves as the stage manager's station.

BOOTH, PROJECTION (booth). Enclosed area near the rear of the auditorium used as a projection room for motion picture theatres. The booth is a good location for high-intensity spotlights used for general coverage or for FOLLOWSPOTS in special productions. In many theatres the booth is also the location for lighting and sound control equipment, providing excellent visibility for the operators. Projection booths used for arc followspots or projection equipment must be designed with fireproof walls. For location, see drawing under BEAM LIGHTS.

BOOTH LIGHTS. ELLIPSOIDAL REFLECTOR SPOTLIGHTS of 1,000- to 3,000-watt capacity (depending upon the THROW) or FOLLOWSPOTS used in the booth location at the rear of the auditorium. See drawing under BEAM LIGHTS.

BORDER (teaser, valance). Canvas, cloth, or any material used to mask the upper portion of the stage from audience view. Borders used to mask BORDER LIGHTS or pipes on which electrical instruments are hung should be given extra flameproofing care and all fabrics should be protected from hot hanging instruments to make certain there is no contact between lights and fabrics. It is the responsibility of the electrician who is hanging equipment to make certain no fabric is in contact with hanging instruments. See FIRECHIEF.

BORDER LIGHT CABLE. Multiple electrical circuits in one flexible sheathing. Color-coded wire makes tracing circuits easy, and the convenience of having cables grouped encourages neatness. See CABLE.

BORDER LIGHT (X-rays). GENERAL LIGHTS usually providing three or four circuits of color for toning and fill light. Dating back to the first gas border light in the United States (installed in New York City's Lafayette Theatre in 1827) and progressing through the early 1900s, border lights have provided the main source of stage illumination by flooding the stage with sufficient light to see the actors. Floodlights, footlights, and border lights were the workhorses of stage lighting until lamps were developed with a concentrated filament that made possible the use of lenses and reflectors. The LIMELIGHT and occasional ARC LIGHT offered special effects. Originally four circuit lights were intended for separate colors in the borders of red, blue, amber, and white. The color green, later to be accepted as a primary, was regarded as far too unflattering for use in the theatre. The white circuit was used primarily for work lights, leaving red, blue, and amber for toning. Early in the twentieth century, Munroe Pevear, founder of the Pevear Color Specialty Company, discovered how to manufacture gelatine colors of exceptional spectral purity, and in 1911 he strongly advocated the use of primary colors, including green, for complete color control. The reluctance of actors to tolerate a green light onstage persisted for many years, and it was not until the late 1930s, when university drama departments accepted Pevear's views on primary colors, that any progress was made in general acceptance. Among old-timers, there are still doubters, but the knowledge is widespread that costumes and settings, composed of many colors, each responding to its own color of light, become much more vibrant under a white light composed of all primaries or dilute primaries.

BOTTLE (bulb, envelope). Term used professionally for the glass portion of LAMPS.

BOUNCE. A diffused light reflected off walls, floors, and props.

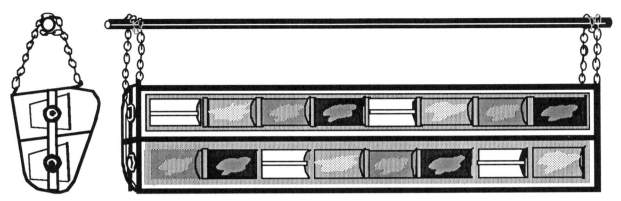

FOUR-CIRCUIT STRIPLIGHTS OF THE EARLY SEVENTIES DESIGNED FOR TUNGSTEN-HALOGEN LAMPS AND USED INTERCHANGEABLY AS BORDER LIGHTS OR CYC LIGHTS. THE TOP AND BOTTOM UNITS CAN BE FOCUSED INDIVIDUALLY, COVERING DIFFERENT AREAS OF THE STAGE, OR EITHER 300-WATT OR 500-WATT LAMPS MAY BE USED, BOTH OF WHICH BURN TOO HOT FOR PRACTICAL USE OF ALL COLOR MEDIA EXCEPT GLASS.

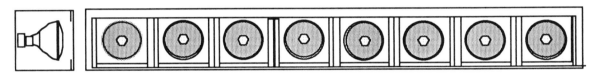

FOUR-CIRCUIT STRIPLIGHTS DESIGNED FOR EITHER PAR 38 150-WATT SEALED BEAM LAMPS OR R 40 150-WATT FLOOD LAMPS AND USED INTERCHANGEABLY AS BORDER LIGHTS, FOOTLIGHTS, OR CYC LIGHTS

BORDER LIGHTS SOMETIMES USED AS STRIPLIGHTS

COMPARTMENT BORDER LIGHTS WITH GLASS REFLECTORS AND METAL FRAMES FOR GELATINE

DOUBLE-ROW, FOUR-CIRCUIT, ROUNDEL BORDER LIGHTS OF THE EARLY TWENTIES

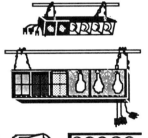

PERIOD BORDER LIGHTS

BOUNCING BARS. British expression for DEAD FOCUS.

BOX BOOM. Temporary FRONT OF THE HOUSE lights in the box seat positions on either side of the proscenium. Locating lights in this position is not legal in some cities; fire inspectors should be consulted. When used, box booms must be secured by guy wires and a shelf or grill placed under anything that could conceivably fall into the audience. The box boom position is similar to the PORTAL position in a theatre with permanent mounting slots.

BOX TRUSS. See TRUSS.

BP. An acronym for BEAM PROJECTOR.

BRANCH CIRCUIT. The final electrical circuit protected by the lowest amperage fuse or breaker. See CIRCUITS.

BREAKER, CIRCUIT. See CIRCUIT BREAKER.

BRIDGE (light bridge). A catwalk or platform hung from the grid just upstage of the proscenium and designed to support lighting instruments and personnel to focus them.

BRIGHAM COLORS. Obsolete. Color media made for lighting instruments by the defunct Brigham Gelatine Company of Randolph, Vermont. Brigham was one of the few companies to make variegated color media (i.e., three or more colors on a base color), useful for fire effects, filtered sunlight, etc. See COLOR MEDIA.

BRIGHTNESS (brilliance, lightness). Intensity, which varies with the illumination a surface receives. Pure white and pure black represent the extremes of brightness from maximum to minimum. Brightness is measured in FOOT-CANDLES.

BRILLIANCE. Better called BRIGHTNESS.

BRUSH. A carbon, graphite, or silver slider placed on the movable arm of a RESISTANCE DIMMER or AUTOTRANSFORMER and designed to vary resistance in the dimmer or voltage in the transformer as it slides over contact points. Both brushes and points need occasional cleaning with ROUGE CLOTH. Alcohol or tuner cleaner may also be used for cleaning electrical points and contacts. Never use oil or grease.

BRUTE. Floodlights made by The Great American Market, Brute lights consist of banks of nine high-intensity LOW-VOLTAGE lamps incorporated in a single instrument. They are available in three different classifications: the Brute, the Mini-Brute, and the Micro-Brute. Each housing contains three groups of three lights each mounted on swivel sticks to provide some focus or concentration of light. High intensity of the tiny Micro-Brute (measuring about 1' square) is provided by 12-volt sealed beam lamps rated at 65 or 75 watts, 1,200-hour life, and 3,150-KELVIN temperature. The low-voltage lamps are wired in series and need no transformer. The concept is reminiscent of the BUNCH LIGHT of the early 1900s.

BTR. An acronym for "big time roadie," a professional colloquialism of self-importance or of derision of other people.

BULB (envelope, bottle). Technically the glass portion of a LAMP but commonly used to describe the entire lamp in a lighting instrument or fixture. Professional theatre uses the term lamp.

BULL SWITCH. The master switch on the old RESISTANCE DIMMER PIANO BOARDS formerly used for ROAD SHOWS and in many Broadway theatres. The bull switch was used for BLACKOUTS as well as for activating or killing the entire board.

BUMP IT (command verb). To increase light intensity suddenly.

BUMP UP (slam up). The act of increasing light intensity suddenly.

BUNCH LIGHT. Obsolete. A floodlight consisting of several small lamps mounted in the same reflector. Bunch lights were developed in the latter part of the nineteenth century when the maximum intensity of a lamp was 16 CANDLEPOWER. The only way to increase intensity was to group several lamps in the same reflector. Several designs were

developed, as shown. It is interesting to note a return to that original concept in the form of the BRUTE and MINI-BRUTE lights.

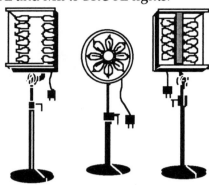

BUNCH LIGHTS OF THE 1900s

BUNDLE (tripe [British usage]). A number of cables tied or taped together to form a single large grouped cable.

BURNDY. An electrical brand name as well as a professional generic term for a solderless connector type of LUG used to connect FEEDERS from the DIMMERS to the COMPANY SWITCH.

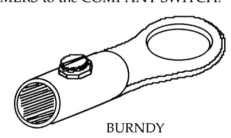

BURNDY

BUS AND TRUCK. The scaled-down version of a road show. Usually the scenery and lighting are reduced to minimum to keep costs down. Presently, the scenery is moved by truck, and the cast and crew fly or, for short distances, travel by bus. See COMPANIES; see also ROAD SHOW LIGHTING.

BUS BAR. A heavy copper bar used as an electrical conductor. Usually found in electrical panels, fuse boxes, and COMPANY SWITCHES.

BX WIRE. Obsolete. Electrical wires or conductors encased in flexible armored steel. Their use is no longer legal, and they have been replaced by GREENFIELD.

BYTE. A unit of digital information comprising "bits" of "on-off" signals. Used in describing the amount of memory associated with COMPUTER BOARDS.

C

CABLE. Rubber-insulated, heavy-duty electrical conductor suitable for theatre use. Because theatrical electrical cable is subject to constant abuse on the stage, extra-heavy insulation is required by the National Electrical Code. The NEC has approved four types of cables for stage use: types S and SO, the preferred rubber insulation; and types ST and STO, the somewhat thinner and less durable plastic insulation. As is the case with other flexible conductors, stranded wire provides the necessary flexibility for the constant reorganization of stage lights. Wire is designated by the gauge (first number, indicating capacity) and the number of conductors within the insulation (second number). Thus, 12/2 with ground (also known as 12/3) is 12-gauge, 2-wire cable plus ground wire, standard for most single-circuit stage uses. For border or beam positions where many circuits are required, special border light cable containing multiple conductors in one flexible sheathing is used. Border light cable is not less expensive per circuit than individual cables, but it is considerably easier to handle and reduces clutter. Circuits are color-coded for easy tracing. Border light cable designated 12/12 with ground means a 12-gauge, 12-wire cable with one common ground (sufficient for six separate, 20-amp grounded circuits). All stage cable is sold by the foot, with a slight discount for 100'–250' reels, and is available in most theatrical supply houses or wholesale electrical companies. The following table gives ampere capacities of various gauges of copper wire:

Wire gauge							
2	4	6	8	10	12	14	16
90	70	50	35	25	20	15	6
Capacity in amps							

Most theatres standardize cables for lighting instruments at 12/3 (12-gauge 3-wire), with 20-amp pin connector PLUGS. A collection of cables 5', 10', 15', 20', 30', 40', 50', and a few 100' long should be made up, labeled, and kept coiled, ready for use. A few TWO-FERS and THREE-FERS should also be on hand for ganging instruments on the same circuit. Heavier cables for projectors, multiple-light circuits, and special high-wattage equipment will undoubtedly be needed from time to time and require additions to be made accordingly. The minimum capacity allowed by NEC for plugs, connectors, and stage cable used for lighting instruments is 20 amps.

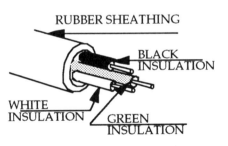

STAGE CABLE

Feeders. Large, single-conductor, rubber-insulated cables capable of powering the dimmer banks when used in the proper multiples. These cables have connectors (UNIPLUGS) at each end. Usually BURNDYS hook into the power panel bus bars of the DIMMERS and into the bus bars of the COMPANY SWITCH. Since long cables can be very heavy, special uniplugs are available to connect shorter lengths together. The following table gives ampere capacities of various gauges of flexible, single-conductor copper wire in hard-service cables:

Wire gauge						
000	00	0	1	2	4	6
200	175	150	130	115	85	65
Capacity in amps						

BX wire or cable. Obsolete and no longer legal in many places. Metal-sheathed wire formerly used for interior wiring, replaced by Greenfield.

Greenfield. Flexible, armored tubing usually used for permanent installations, although large diameters are sometimes used to run cables through walls on a temporary basis.

Lamp cord (zip cord, rip cord). A light-duty, rubber- or plastic-covered wire available in 16 and 18 gauge. Permitted in the theatre only as found on needed prop lamps, appliances, or for speaker wires on sound systems.

Romex wire. Trade name for solid copper wire with a plastic covering, used for permanent interior wiring. Romex will bend but is not very flexible and is therefore not suitable for temporary use.

Shielded wire. Copper wire covered with insulation plus a braided metal shield, used for amplifiers, computers, and other electronic equipment to reduce radio frequency disturbances. To further avoid potential disturbances, shielded wire should not be run next to power lines of 110 volts or higher.

CABLE BOX. Term used in professional theatre for boxes on casters used to transport cable from one location to another.

CABLE CLAMP. See under CLAMPS.

CABLE HOOK. A wire hook on a light STANDARD used to hang excess coiled cable.

CABLE LOCK. A Velcro ribbon used to tie coiled cables and, occasionally, to tie PIN CONNECTORS together.

CABLE PIPE. See CROSSOVER PIPE.

CAD. See COMPUTER-ASSISTED DESIGN.

CAGE. A chain-link fence or expanded metal enclosure sometimes used to separate permanent lighting control or sound control installations from the stage.

CALCIUM LIGHT. Obsolete. An early followspot using as its light source a cylinder of lime heated to incandescence by an oxygen-hydrogen flame. See LIMELIGHT.

CALIBAN FLOOD. Obsolete. An early floodlight using a PARABOLIC REFLECTOR and SPILL RINGS. This was the first stage light to use the then new nitrogen-filled, 1,000-watt incandescent lamps. The caliban flood (an adaptation of the ARC LIGHT GALLERY REFLECTOR) was built for and named after the production *Caliban* staged by Percy MacKaye at the stadium of the College of the City of New York in 1916. The gallery reflector and the caliban flood were precursors of the present BEAM PROJECTOR.

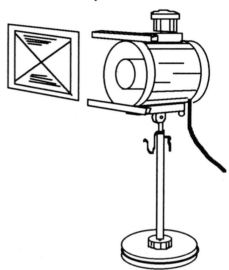

FIRST STAGE LIGHT TO USE
1,000-WATT INCANDESCENT
LAMP (CA. 1916)
CALIBAN FLOOD

CALIBRATE. On some dimmer systems it is necessary to set (adjust) voltage levels to achieve proper DIMMER CURVES.

CALIBRATION. System of placing numbers beside DIMMER or POTENTIOMETER handles so accurate light levels may be read and recorded.

CANCEL (command verb) (kill, strike). To remove a particular light or delete a cue.

CANDELA. Since 1979 the international standard of luminous intensity; 1 footcandle. See also LUMEN.

CANDELABRA BASE. A socket or base for a lamp, slightly smaller than the medium base (standard household lamp base). Usually found in wall brackets, large Christmas tree lights, or chandeliers. See **Base** under LAMPS.

CANDLEPOWER. Luminous intensity. See FOOT-CANDLE; ILLUMINATION; LUMEN.

CAPACITY. The amount of current a conductor can safely carry. Usually used in reference to dimmers or wire. See also AMPERE.

CAPCOLITE (embryo spot, inky). Obsolete. Trade name for Capitol Stage Lighting Company's 3" fresnel spotlights designed for 75- to 150-watt G 16 lamps. Its compact size made it particularly useful for short THROWS in tight quarters. PARcans are possible substitutes for the old Capcolite. See INKY.

CAPCOLITE

CAPITOL STAGE LIGHTING COMANY. Obsolete. Manufacturer and distributor of stage lighting equipment.

CARBON ARC. The carbon arc was the light source for many types of FLOODLIGHTS and SPOTLIGHTS from the late nineteenth century to the early twentieth century. See ARC LIGHTS; FOLLOWSPOT.

CARBONS (trim). Positive and negative carbon rods used as electrodes between which a current jumps to form the light source in ARC LIGHTS and arc FOLLOWSPOTS.

CARBORUNDUM PAPER. An abrasive paper sold in different grits and used for sanding and cleaning. Use a number 6/0 grade for improving electrical contacts between brushes and rheostat dimmer or autotransformer contacts. See BRUSH.

CARPENTER'S PIPE. See CROSSOVER PIPE.

CARTRIDGE. A mount or holder for a dimmer BRUSH.

CARTRIDGE FUSE. A cylindrical-shaped electrical FUSE. Fuses of less than 5-amp or more than 30-amp capacity are often the cartridge type.

CATWALK (bridge). A platform or walkway suspended from the stage GRID or ceiling or in the FRONT OF THE HOUSE position and used to hang, focus, and service lighting instruments.

C-CLAMP. A clamp shaped like a letter "C," designed to fasten lighting instruments to PIPE BATTENS or STANDARDS. See under CLAMPS.

C-CYC. See under **CYC.**

CEILING SLOT. Opening in the ceiling of an auditorium through which lighting instruments may be focused on the stage. This mounting position is considered ANTEPROSCENIUM.

CENTERLINE

Drawing. A broken (dot-dash) line drawn to bisect a drawing. When applied to a stage, the centerline of the stage and the CURTAIN LINE are used as reference points for placing scenery, props, and lights on the stage and apron. These two lines are usually used to locate the FOCUSING CLOTH.

Rigging. The middle line of a three-line or five-line flying system.

CENTRAL STAGE. A stage surrounded by audience. See ARENA STAGE LIGHTING.

CENTURY LIGHTING COMPANY. Obsolete. A manufacturer of lighting instruments, accessories, and control boards. The name LEKO, now used as a generic term for ELLIPSOIDAL REFLECTOR SPOTLIGHTS, originated with this firm, which became Century Strand in the 1960s and finally Strand Lighting in the 1980s.

CENTURY WRENCH. A special wrench designed to fit all bolt heads on Century Lighting instruments.

CHAIN

Furnace chain. Sometimes used to tie COLOR FRAMES to lighting instruments.

Safety chain. A length of chain fastened to a spotlight or other hanging object to secure it to a wall, BATTEN, or ceiling, and used as a safety device. Either #2/0 passing link chain (450-lb test) or #2/0 straight link coil chain (495-lb test) will serve well. 1/8" wire rope (340-lb test) will also work if a NICOPRESS crimper and sleeve are used for fastening.

CHAIN HANGER. The only means of hanging lighting equipment prior to the invention of C-CLAMPS and YOKE CLAMPS in the early 1920s. BORDER LIGHTS and FLOODLIGHTS of that period came equipped with a length of chain fastened to each end of the instruments; the chains were detached, wrapped around the PIPE BATTEN two or three times to keep a precise setting, and then reattached. Occasionally, chain hangers are still seen on border lights. The first spotlights to be flown in the border position were chain-suspended by a ring mounted at the back of the instrument, creating a "DOWNLIGHT" of uncertain stability. See YOKE.

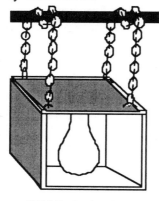

CHAIN HANGER

CHANNEL. See under COMPUTER LIGHT BOARD TERMINOLOGY.

CHASER. Turns individual lamps on or off sequentially by mechanical or electronic control. See also SPECIAL EFFECTS.

CHEAT (verb)

    Dimmer. To move a dimmer setting up or down from its prescribed setting.

    Instrument. To move the focus of an instrument slightly off its intended area. Often used to avoid SPILL on the set.

CHEAT SHEET. A listing of dimmers and instruments controlled by them plus pertinent data prepared by the lighting designer to be used for quick reference at rehearsals. See DESIGN FOR LIGHTING.

CHOPPER (cutoff, douser). Handle-controlled metal plates mounted within a followspot and designed to close against each other horizontally, blocking the gate through which light travels. On some older followspots the chopper not only acted as a BLACKOUT device but also as a STRIP-OUT device, allowing the width of the beam to be increased while maintaining a constant height.

CHROMA. The amount of pure color within a HUE. The chroma of a GELLED spotlight will be altered as the intensity of the lamp is varied by a dimmer. At low intensities, the filament glows red, and as the intensity gradually increases, the filament color changes to the white-yellow of full intensity. See COLOR.

CINABEX. Obsolete. A trade name for color media.

CINEMOID. Trade name for color media manufactured by Rank Strand Ltd. of England. Universally available for stage lighting. See COLOR MEDIA. See Selected List of Manufacturers and Distributors in back of book.

CIRCLE THEATRE. A stage surrounded by audience. See ARENA STAGE LIGHTING.

CIRCUIT BREAKER. A device designed to give the same protection to a circuit as a fuse except the circuit breaker may be reset when blown. Circuit breakers resemble regular electrical switches in appearance. Some types activate when an overload heats two metals with different coefficients of heat expansion, thus triggering the switch. Other types are activated by an electric magnet or solenoid.

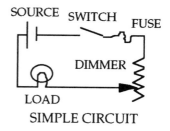

CIRCUIT BREAKER

CIRCUITING. Connecting lighting instruments to outlets, outlets to dimmers, dimmers to controls, etc.

CIRCUITS. The complete path of a current, from the electrical source (LINE) through the lamp (LOAD) and back to the source, including SWITCHES, FUSES, and DIMMERS.

SIMPLE CIRCUIT

Overview

    Homes. Standard household electrical installations are **Three-wire, single phase** (see illustration under three-wire, single-phase). The wires enter the house at the entrance panel, where they are subdivided into two types of circuits. The higher voltage, 240 volts, is taken from the two

HOT legs of the power line. This is used for hot-water heaters, electric stoves, clothes dryers, and baseboard heaters. The lower voltage, 120 volts, is taken from one hot LEG and the neutral (common) and serves the rest of the house for outlets, lighting, small appliances, etc. In wiring the lower voltage **Branch circuits**, effort is made to anticipate and equalize the loads from each of the legs.

Theatre. In theatre **Four-wire, three-phase** 208-volt power lines enter the MAIN power panel and, as in the home, are split into three kinds of branch circuits. The heavy-duty circuits used for motors are three-phase circuits. The lighter duty circuit is the higher voltage, 220-volt circuit taken from two hot legs and is used for hot-water tanks, heavy-duty power tools, electric stoves, and clothes dryers. The lower voltage, 120 volts, is taken from one hot leg and the neutral (common) and serves the rest of the building for stage lighting, architectural lighting, small appliances, and outlets. Once again, in wiring the lower voltage **Branch circuits**, effort is made to equalize the loads from each of the hot legs.

Types of entrance wiring. In the order of complexity with simplest first:

Two-wire, single-phase circuit. One hot leg with a neutral (common) wire. This was the entrance wiring into homes in the first half of the twentieth century. It is now the normal branch circuit of a 120-volt circuit from a 208–240 volt circuit.

Three-wire, single-phase circuit. Two hot legs with a neutral (common) wire. A 110-volt potential exists between either of the hot legs and the neutral wire, and a 220-volt potential exists between the two hot legs. The neutral line is the same gauge as the other two lines but *must not be fused.* Trace the circuitry in the diagram, and it will be found that if a neutral wire is fused and if it should blow, all circuits would suddenly become 220 volts instead of 110 volts, resulting in burned-out equipment.

Four-wire, three-phase circuit. A circuit involving three hot legs and one neutral (common) wire serving all three lines. The potential between any hot leg and the neutral wire is 120 volts and that between any two hot legs is 208 volts. Three-phase services offer the greatest capacity for the lowest initial installation cost, and three-phase

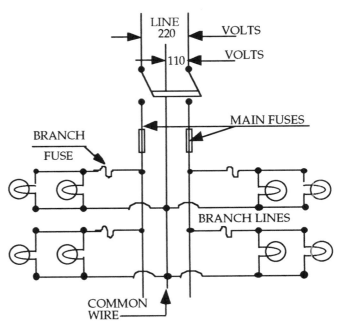

THREE-WIRE, SINGLE-PHASE CIRCUIT

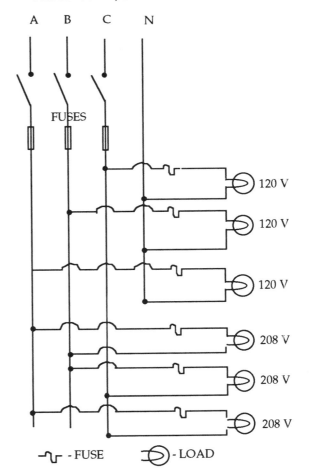

FOUR-WIRE, THREE-PHASE CIRCUIT

31

motors are both cheaper and smaller than single-phase motors of equal horsepower. The stage electrician should be aware that occasional installations using only 208 volts may omit the neutral wire in the service panel, thus making it appear to be a three-wire, single-phase circuit; this rarely happens with the COMPANY PATCH but should be checked with a VOM to be certain. A fuse is never placed on the neutral. Always use a voltmeter or WIGGY to check the voltage between wires before installing any equipment.

Other circuits

Branch circuit (branch line). The final electrical circuit protected by the lowest-amperage fuse or circuit breaker. Most branch lines are two-wire, single-phase. See illustration under **Three-wire, single-phase circuit.**

Hot circuit (open circuit, live wire, live circuit). An electrical circuit carrying a current. Be doubly careful to make certain that a circuit is turned off before plugging in lighting instruments, making any changes in wiring, or baring any insulated wire.

Parallel circuit. A circuit in which the current flows independently through each socket or outlet. For the most part, parallel circuits are used for GANGING lights in the theatre. (See **Series circuit** following.) Batteries wired in a parallel circuit (positives to positives and negatives to negatives) produce no change in voltage but an increase in the amperage equal to the sum total of the amperage of each battery in the circuit.

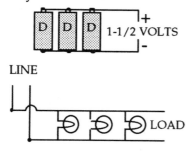

PARALLEL CIRCUITS

Series circuit. Equipment wired to form a part of the conductor (e.g., a series of lamp sockets with alternate binding posts connected so current must flow through each lamp in order to complete the circuit). Thus, in a 110-volt circuit wired in series with 10 lamps of equal wattage, the voltage

measured at each lamp would be 11 volts, and intensity would be lessened accordingly. The increasing popularity of low-voltage lamps has resulted in wiring these lamps in series instead of using TRANSFORMERS to reduce voltage. BRUTE lights and certain STRIPLIGHTS are examples. Switches, fuses, and most dimmers are placed in series with the lights they control. Batteries wired in a series circuit (positive to negative to positive, etc.) increase voltage to the sum total of the voltage of each battery but produce no change in the amperage.

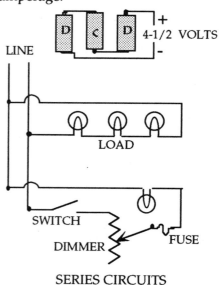

SERIES CIRCUITS

Short circuit. To complete an open circuit by a SHUNT of low resistance. Short-circuiting occurs when worn insulation allows bare wires to touch, when a cable is accidentally cut, when the wires of an open circuit are handled carelessly, etc. The results of a short circuit are usually blown fuses or tripped circuit breakers, but burned-out equipment can also occur, or if fuses of higher capacity than intended in the circuit are substituted, electrical fires may be started. Always try to determine the cause of a short circuit before replacing a fuse or resetting a breaker. Replace fuses with the correct size to protect the circuit. On rare occasions, fuses will blow as a result of fatigue for no apparent cause, but never assume this.

Three-way circuit. A circuit in which two switches control the same light or group of lights. Switches used in these circuits are known as three-way switches.

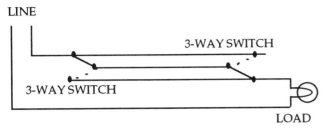

THREE-WAY SWITCH CIRCUIT

CIRCUIT TESTER. See CONTINUITY TESTER; MULTIMETER; NEON CIRCUIT TESTER; VOM; WIGGY.

CLAMPS. Devices designed to fasten things together or to fasten electrical instruments to pipes.

    Cable clamp. A small metal clip (NICOPRESS sleeve) used to hold cable or wire to a ceiling or wall. Usually used in permanent installations.

    C-clamp (pipe clamp). Used on lighting equipment to fasten equipment to pipe battens or standards.

    G-clamp (bar clamp [British usage]). Similar to the **C-clamp.**

    Sure clamp. Light batten clamp patented by J. R. Clancy.

    Wire rope clamp (clip, crosby, fist grip clip). A U-shaped bolt with a yoke designed to clamp wire rope or cables together.

    Yoke clamp (bridge clamp). A clamp made in two pieces to grip a pipe from two sides. Used to fasten spotlight to sidearms or hangers to pipe battens.

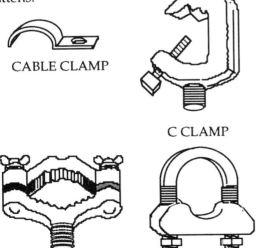

CABLE CLAMP

C CLAMP

YOKE CLAMP   WIRE ROPE CLAMP

CLEANUP CALL. A work call for the light crew, usually announced at a dress rehearsal and prompted by the need for further adjustments of lighting equipment, color, cues, or related problems.

CLEAR. See under COMPUTER LIGHT BOARD TERMINOLOGY.

CLEAR PLEASE (command verb). Warning that curtain is going up, crew is to leave the stage, and all personnel are to get ready for coming cues. Usually the next command is "places."

CLIP, TERMINAL (gator clip). Fastener with spring and jaws, used as a temporary electrical contact for a terminal. Also called ALLIGATOR CLIP.

GATOR CLIP

CLOUD EFFECTS. See PROJECTED SCENERY.

CLOUDS. Partial ceiling pieces suspended in auditoriums to help reflect sound. Clouds are often used to hide CATWALKS providing access to lighting instruments for FRONT OF THE HOUSE lighting.

CODE. Refers to city, state, or national building and electrical regulations for the installation of wiring and equipment. Often city codes differ from state and/or national codes. Check with local architects, contractors, or building authorities. See also FIRE CODE; NATIONAL ELECTRICAL CODE; NATIONAL UNDERWRITERS CODE.

COEFFICIENT OF REFLECTION. The proportion of light reflected off a given surface if lighted with white light. Similar to the term "value" for pigments. The following are examples of the reflective quality of various colors: white, 70%–90%; dark red, 10%–15%; dark blue, 3%–10%; dark green, 17%–20%; and black, 1%–5%.

COHERENT LIGHT. Light of the same wavelength, all waves being in phase and polarized. Lasers are coherent light. See LASER.

COLOR

    Light primaries. Red, blue, green.

    Light secondaries. Magenta, blue-green (cyan), yellow.

    Pigment primaries. Red, blue, and yellow.

    Pigment secondaries. Purple, green, orange.

    Warm colors. Red, yellow, and combinations.

    Cool colors. Blue, green, and combinations.

COLOR BEAM. Obsolete. Trade name for a colored reflector lamp from the 1950s.

COLOR CHANGERS. Mechanical methods of changing colors within or in front of instruments. See BOOMERANG; COLOR WHEEL; SCROLL COLOR CHANGER.

COLOR CODE

Cables. In multiple-conductor cables, each wire is given a different color insulation to simplify tracing circuits or wires.

Scenes. In multiple-scene shows SPIKE MARKS are often color-coded to a scene so that furniture may be placed on the proper spot for its scene.

COLOR COMPARISON. The following lists show colors from various manufacturers, going from light to dark and with generic names added. Only a few are identical matches. Since color definitions are dependent on the viewer's eyes, the chart is highly subjective. Because many of the colors listed actually have more red, blue, gray, or other color in them than the color name given next to them implies, this list is just a guide.

Color	GAM	Lee	Olesen	Roscolux	Roscolene	Cinemoid	Transmission percentage
No color straw				804			
Pale Straw	510	159			06		90%
		212	03		07	50	
		HT007	09				
Yellowing	470					40	
	460	HT010			10		
Lemon yellow	480	101			12		85%
			05				
			10		11	02	
	450	102	07	806			80%
			08	807 810 809			
Dark lemon							
No color amber	440	205			08		80%
	360						
					09	03	
Oranging	385	HT009					
		204					

Color	GAM	Lee	Olesen	Roscolene	Roscolux	Cinemoid	Transmission percentage
Light amber	343	147		811	18		70%
	375	134		813			
	335					33	
	350	105	18	815	21	05	50%
			19	817			
Dark amber	345	HT021					40%
Dark red amber	315				23		35%
Pale pink amber	363						85%
	364						
	365	103					80%
		206					
Gold	340	162			02		80%
		152		803	04		
	325	HT004	26		304	51	
	305	151				52	70%
		176	27	802	01		
Pale pink salmon				802			
Deep pink salmon					35		
No color pink	155			825	33		70%
		153	30				
	160					09	
	190		31	834	34	07	
	195			826			
Medium pink	260	157			31	57	50%
			33				
Bright pink					32	66	
Orange pink	320		27				45%
Orange red	290		21				30%
Red	280	164			19		
			24		25		
	270				26	06	
	245	106		821			
	250		25	823	27	14	10%
Dark Red							
Pale red magentas	105	110				10	60%
	130				36		
		002			44		
	110		38			11	25%

Color	GAM	Lee	Olesen	Roscolene	Roscolux	Cinemoid	Transmission percentage
Magenta	120						20%
	150	328		828	344		
					45	13	
			37	832	46		
Red Magenta	220	148					20%
				837			
		113					
Pale yellow green	520						85%
	540	138			87		
			67		88	38	
						21	
Medium yellow green	570			878			45%
Medium green	660	122			89		35%
		121				23	
	655		68		70	68	10%
					389		
			70	871		24	
	650	124	71	874			
		139				91	5%
Dark green							
Pale green blue	680						35%
	685				93		
			65				
Deep green blue	690	116			95	016	15%
				877			
Pale blue green			61				
	720						55%
			47	849		17	
	730	117					
					73	15	
	710						15%
	760					16	
Deep blue green							
Pale grayed blue	870						75%
	885						
	830	202					
	820				60		
Grayed blue	842				62	67	45%
Light blue	888						50%
		201					
	860						
	882						
Medium blue	848						
	847				78		
		132				32	
				862			
				862			
				863			
	850	119			83	19	5%
Continuing to Darker Blue	890	195	49		85		

Color	GAM	Lee	Olesen	Roscolene	Roscolux	Cinemoid	Transmission percentage
	905	120		866	383		
Very dark blue						20	1%
Pale red lavender	980				51		50%
						36	
	970	136	43	840			
		170			52		25%
					47		
					48		
				838			
	990			829		26	
					49		
Deep red lavender	995	126					5%
No color blue lavender	920				53		65%
					54		
						42	
	940	137		841	55		
		194			356		
	960						20%
				844	57	42	
			45		58		
		180					
Medium blue purple	948			843			
	945				56		2%
Deep blue purple	950						
Pale aqua	780				70		25%
				853	72		
	770				71		
	740	118					
		143					
Medium aqua	750	144	53				15%
		183					
Light blue blue green	815	196	54				
		161				61	
	840				64		
					67	41	20%
	810			851			
				856			
				859	68		
					81		
Medium blue blue green	835	132	48	857	80	32	5%
					79	63	
Chocolate			73	882			
	330				99	56	
		156					
		207					
		208					
Light grey	1514						65%
	1515	209					

COLOR CORRECTION. Color media and screens used to adjust the output of light to achieve changes in COLOR TEMPERATURE. Lee filter 204 changes daylight to 3,200 K; Lee filter 201 changes tungsten (3,200 K) to daylight (5,700 K). In addition to color correction there are filters which are used for other effects, such as reducing light transmission without changing color. GAM 1515 neutral density filter is one of the latter filters; it reduces light by 1 stop in a camera aperture.

COLOR FRAME (gel frame). Metal, specially treated cardboard, or wooden frames designed to hold color media in front of lighting units. Sizes vary according to manufacturers, but frames are often interchangeable from one manufacturer's equipment to that of another. Untreated cardboard is a fire hazard.

COLORINE. See LAMP DIP.

COLOR KEY CHART. A chart showing the chosen color scheme for a production, including the media, code number, and direction from which the color will come. See DESIGN FOR LIGHTING.

COLOR MEDIA (filter, gel, medium). Transparent material—gelatine, glass, or plastic—used to color a light beam. The earliest color media for theatre lighting consisted of bottles of colored water placed in front of candles or lamps. Later, colored silk was hung in front of the gas flame BORDER LIGHTS, and elaborate rollers were constructed to transfer silks of diferent colors from one roller to another, thus providing gradual color changes onstage. Present-day designers have three choices of color media: colored glass, gelatine, and plastic (acetates and polyesters). The choice of manufacturer is governed by many considerations. Color is obviously the prime reason for choice since not every brand has the same hues available. Heat resistance can be important depending on the type of instrument and lamp to be used. Dye stability can be a problem in some brands. Most often a designer will use colors and types of media from several manufacturers, with one brand being a slight favorite for most of their work. Sometimes these color media decisions are based on such simple facts as which supplier can get the order delivered overnight via UPS. The most common trade names for lighting color filters include GAM, by Great American Market; Lee Filters, by Lee; Dura by Olesen; Roscogel, Roscolene, and Roscolux, by Rosco Laboratories; Cinemoid, by Strand Corp. See Selected List of Manufacturers and Distributors in back of book.

Colored glass. This medium is fade proof and therefore the most durable. However, because it is somewhat fragile and available in a limited number of colors, it is the least used of the color media. Roundels are the most frequently seen glass filters found in BORDER LIGHTS and FOOTLIGHTS. Available colors are red, blue, green, amber, and a minimal selection of tints.

Strip glass. Thin sheets of very fragile colored glass cut in about 1" widths to allow for expansion from heat inherent in TUNGSTEN-HALOGEN LAMPS, used in BORDER LIGHTS, CYC LIGHTS, and FOOTLIGHTS. Available colors are red, blue, green, amber, and a minimal selection of tints. Not as readily available as gel and plastic but essential for certain high-intensity instruments that may generate enough heat to literally char or melt other media. Strip glass offers more color choices than roundels but considerably fewer than gel and plastic filters. Available through full-service supply houses.

Gelatine (gel) The cheapest form of color medium, made of animal or grain jelly mixed with synthetic dyes. It comes in almost 100 different colors and is cast in sheets approximately 20" x 24". Because gel fades rapidly (almost instantaneously in front of some high-intensity tungsten-halogen lamps), becomes brittle over a short period of time, and turns into a glob when wet, it is losing favor as a color medium.

Plastics. Plastics used as color media are usually polyester- or acetate-based plastics. Polyester is the newer color base and offers more heat resistance than acetate. Although more expensive than other colors (except glass), higher TRANSMISSION FACTORS, greater purity of color, and availability of new hues make polyester colors a favored choice for washes, cyc lights, and various other background lighting. It is important to note that even this heat-resistant medium is not as good as glass in close proximity to high-output lamps. Both acetate and polyester are strong, waterproof, and much more resistant to color fading than gelatine. However, despite claims, even polyester colors will fade and tend to warp with extended use. Pale colors and tints resist fade much longer than darker, saturated colors. Blues are notorious for fading and burning out quickly. Most manufacturers are very careful about color control, and for the most part, there is little variation between batch lots. However, be aware that the names of colors vary a great deal between different manufacturers. Thus "special lavender" will vary by several shades between Roscolene and Roscolux and may be completely different colors in Rosco and Lee filters.

Joining colors. Acetone may be used as a solvent to join two pieces of plastic media for special color effects. Avoid extended inhalation or skin contact with acetone; see SAFETY. Gelatine can be easily variegated by wetting one color with water and sticking it on a base color. Composite colors and VARIEGATED GEL both utilize the subtractive method of COLOR MIXING to vary the color. Available in 20" x 24" sheets as well as 24" x 50' rolls. See CINEMOID; GELATINE.

COLOR MIXING. Given proper control, any color in the spectrum may be made by mixing the primaries. Primary colors are those colors that cannot be made from other colors in the system but may be used together to make any other color within that system. Red, green, and blue are considered the colors fitting this definition for primaries of light, and red, yellow, and blue are considered the colors fitting the definition for the primaries of pigment. Technically, the wavelengths of the primaries do not coincide exactly with the generic names. In addition to the two sets of primary colors (one for light and one for pigment) there are two separate methods of mixing colors: the **Additive method**, which with proper mixing produces white light, and the **Subtractive method**, which with proper mixing blocks the passage of all light.

Additive method. Producing different colors by mixing the light beams of colored lights. If we could assume equal intensity and equal purity of color, a red light, green light, and blue light focused on a white surface would produce a white light. Under ideal conditions, varying the intensity of these three colors should produce any color of the spectrum, and in reality, a great variety of colors can be produced in this way. However, dimming cools the filament of the lamp, causing it to yellow and redden, thereby altering the expected color. In spite of these variations, the use of the three-color

system for toning, blending, and color control is common procedure, and variations are either compensated for or tolerated.

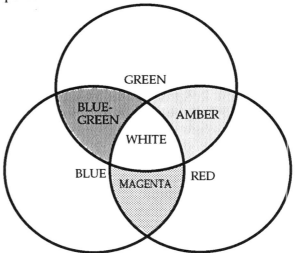

OVERLAPPING POOLS OF PRIMARY LIGHT COLORS
ADDITIVE MIXING

Subtractive method. With pigments, a certain color will absorb (or subtract) some colors from the spectrum and reflect others. When subtractive mixing is applied to color filters, each filter will allow its own color to pass through, subtracting the others. The results of overlapping filters of the primary colors (red, green, and blue) are shown in the diagram. Combining other color filters produces similar results. For example, when blue-green and pink are placed in the same color frame, the pink will cancel some of the green spectrum, making the blue-green a little bluer.

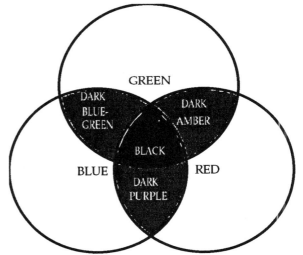

OVERLAPPING PRIMARY LIGHT COLOR SAMPLES
SUBTRACTIVE MIXING

COLOR SCHEMES

Colors for areas. Since the function of area spotlights is to light actors, colors are chosen which will allow a high degree of light transmission (see TRANSMISSION FACTOR). Colors suitable for area lighting include tints of pink, amber, straw, blue, lavender, gray, and chocolate. Darker shades of straw and amber tend to turn skin pigments yellow, giving a sickly appearance. As every fading actor and actress knows, the most flattering and youthful colors include pink, lavender, and light blue. Certain colors should be avoided for certain skin tones: blues for black skin, lemons for yellow skin, greens for white skin. The three-dimensional effect resulting from using warm colors in spotlights from one side of the stage and cool colors from the other side offers the lighting designer a wide choice of color combinations. Basically, TINTS will be used for better transmission of light, and extreme contrasts of colors will be avoided. The table below gives a few commonly used combinations, with code numbers as listed in six different color swatch books from five different manufacturers. Each company makes many HUES of color media; these are just a few examples. Each suggested combination is meant to cover each acting area with the warmer color from one side of the stage and the cooler color from the other.

Type of scene and color	GAM	Lee	Roscolene	Roscolux
Warm				
Flesh pink	190	110	834	34
Pale gold	305	151	803	04
Cool				
Light blue	740	118	850	71
Blue lav	940	137	841	58
Bright day				
Light pink	155	153	825	33
Pale straw	440	009	804	06
Day				
Red lav	970	136	840	52
Pale gold	152	305	803	02
Dark day				
Gray	1516	210	880	97
Chocolate	330	156	882	99

Color combinations for McCandless system of lighting. The following are combinations which produce reasonable results. Numbers are Roscolene code numbers.

Cool colors	Warm colors					
	802	804	805	825	826	842
842	E	G	G	E	E	Do not use
849	E	G	G	E	E	G
850	E	F	F	G	E	G
851	G	F	F	F	G	F
854	G	F	F	F	G	F

E = excellent, G = good, F = fair.

Border lights or blending colors. Pigments may either absorb or reflect colored light. They cannot add wavelengths to create new colors that are not there originally. The brilliance of a color is enhanced when seen under lights containing its own color. In other words, red colors reflect red light and absorb all other colors, blue colors reflect blue light and absorb all other colors, etc. For this reason the near white light made from primary, secondary, or dilute primary colors is preferred for stage use because scenery and costumes reflecting their own colors become much more vibrant and exciting than they would appear under a plain white incandescent light. See also BORDER LIGHTS.

Primary colors of light. Red, green, and blue in equal intensities will produce white light. However, perfect conditions for this are seldom found outside laboratories. Variables found onstage include impure colors, yellow inherent in the incandescent lamp, filaments reddening as lights are dimmed, and light loss due to the density of pure colors, up to 99% for urban blue, but varying with each color.

Primaries	GAM	Lee	Roscolene	Roscolux
Red	250	106	823	27
Green	655	139	874	91
Blue	850	119	866	80

Secondary colors. Magenta, blue-green, and amber are sometimes used in border lights, but because of the limited amount of red present in the secondaries, the spectral range of this combination is limited. The colors are nevertheless popular in front-of-the-house color washes.

Secondaries	GAM	Lee	Roscolene	Roscolux
Magenta	220	148	832	46
Blue-green	690	116	877	95
Amber	350	105	815	21

Dilute primary colors of light. Because of the high density and low light transmission of primary colors, many designers and technicians prefer to use the so-called dilute primaries, which allow much more light to reach the stage. Dilute primary colors include light red, medium green, and medium blue. Varying intensities of these three colors will produce a basic white as well as a wide spectral range of colors, making them useful as color washes from either overhead or the front of the house.

Dilutes	GAM	Lee	Roscolene	Roscolux
Light red	245	106	821	26
Medium green	655	121	871	70
Medium blue	850	119	863	83

Cyclorama lighting. Sky cycs are best lighted with enough hanging FLOODLIGHTS, BORDER LIGHTS, SCOOPS, or the newer CYC STRIPS to cover the cyc evenly in the colors appropriate for the production. Portable STRIPLIGHTS or floodlights on the floor are needed to provide HORIZON LIGHT. Using no color media on a sky cyc is likely to suggest a dull, uninteresting cloth background rather than the realistic sky intended. Colors should be provided, often in gradations from light on the horizon to darker blue from above. To provide sufficient change for full-color sky effects, lights on the floor and in the overhead position

should be in at least three, preferably four, circuits, one for each primary or dilute primary plus an extra circuit for blue since it has a lower transmission factor. If equipment is not available for three different circuits, or if the production calls for only one kind of sky, some choices for day and night skies are suggested in the chart below. The numbers in each line represent the same colors but the manufacturers do not always use the same generic names listed in the left column.

Sky type	GAM	Lee	Roscolene	Roscolux
Daylight sky				
Day blue	815	161	851	64
Steel blue	730	117	849	73
Night sky				
Urban blue	905	120	866	383
Moon blue	690	116	877	95

Colors for creating atmosphere. This is a very subjective area dealing with, for example, the colors found in different climatic zones. The play Mr. Roberts calls for the intense-sun effects found in the South Pacific at sea. One solution was to use three colors to give stark sun (#807), hot skin tones (#813), and the blue-green of the sea air (#854). The show was triple hung for the deck scenes. In other productions, hot, humid, tropical rain scenes worked well with double-hung colors: hot, damp skin tones (#815) and a blue-green quality to the air suggesting muggy sea air (#854). In the other extreme, for arctic cold, colors such as #855 for frigid air, white light for a bit of cold skin color, and a third color to set the mood of the play work well. The colors mentioned here are Roscolene colors; see lists under COLOR COMPARISON for approximations from other manufacturers.

COLOR SPECTRUM. The color spectrum is composed of various wavelengths of light from ultraviolet to infrared. Even though blue is a small portion of the visible spectrum, when the combined light from the lower third of the visible spectrum strikes the eye, we see the color blue. Similarly, when the combined light from the center

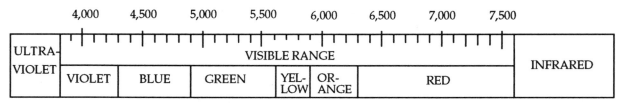

WAVELENGTH IN ANGSTROM UNITS
(ONE TEN-MILLIONTH OF A MILLIMETER)
COLOR SPECTRUM

third of the spectrum strikes the eye, we see green, and the combined light from the upper third registers as red. These three colors are the light primaries. Color media sample books often give the wavelength of each color in NANOMETERS (nm), equal to one billionth of a meter. The ANGSTROM, equal to one ten-billionth of a meter, has also been a common measurement for wavelengths.

COLOR SYMBOLISM

Black. Considered subdued, depressing, solemn, and profound. In Western society it signifies sorrow, gloom, and death. The fear of darkness (therefore black) has been associated with secrecy, terror, and evil since the beginning of time. If used carefully, particularly with white, black can achieve a very chic and smart formality.

Blue. A cool color considered serene, passive, tranquil, nonsensuous, expansive, and aristocratic. Often considered a spiritual color, blue does not seem to press in on us. Because of its atmospheric associations, blue can be cold and disembodied, evoking expanse, distance, and boundlessness. In church it can signify sincerity and hope. The elite, aware of the aloofness inherent in the color, developed the expressions of "blue-blooded," signifying aristocracy, and "true blue," meaning faithful or loyal.

Green. Considered soothing and suggests serenity, tranquility, and hope. The olive branch is a symbol of peace; the laurel wreath, a symbol of immortality. Compared with other colors, green is relatively neutral in its emotional effect, tending to be more passive than active. Derived from the Aryan word meaning "to grow," certain religions associate it with faith, immortality, and contemplation. At Easter green symbolizes the resurrection in the Christian religion. Pale green is the color of baptism. In common usage it can express freshness, raw callow youth, and immaturity. Despite its overall favorable symbolism, green is the most unflattering of all colors to the complexion.

Purple. Suggests pomp, royalty, and richness and is considered a soothing color. Purple combines many of the attributes symbolized by the red and blue from which it comes. Worth its weight in gold, purple dye was once made from a Mediterranean sea snail and used to color the robes of Roman emperors. Homer used purple to express death and sadness, and actors in theatrical performances of the Odyssey often wear the color to symbolize the sea-wanderings of Ulysses.

Red. A warm color with great emotional appeal and power of attraction. It is associated with passion, anarchy, classical art, rage, strife, danger, courage, virility, sex, defiance, and violence. Large expanses of red can produce mental fatigue and generate a longing for its complement, blue-green.

White. A positive, stimulating, luminous, airy, light, and delicate color. Purity, chastity, innocence, and truth, all come to mind with white, hence the symbol of the "White Knight." However, white is also the color of the flag of surrender. In China white is associated with mourning and bereavement.

Yellow. Considered masculine, splendid, radiant, cheerful, gay, lively, and vivid. A sacred hue in both Eastern and Western civilizations, where it is often used in the form of gold leaf. Darker or more neutral shades of yellow along with greenish tinges connote sickness, disease, indecency, cowardice, jealousy, envy, deceit, and treachery (yellow dog, yellow streak). In tenth-century France the doors of traitors and criminals were painted yellow. Judas Iscariot has been pictured clad in yellow clothing.

COLOR TEMPERATURE. The color of light as determined by temperature. Each color of the spectrum has a different wavelength. When metal is heated it emits energy; the hotter it becomes, the shorter the wavelength of energy. At a given temperature, the wavelength is visible as dull red, and as heating continues, the color progresses from a light red, through orange, and eventually to white, thus establishing a correlation between color (wavelength) and temperature. Because colors and temperatures vary with the metal tested, a hypothetical body with known incandescent qualities that can be mathematically computed was chosen by scientists to be a basis for comparison of color and temperature. This is known as the *standard blackbody* or *perfect radiator.* By heating the blackbody and using a spectrometer to measure the wavelengths of light, the precise color may be determined at any given temperature. To avoid confusion with other temperature measurements, scientists agreed to use the KELVIN SCALE for color measurements, and hence the temperatures of bodies emitting light are expressed in kelvins (no degree symbol is used with kelvin). Absolute zero is -273.15° Celsius, or 0 K (kelvin). Color temperatures are of critical importance to color photography and television, where faithful color reproduction depends upon the exact color content of the so-called white light the camera operator uses on the subject. Color temperatures are not as critical in theatre because the human eye is much more forgiving than the camera lens. However, there are certain facts that are of interest and use. Visible light begins at about 600 K. The normal temperature range of gas-filled spotlight lamps is between 2,750 and 3,100 K, and the normal range of tungsten-halogen lamps is between 3,000 and 3,400 K. The color of light at these temperatures is compared with the color of sunlight from 40 minutes to 1 hour after sunrise. Warm colors are within the 1,800–3,500 K range; temperatures above that are cool colors, progressing from the palest of blues at 3,500 K to the blue of a clear daylight sky at 28,000 K. In lamp catalogues, color temperatures are given for stage, studio, and TV lamps, and although it is not necessary to choose matching temperatures for all spotlights used in a given show, it will be discovered that certain color media will appear altered if temperatures of lamps vary too much. It will also be noted that when lights are dimmed, color temperatures drop, and the color of light becomes "warmer" (redder). There is, then, a kind of inverse relationship between color and temperature; the hotter the lamp, the cooler the color, and the cooler the lamp, the warmer the color. Also, color temperatures are of interest to the budget-minded; generally speaking, the higher the intensity of the lamp, the higher the color temperature and, therefore, the shorter the rated life of the lamp and the more susceptible the color filter to fading—just one more trade-off decision for the technician.

COLOR WASH

Front of the house (FOH). FOH ELLIPSOIDAL REFLECTOR SPOTLIGHTS equipped with color media and focused on the stage at a fairly flat angle provide color wash. The function of the color wash is twofold: to blend area lighting and to tone the setting and action with a color appropriate to the play. Dilute primary colors (light red, medium blue, and medium green, see charts under COLOR SCHEMES) are sometimes used to provide a wide variety of combinations that may fit the mood of many different scenes. For lighter, brighter shows, musicals, or presentationals, the secondary colors are sometimes used.

Onstage. FRESNEL LIGHTS, existing BORDERLIGHTS, or overhead SCOOPS may be used to provide upstage color washes. These should be carefully blended in with the FOH color washes to give a smooth effect from downstage to upstage.

COLOR WHEEL

Color media. An old form of BOOMERANG designed to fit into the color frame slots in the front of a spotlight and used for rapid changes of color. The function of the color wheel is largely assumed by built-in boomerangs found in most followspots made within the past forty years. Boomerangs are used primarily for musicals, opera, dance, ice shows, concerts, and extravaganzas. Miniature

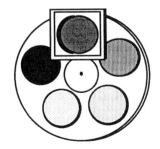

COLOR WHEEL ATTACHMENT
FOR SPOTLIGHT

color wheels, usually motorized, are sometimes found in certain brands of **Sweepers** (see under SPECIAL EFFECTS). The newest form of boomerang is the SCROLL COLOR CHANGER.

Color relationships. Diagrams used to represent the relationships between colors are also called color wheels. There are two color wheels, one based on the primary colors of light (red, green, and blue) and the other based on the primary colors of pigments (red, yellow, and blue). Three spotlights, each with a different primary color medium and focused on a single white surface, will produce an approximately white light. On the other hand, if those same three colors are placed in front of one spotlight, each color will allow the passage of only its own wavelength, thus resulting in a total blockage of light. See also COLOR MIXING.

COMPANIES. Very often ROAD SHOWS have more than one group on tour at a time; these are called companies. The groups may be referred to as the "A company," "B company," or sometimes the red or blue company. In conversation one might hear: "The A company of *Cats* had an interesting sound board using a joystick." See also BUS AND TRUCK.

COMPANY PATCH (transfer box). A panel backstage that allows a road show to patch into the permanent wiring circuits in a theatre and then terminates in remote areas such as the rail and booth positions. Recessed male PIN CONNECTORS in the company patch attach to the theatre's internal wiring and go to remote locations (see illustration). A standard male (LINE) to female

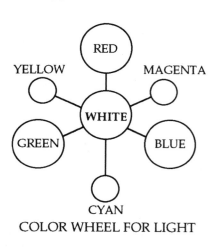

COLOR WHEEL FOR LIGHT

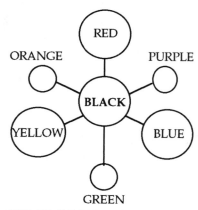

COLOR WHEEL FOR PIGMENTS

COMMAND. See under COMPUTER LIGHT BOARD TERMINOLOGY.

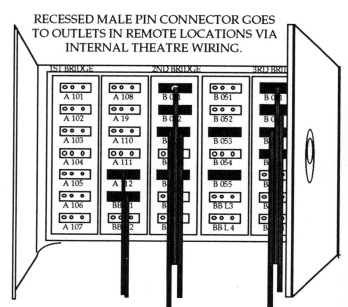

RECESSED MALE PIN CONNECTOR GOES TO OUTLETS IN REMOTE LOCATIONS VIA INTERNAL THEATRE WIRING.

FEMALE PIN CONNECTOR ON CABLE IS TEMPORARY WIRING GOING TO ROAD BOARD.

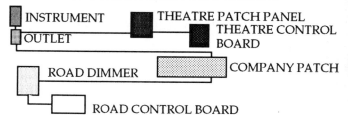

TEMPORARY WIRING CABLE WITH PIN CONNECTORS

COMPANY PATCH

(LOAD) pin connector CABLE connects the road show dimmer to the company patch. When not being used, a short JUMPER connects the company patch to the theatre's PATCH PANEL and DIMMER. Utilizing a company patch saves the touring company many hundreds of feet of cable runs plus many hours of set-in and strike time.

COMPANY SWITCH (company panel). Auxiliary electrical panel used as the power supply for portable dimmer hookups. An essential installation for theatres catering to road shows with their own lighting equipment. Electricity is available on large copper BUS BARS which are drilled and tapped to accommodate the BURNDYS attached to the ends of the FEEDERS. The doors enclosing the switch usually have electrical interlocks which allow the

bus bars to be energized only when the doors are closed, thus providing a DEAD FRONT situation. The company switch is usually located on the service side of the stage and provides three-phase alternating current ranging between 400 and 2,400 amps per LEG. See also **Four-wire, three-phase** under CIRCUIT.

COMPARTMENTALIZED LIGHTS. BORDER LIGHTS, FOOTLIGHTS, and STRIPLIGHTS designed with separate compartments for each lamp, thus maintaining color purity for the individual circuits. Each compartment is equipped with its own slot for color frames. First introduced in equipment catalogues ca. 1903.

COMPLEMENTARY COLORS. Opposite colors on the COLOR WHEEL. For example, on the light color wheel, complementary colors are red and cyan, blue and amber, magenta and green. With the ADDITIVE METHOD OF COLOR MIXTURE, complementary colors of light form white. With the SUBTRACTIVE METHOD OF COLOR MIXTURE on the pigment color wheel, complementary colors form black. See also COLOR SCHEMES.

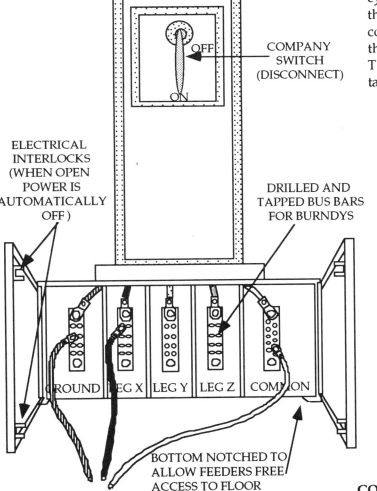

COMPANY SWITCH (DISCONNECT)

ELECTRICAL INTERLOCKS (WHEN OPEN POWER IS AUTOMATICALLY OFF)

DRILLED AND TAPPED BUS BARS FOR BURNDYS

GROUND LEG X LEG Y LEG Z COMMON

BOTTOM NOTCHED TO ALLOW FEEDERS FREE ACCESS TO FLOOR

COMPANY SWITCH

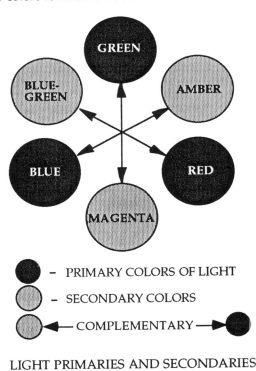

PRIMARY COLORS OF LIGHT

SECONDARY COLORS

COMPLEMENTARY

LIGHT PRIMARIES AND SECONDARIES

COMPLEMENTARY TINT SYSTEM. Another term for **McCandless formula** (see under PROSCENIUM STAGE LIGHTING).

COMPOSITION. Grouping of component parts to form a unified whole. It is the responsibility of the director to place props and actors on the stage in a manner appropriate to both the visual and practical aspects of the play, but since nothing is visible on that stage without light, the lighting designer is responsible for revealing, emphasizing, or subordinating anything and everything on the stage. For this reason, among others, close cooperation and mutual understanding of goals between director and lighting designer are essential. The final word is always the director's (except in opera, where the conductor's word is final).

COMPUTER-ASSISTED DESIGN (CAD). Computer drafting programs using "tools," as one would when drafting by hand, to make drawings to be outputted to a PLOTTER. CAD programs are designed for various groups: architects, engineers, cartographers, etc. The programs have a high accuracy potential and when combined with a plotter fairly large drawings can be outputted. One of the primary advantages of CAD is the ability to have data relating to the drawings (relational data base) stored within the program, allowing information concerning the drawing to be called up at will. Using a computer for drawing has many benefits, but perhaps the speed and the ability to change parts of a drawing easily are the greatest features. CAD programs can also produce drawings on various types of printers, enlarge or reduce accurately, and have precision that few drafters can equal. Special lighting programs are available in both IBM-PC and Macintosh formats. These programs show floor plan and section drawings and can automatically produce various schedules based on data and instruments used in the drawings. Rosco's Candlepower (Macintosh), Stagelights and Lightwright (PC), along with Heintz's MacLux and JCN's Argus (both Macintosh) are but a few of the programs available. Some of these programs are very sophisticated and expensive and may have all kinds of bells and whistles. They may output to printers or plotters, depending on the program.

COMPUTER BOARD (microprocessor). A lighting control system with a microprocessor at its heart, usually associated with memory systems. See CONTROL BOARDS AND CONSOLES.

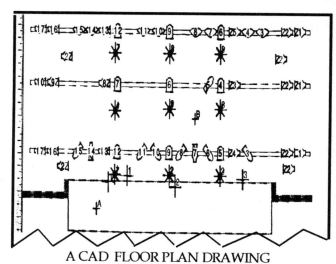

A CAD FLOOR PLAN DRAWING

CHANNEL HOOKUP SCHEDULE

CHAN.	DIM.	UNIT POSITION	INSTRUMENT TYPE	LAMP	PURPOSE	COLOR
		#1 2nd House pipe	Altman 6x9 ERS	500w	Front 3	
		#2 2nd House pipe	Altman 6x9 ERS	500w	Front 2	
		#3 2nd House pipe	Altman 6x9 ERS	500w	Front 1	
1	3	#3 1st House pipe	Altman 6x12 ERS	750w	Area 1 left	62
1	7	#7 1st House pipe	Altman 6x12 ERS	750w	Area 1 right	62
2	2	#2 1st House pipe	Altman 6x12 ERS	750w	Area 2 left	62
2	5	#5 1st House pipe	Altman 6x12 ERS	750w	Area 2 right	62
3	1	#1 1st House pipe	Altman 6x12 ERS	750w	Area 3 left	62
3	4	#4 1st House pipe	Altman 6x12 ERS	750w	Area 3 right	62
4	19	#15 1st Electric	Altman 6x9 ERS	750w	Area 4 right	62
4	21	#10 1st Electric	Altman 6x9 ERS	750w	Area 4 left	62
4	36	#5 3rd Electric	Altman 6x12 ERS	750w	Side 7 left	62
5	27	#2 Stage boom right 1	Altman 6x12 ERS	750w	Side 1 right	62

TYPICAL HOOKUP SHEET FROM CAD

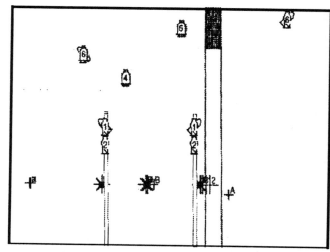

TYPE OF CAD SECTION DRAWING

THE 3 EXAMPLES ABOVE ARE ALL SCANNED FROM SIMPLE DRAWINGS GENERATED FROM A LIGHTING CAD PROGRAM (ARGUS)

COMPUTER LIGHT BOARD TERMINOLOGY.

It is noteworthy that the terminology differs from one brand of light board to another.

Backup. An auxiliary that allows a takeover (usually manual) in case the primary system malfunctions completely. On some systems the backup is actually another microprocessor separate from the primary control. The term is also used for making copies of data and saving them on floppy disks.

Blind recording. Programming a board without actually seeing the lighting on stage. Often used as a starting point and then modified during rehearsal.

Channel. An individual control unit. Often used to describe the size of a system, for example, 60 channels in use on a 120-channel system.

Clear. To erase a given unit of information.

Command. An order given by typing instructions on the keyboard or by hitting specific command keys on the keyboard.

Contactor. Remote, electromagnetically controlled switch.

Controller. Usually a small potentiometer used to control one or more groupings of dimmers, controllers, or channels. To some electricians, it means the control of dimmers. The word "dimmer" is sometimes incorrectly used for "controller."

Cross-fade. The process of simultaneously fading one cue out and another cue in.

Cross-fader. A device, often a dimmer, used to fade one cue out as a second cue fades in.

CRT (display, mimic, monitor, screen). An acronym for cathode ray tube, the screen used for TV and computer monitors.

Delay. Holding or stopping a cue movement to achieve a certain effect. A technique often performed by a split fader. This is necessary when an unexpected happening occurs and forces holding up a cue a few seconds.

Delete. Remove a given cue, group of cues, or parts within a cue.

Diagnostics. The ability of a computer board to self-test its many functions and controls.

Display (CRT, cathode ray tube, mimic, monitor, screen). A screen on which information is viewed; looks like a TV screen.

Fade profile (profile fade). The ability of some control boards or consoles to shape a fade up or down in a nonlinear manner. With this capability a designer may have fades that start slowly and speed up to a SLAM OUT, all done by preset and thus able to be duplicated for every performance. See **Real-time fades**.

Floppy disk (floppy). A magnetic record used to store and to retrieve data from a microprocessor board.

Glitch (surge). A power fluctuation that, in the case of computer or microprocessor lighting controls, may be the equivalent of a random command, causing control boards to act unpredictably. Using a line or surge filter will often help prevent glitches.

Headroom. The amount of space available for additional cues in memory. See also **Memory available**.

Highlighting (reverse video). The screen has white letters or symbols on a black background. The shaded area shows a particular piece of information on the display screen. Varies slightly with manufacturer.

Inserting. Adding additional cues within existing cues. See **Part**.

Keypad. A grouping of keys used to control computers. The keys have numbers and symbols on them.

Level wheel (rate wheel, wheel). A device that acts like a potentiometer with no stops. Used to raise or lower intensity of individual or groups of channels. Often used in prerecording or playback situations.

Library. A method of storing switchboard information on either floppy disks or tapes. Not all computer light boards have this capability.

Live recording. Setting up a viewed lighting situation on stage and then recording it. See also **Blind recording**.

Locked. A method of protecting a recorded cue from being wiped out or accidentally recorded over. A key switch is often used for this purpose. Floppy disks can also be locked so cues cannot be recorded over accidently.

Manual override. The ability to switch to manual control at any time during a cue or before a cue. A necessary feature of any automated board.

Memory available. The number of cues available for use or, depending upon the system, the number of cues already used. Sometimes this is referred to in percentage of memory rather than number of cues.

Memory limit. Some light control systems are equipped with an override feature that allows the operator to delete certain portions of the memory of a cue temporarily. This may be used, for example, to turn off one instrument that has been accidentally knocked out of focus.

Mode. An operational function to give certain commands or view displays. Patch, master, submaster, and record are considered modes of operation.

Multiplexing. Sending the control signals from computer to dimmers by one or two cables rather than over individual dimmer control wires.

Page (cue page, cue sheet). A series of cues shown on the display screen of a computer light board is referred to as a page.

Part. Adding different components within a cue. In nondigital devices, when cues or parts of cues are added, the method is cue 1, cue 1a, cue 1b, cue 1c, cue 2, etc.; with digital devices, it is cue 1, cue 1.1, cue 1.2, cue 2, etc. Within the framework of any one cue or part of a cue, any number of parts may be added, depending upon the system.

Patch at level. A feature of some electronic control systems making it possible to balance the intensity of a dim instrument and a bright instrument before entering their control into a single channel. This works only if a DIMMER PER CIRCUIT technology is in use.

Preset. A system by which one series of dimmers is assigned given light intensities for one scene while another series of dimmers is assigned different light intensities for the next scene. A single control can be used to **cross-fade** from one cue to the other. The term also refers to a type of computer light board; see PRESET BOARD.

Preview (previewing cues). A method of viewing past or present cues without actually changing existing intensities onstage at the moment; for example, when preset 5 is in progress onstage, the operator can view preset 3 to see what was wrong with that cue without changing the stage lighting at the moment.

Programmable patch. Electronic patching featured in some computer light boards allowing various dimmers to be patched to any control channel. See **Patch at level.**

Rate wheel. See **Level wheel.**

Real-time fades. The ability of a board to let an operator do a manually controlled fade, record it, and play it back within a production upon demand. The advantage of this capability is that not only the time but the nonlinear qualities of any fade or cross-fade can be stored.

Record. To store a given unit of information for future use.

Reverse video. See **Highlighting.**

Sequencing (sequence mode). A method of assigning cue numbers to faders. May be accomplished manually or automatically depending upon the system.

Split fader. Two submaster dimmers allowing simultaneous fading up of one cue and down of another at different speeds, even permitting a lag or hold in either cue.

Step. The moving from one part of a cue to another or from one cue to another. Often used to describe parts of a sequential cue; CHASERS use many steps as part of their sequencing. One might give a command, "Step the chase cue to make it flow forward and backward."

Symbols. Some typical symbols found on keyboards:

+   "Plus" or "and" symbol, e.g., channel 3 + 5 + 8 at (intensity, level of) 5.

@   "At," e.g., channel 70 @ (level of) 80.

F   Full intensity, e.g., channel 2 F.

*   "Execute." Command to do it now.

>   "Through," indicating a range, e.g., channels 3 > 8 at (level of) 5.

↑   Raise intensity level.

↓   Lower intensity level.

X C   Erase or clear.

Timed fade. A fade up or down at a predetermined speed set on the control board timer. Calibrated in both seconds and minutes, these timers are features of most computer boards. Timed fades can be programmed to happen within parts of a second or many seconds, some up to many minutes.

Tracking. The ability to add or remove instruments from cues as well as change intensity levels of instruments by changing one cue and commanding it to "track" through the rest of the cues. This can be a very useful feature when making emergency alterations in the middle of a show.

CONCAVE-CONVEX. A LENS used as a component part of a multi-element OBJECTIVE LENS.

CONCENTRATED FILAMENT. See **Filaments** under LAMPS.

CONCERT BORDER. Border lights mounted on the first electric pipe upstage of the proscenium. See BORDER LIGHTS; ELECTRICS.

CONCERT LIGHTING. Usually these productions are road shows featuring a star or lead group. These shows include rock groups, solo singers with backups, comedians, country western shows, gospel singers, evangelists, etc. Performances are located anywhere imaginable—from a cornfield in Iowa to an opera house in Spokane or a casino in Las Vegas. Lighting concerts for individual artists or groups has become a very specialized task. There are no prescribed or predetermined FORMULAS since the lighting is for effect and the only limit is in the mind of the designer.

Practice. Many of these shows are self-contained and use a TRUSS staging that holds large numbers of instruments and special effects. In overhead truss arrangements the lights are often carried within the truss in rough prefocus. With the instruments protected inside the truss and a very precise HANG, it is possible that only a touch-up focus will be necessary during the set-in. The lighting is usually from four sides, often with FOLLOW-SPOTS from the back of the truss and followspots from the BOOTH. PARcans are usually the instruments of choice, though they are seldom used as single units but rather as BANKS of lights. ELLIPSOIDALS are used for tight and close focusing or for the necessary FRAMING. If house units are used, they are usually general or wash lights. Often sweepers, strobes, and other SPECIAL EFFECTS are used. CYC LIGHTING is common, using both conventional COLOR WASHES and effects. GOBO projections are often used, adding not only effects but texturing as well.

Color. A wide variety of colors are used for concerts, including tints for facial colors on the star. Atmosphere is provided with BATTERIES of heavy color washes, both in primary and in secondary colors. Color comes from all sides and straight down. Some shows even have translucent floors lighted in color from below. See **Acrylic** under PLASTICS.

Control. The complexity of control necessary is usually directly related to the "name" of the star or group. It is always a matter of monies available, with the priorities being sound, lighting instruments, and then control. The big name shows have the latest in control equipment and enormous numbers of special effects and instruments. A show staged outdoors can easily have 1,000–1,500 instruments with 999 dimmers and miles of cable.

CONDENSER LENS. One or more lenses used to concentrate, or bring together, rays of light. Condenser lenses are used in projection equipment to concentrate an even distribution of light on slides. Because a single lens of short enough FOCAL LENGTH for this job is usually too thick to withstand the heat from the projector lamp, two lenses are generally required, and in the case of extreme heat, three condenser lenses may be necessary.

CONDUCTOR. A wire or bus bar used to transmit electricity. No material is a perfect conductor just as no material is a perfect insulator. The best electric conductors are silver, gold, copper, and aluminum. Obviously, silver and gold are too expensive for common use, and aluminum tends to become brittle over a period of time, hence the widespread use of copper. Water is also a good conductor, which accounts for the warnings against the use of wet electrical equipment or working with electrical equipment near water. The best nonconductors used for insulation include rubber, most plastics, glass, ceramics, and wood. See also INSULATOR; CABLE.

CONDUIT (thin wall, EMT). A lightweight, thin-walled metal pipe used to carry electric wires for permanent wiring. See EMT.

CONNECTION. A temporary electrical connection is made with electrical plugs that may be disconnected at any time. A permanent electrical connection may be made with a solderless connector or with the older method using splice, solder, and taping the joint.

CONNECTING STRIP. See RACEWAY.

CONNECTOR, PIN. See PIN CONNECTOR.

CONNECTOR (plug). Temporary connections of cables, instruments, and outlets. Several different styles are used on the stage. See PLUGS.

CONNECTOR, SOLDERLESS (wire nuts). Joining wires by twisting together and then using the solderless connector. The strands of wire should be twisted clockwise and the connector turned in the same direction and tightened like a nut by hand. Some connectors use a bolt or setscrew to tighten the wire. See BURNDY.

CONSOLE. Control center for lights, sound, etc. See CONTROL BOARDS AND CONSOLES.

CONTACTOR. An electromagnetically controlled relay often placed in a remote location so the noise it makes won't be distracting. The control switch is usually located in a convenient place for use by the proper person.

CONTINUITY TESTER. Any of a number of testing devices used to detect a break in a circuit. A simple continuity tester can be made with a battery and a buzzer, bell, or lamp. A more versatile combination of voltmeter, ammeter, and continuity tester is available at a reasonable price from radio supply and hardware stores. See also MULTIMETER; VOM; WIGGY.

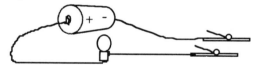

CONTINUITY TESTER

CONTROL BOARDS AND CONSOLES. A great variety of dimmers and configurations of controls used to vary intensities of stage lights. Four major categories of boards represent the evolution of light control during this century: switchboards, light boards, control boards, and consoles.

Switchboard. The oldest type of electrical control. Originally a group of KNIFE SWITCHES mounted on an insulator such as marble or asbestos board and known as "live front boards." Later the knife switches were enclosed to make a "dead front board" and resistance dimmers were added. In the last stage of development mechanical interlocking, mastering, and submastering were integrated into these units, but they were still commonly referred to as switchboards. Piano boards were the ultimate in this classification. See also DIMMERS; SWITCHBOARD.

Light board (board). Any kind of lighting control from knife switch to computer boards and everything in between. See also DIMMERS.

Control board (board). A remote control board, preset, or microprocessor that is not built into a piece of furniture. The remote control board is usually smaller and more portable than the console and generally is placed on a desk or table.

Console (board). A remote control light board, preset, or microprocessing device built into a desk unit.

CONTROL CIRCUIT (controller)

A circuit used to control another circuit or group of circuits.

A dimmer or potentiometer used to control a light.

A potentiometer used to control a dimmer.

CONTROLLER

Usually a small potentiometer used to control one or more groupings of dimmers, controllers, or channels.

The electrician who has control of the dimmers.

CONTROL ROOM (booth). Designated space for control boards, sound, and/or lights; on occasion, the stage manager's station as well.

CONVENIENCE OUTLET (duplex receptacle, handy box). The common household double-outlet wall receptacle, for 120-volt applications. Also called an Edison outlet. In homes, they are usually located every 12 feet or so.

CONVENIENCE OUTLET AND ADAPTOR

CONVEX LENS. See **Plano-convex lens** under LENSES.

COOL COLORS. Blues, greens, and combinations are considered cool colors. See under COLOR; COLOR SCHEMES.

CORD LOCKS. 1-inch wide strips of Velcro, fastened to one end of an electrical cable and used to tie the cable when coiled and to secure pin connectors to each other.

CORD TIES. Venetian blind or sash cord used to tie cables in a coil.

CORE. Soft iron bar or lamination forming the center of a TRANSFORMER or autotransformer dimmer.

CORE, SOLDER. See SOLDER.

COUNT. Time in seconds for the duration of a cue. When counted aloud, the two most common methods of maintaining consistency are to count "one thousand one, one thousand two" or "one chimpanzee, two chimpanzee," etc. A more acurate method is for the stage manager to hold a stopwatch and count aloud over the intercom.

COVE LIGHTS. Lighting instruments placed in vertical slots in the sidewall of the auditorium. A permanent installation in the BOX BOOM position. See PORTAL LIGHTS.

CRADLE

   Curved support used to help hold the center of flying electrical lines.

   Obsolete. A metal frame in first border position in which BABY SPOTS were mounted. This idea has been revived in the TRUSS concept, where spots are mounted in portable trusses, prefocused, transported, and set up as individual units for each show.

CRESSET. One of the earliest light sources known to be used in theatre. Records dating back to 1325 tell of using pine knots, pitch, oils, or resin-soaked rope as fuel to burn in the cresset when lighting the stage.

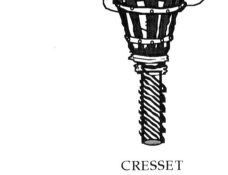

CRESSET

CROSS-FADE (command verb). The process of simultaneously fading one cue out as another cue is faded in.

CROSS-FADER. A dimming device used to fade one cue out as a second cue is faded in. See under COMPUTER LIGHT BOARD TERMINOLOGY; PRESET BOARD.

CROSSLIGHTING. Lighting from wing positions onstage or from the PORTAL or BOX POSITION in the proscenium. To keep the light intensity approximately the same across the stage, different-sized instruments are used, as shown in the illustration. See also **Sidelighting** under LIGHTING PRACTICE.

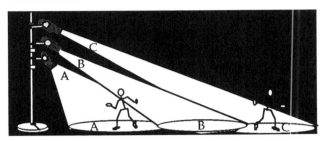

A - 4 1/2" ELLIPSOIDAL
B - 6" x 9" ELLIPSOIDAL
C - 6" x 12" ELLIPSOIDAL
ALTERNATE
A – 6" FRESNEL WIDE FOCUS
B – 6" FRESNEL MED. FOCUS
C – 8" FRESNEL NAR. FOCUS
BLEND CAREFULLY AND FOCUS LIGHTS HIGH
ENOUGH FOR THE LONG THROW ACROSS STAGE
CROSSLIGHTING

CROSSOVER PIPE (carpenter's pipe, cable pipe). A pipe and set of lines from the fly system dedicated to carrying lighting cables from one side of the stage to the other, used on road shows.

CROSS-SECTION DRAWING (section). A drawing made at right angles to the main axis of a three-dimensional object. Cross-section drawings are the only method of determining TRIM height for borders and light pipes prior to the set-in. See SIGHTLINE.

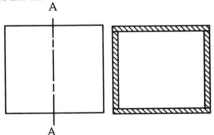

SECTION OF BOX THROUGH A-A

CRT. Cathode ray tube. See under COMPUTER LIGHT BOARD TERMINOLOGY.

CUE. All cues given during the course of a show are the responsibility of the stage manager. For the most part these are verbal cues given over an intercom system linking lights, sound, flies, orchestra, and any department involved in running the show. Cues are first given as warnings a predefined time ahead, and on the actual cue, the word "go" ("hit" is often used for FOLLOWSPOTS) is used to activate. For example, a sample cue to a followspot operator might be "Warning: followspot number 2; frame 3 (number 3 from front); head and shoulder spot on Billy's entrance down right." On the cue, 10–15 seconds later: "Followspot 2: Hit." Another example: "Warning: Cue 15, lights, sound, and carpenter"; 15–30 seconds later on cue: "Cue 15: Go." Another method of doing the latter cue, via cue lights, is to announce "Warning: Cue 15, lights, sound, and carpenter" (and then turn on the cue lights for the three departments). On cue 15–30 seconds later, turn off the cue lights and the cue will "go." One of the benefits of using cue lights is the ability to delay a part of a cue by simply turning off one or more lights after the others. See also **Part** under COMPUTER LIGHT BOARD TERMINOLOGY.

CUE CARD. Many electricians and technical directors consider cards (usually 3" x 5") an easier method of organizing the cue information. A common method of writing the card shows the cue number, dimmers involved, the direction of the move, the new numerical setting of the move, and the count for the move. See FOLLOWER.

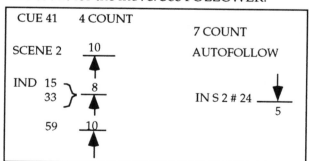

THIS IS CUE 41: THE FIRST PART, SCENE 2 MASTER GOES TO 10 IN 4 SECONDS, INDEPENDENT CONTROLLER 15 AND 33 UP TO 8 AND INDEPENDENT 59 UP TO 10 AT THE SAME TIME WITHIN THE 4 COUNT. UPON COMPLETION OF THE FIRST PART OF THE CUE, COUNT 7 SECONDS DELAY AND AS AN AUTOMATIC FOLLOWER IN SCENE 2 CONTROLLER 24 GOES DOWN TO A READING OF 5 ON A COUNT OF 5 WHICH IS THE DEFAULT COUNT IF NO COUNT IS GIVEN.

                       CUE CARD

CUE LIGHTS. A system of lights and switches with controls at the stage manager's station allowing him or her to signal cues to other members of the crew. A good cuing system will have two lights in parallel on a circuit at each workstation in case one burns out. The normal procedure is for the stage manager to give a vocal warning over the intercom system as he or she turns the cue light on, followed in 15–30 seconds by the "go" cue, which may be verbal or simply involve turning the cue light off. Red is often used for the electrician, green for the sound person, blue for carpenters, and orange for fly operators. See also CUE.

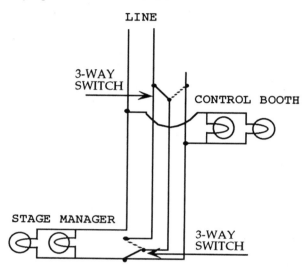

TWO-WAY CONTROL
SIGNAL LIGHT

Arsenic and Old Lace		Sht 7 of 20
Cue 38 on 7 count	Ind 15-4 Ind 33-6	
Cue 39 10 count	Scene 1-5	
Cue 40 15 count	Scene 1-out	
Cue 41 4 count	Scene 2-Full In Ind #15 & In Ind #59-Full Count 7 then Autofollower on 5 count in Scene 2	
Cue 41 A count	Scene 2-5	

CUE SHEET

CUE SHEET. Notations for stage manager, electrician, or sound person pertaining to light changes, sound cues, etc.

CUING SYSTEM. Often a combination of voice calls and lights. See CUE CARD; CUE LIGHTS.

CURRENT. The rate of flow of electricity, expressed in amps. See also AMPERE.

CURTAIN CALL (bows). The final audience approbation accorded performers at the end of their performance. In general, lights are brought to full intensity for the call, and if a curtain is used, those lights from the FRONT OF THE HOUSE striking the curtain in objectionable patterns should be dimmed out as the curtain is lowered and brought back up again when it rises. This probably will require at least one preset on the board and may easily be overlooked in rehearsals. Individual calls, beginning with lesser roles and progressing to the stars, often start with a center concentration of light and build to full-stage coverage at the final ensemble bow. Most productions requiring a followspot will take full advantage of its potential for focusing attention for the curtain call, especially when the principals come forward from the ensemble for their final applause. Some kinds of productions (ice shows, for example) develop traditional lighting patterns for curtain calls like the figure eight BALLYHOO from followspots.

CURTAIN GOING UP. Warning given by stage manager to actors and technicians that the scene is about to begin.

CURTAIN LINE

A line drawn on the stage floor marking the curtain location when closed.

A dashed line drawn on a light plot used with the CENTERLINE to give two points of reference for FOCUS measurements and the FOCUSING CLOTH.

CURTAINS. Draperies separating the stage from the auditorium. The HOUSE CURTAIN, or grand drape, is the permanently installed curtain for a given theatre. The house curtain may also be used as an ACT CURTAIN. A show curtain is specially made for a given production.

CUTOFF. Framing shutters in ELLIPSOIDAL REFLECTOR SPOTLIGHTS used to shape and size a light beam. See also DOUSER; **Barndoor** under LIGHT SPILL CONTROL; STRIP OUT.

CUTOFF, ELECTRICAL. A switch for one portion of a given circuit.

CYAN. A secondary color in lighting. A blue-green color; complement of red. See COLOR MIXING.

CYC (cyclorama). A surface used as a sky background or as a screen for projections of skylines, clouds, gobos, slides, motion pictures, etc. A cyc may be made of canvas, muslin, scrim, filled scrim, or plastic screen material (either front or rear projecting), or it can be a permanent installation made of plaster. It can be a fairly small drop representing sky outside a picture window, a flat drop like sky upstage, a modest C-shaped unit barely coming downstage, or a huge U-shaped unit coming almost downstage to the proscenium.

C-cyc (curved cyc, full cyc, surround a cyc). A cyclorama shaped somewhat like the letter "C" or "U" enclosing the acting area either partially or completely. May be used as a sky cyc or a projection cyc.

Linnebach cyc. Designed and invented in the early twentieth century by Adolphe Linnebach (1876–1963). Hung on a curved track and rolled on a cone at one side of the stage when not needed.

Plaster cyc. See PLASTER CYC.

Projection cyc. See PROJECTION SCREEN.

Roll cyc. A cloth backdrop which is sandwiched between wooden battens both top and bottom. To get it out of the way the cyc is rolled up on the bottom batten and tied to the top wood batten or to the pipe batten which supports all.

Sky cyc. An expanse of cloth, stretched on a four-sided frame. The most common colors for skys are light blue, white, and light gray. When lighted it can resemble the sky. See also Cyclorama Lighting under COLOR SCHEMES.

Straight cyc. The only difference from C-cyc above is that this sky representation is flat on a straight frame. A canvas, muslin, or scrim drop used for a sky backdrop.

Traveling cyc. A special background which rolls from a large holding spool on one side of the stage to the spool on the other side of the stage.

Trip cyc. A cyc which is tripped up to get it out of the way when not in use.

CYC LIGHTS (cyclorama lights). BORDER LIGHTS, FLOODLIGHTS, and STRIPLIGHTS used to illuminate the cyc. On some stages, floor lights are referred to as cyc foots. For use of color on cycloramas see **Cyclorama lighting** under COLOR SCHEMES. See also CYC STRIP.

CYCLORAMA DRAPES. The basic drapes surrounding the stage consisting of legs, borders, tabs, and backdrops (the last should not be confused with the sky cyc). Cyclorama drapes are often referred to by the color of the fabric (e.g., the blacks, the blues, the browns).

CYC STRIP. Trade name for Colortran striplight packaged in 1, 2, 3, 4, 6, or 9 compartments to each strip, designed to accommodate a variety of TUNGSTEN-HALOGEN LAMPS and intended for either overhead or horizon cyc lighting.

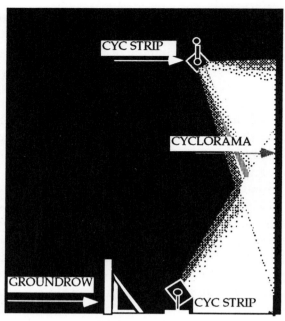

CYC LIGHTING

LEE COLORTRAN
3-UNIT CYC STRIPLIGHTS

D

DANCE FLOOR. A resilient surface made of a variety of materials designed to protect the dancer's limbs from injury. A floating floor is a wooden floor on flexible joists which allow some "give" beneath the feet. D'ANSER is a modular flooring system; HARLEQUIN is a roll-type floor covering.

DANCE THEATRE LIGHTING. Dance covers a variety of artistic performances from ethnic, folk, gymnastic, jazz, tap, and modern, to production, mime, martial arts, and dance entertainment. As with other forms of theatre, designers should rely on the particular type of dance program to determine their approach to lighting the production and the DESIGN FOR LIGHTING should be dictated by the choreography. Lights must enhance and complement the production rather than detract. Many of the standard basics of LIGHTING PRACTICE are used for this type of production. The stage setting for dance usually consists of a set of soft LEGS and a BACKDROP or CYC as well as a DANCE FLOOR designed and constructed for resiliency. It is possible to take advantage of reflective-surface floors to augment planned lighting, but as with BALLET LIGHTING, the designer must be aware of the possibility of reflected light spilling into unwanted areas.

Practice. Because of the fluidity of the dance, area lighting is not as predominant a concept as in other TYPES OF SHOWS. Every position in which a lighting instrument can be hung is a potential mounting position. SIDELIGHTS—hung on ELECTRICS, LADDERS, and TREES with SHIN BUSTERS on BOOMS—may be BEAM PROJECTORS, ELLIPSOIDAL REFLECTOR SPOTLIGHTS, FRESNELS, or PARcans depending on the degree of blending required. Follow the guidelines for ballet lighting for the choice of instruments and the placement of sidelights. Fairly high

intensity lights are preferred for backlighting, especially if they are to be used in part for toning. If saturated colors are planned, BANKS of lights may be needed to compensate for the lower light transmission. FOLLOWSPOTS are usually needed to focus attention on the principals, helping to separate leads from the ensemble. If projections or cyc colors are planned, followspots are best placed at steep angles to prevent background spill. It may also help to place followspots behind or to the side of the action where they may be used in SOFT FOCUS to better highlight the performer and call less attention to the lights themselves. Followspot operators need to be trained for difficult PICKUPS, fast moves, and instant tromboning in and out. If a CYCLORAMA is used for PROJECTED SCENERY, the PROJECTOR should be of sufficient size and intensity to fill the screen. If the background is to be sky, CYC LIGHTS will be needed for the overhead position. STRIPLIGHTS are needed on the floor, preferably in four circuits each, providing maximum color variation for the background. Projecting silhouettes onto a front-mounted screen or scrim from upstage spotlights can work for some sequences. Variations in lighting the dance are as limitless as the imagination, although moderation of any special effect is paramount. If fresnels, PARcans, and projections are to be used, be prepared to use LIGHT SPILL CONTROL devices to protect the cyc.

Color. Historically color for dance has been TINTS because of the chronic lack of money and equipment experienced by many companies. Usually, with the availability of more instruments and control, much bolder use of color becomes the rule. Toning colors are often used to set the overall mood of the dance, either from BORDER LIGHTS, sidelights, or COLOR WASHES, although if the latter are used from the FOH, they should be set at steeper angles than usual to avoid spilling onto the background. If equipment is available, it is a good idea to double the crosslights used from wing positions so that warm and cool color circuits may be included in each set of wing lights, offering greater variety and color control. POOLS of color and individual backlighting pools are popular in modern dance. See COLOR SCHEMES.

Control. Maximum control is desirable with dance lighting. In order to achieve effective lighting and maximum variety, separate color control of each side of the stage is essential—of course, DIMMER PER CIRCUIT is the ideal. Again, as with ballet, so much of the overall effect of dance lighting depends upon the board operator's precise execution and timing that it is necessary for the person calling cues to be thoroughly familiar with the music and movement and be very aware of the choreographer's interpretation and to allow a great deal of time for lighting rehearsals.

D'ANSER. A trade name for a modular dance flooring system which can be laid on any hard surface. This system is a floating floor and is available in 4' x 8' all-wood units.

DARK (dark house). A theatre with no show playing is said to be dark. A theatre may be dark for one night, for a week, or for an extended period between productions.

DAVIS BOARD. Obsolete. Trade name for a versatile, compact, portable, AUTOTRANSFORMER dimmer package operating six circuits from a single core and coil. Originally available as single packages or permanently mounted in units of either 6,000-watt or 12,000-watt capacities.

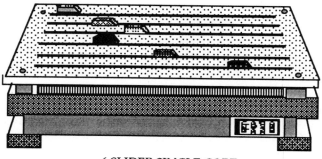

6 SLIDER SINGLE CORE
AUTOTRANSFORMER
DAVIS DIMMER

DC. Abbreviation for DIRECT CURRENT.

DEAD CIRCUIT. A circuit with no current flowing in it. Make certain all circuits are dead before changing lamps or plugs or adding loads.

DEAD FOCUS (bouncing bars [British usage]). Focusing a spotlight mounted on a pipe batten while still at floor level. The procedure is to bring in the light batten to the DECK and rough aim the spotlight, return the batten to show position, and check the focus. The process is repeated until the correct focus is achieved. An experienced lighting person will be able to make a fair approximation of the true setting by dead focusing. However, if very precise focus is essential, it is much faster to use a ladder. During the initial HANG it is helpful to roughly aim the lights to minimize ladder-work later.

DEAD FRONT. Said of a switchboard or electrical panel having no exposed wires or parts carrying a current. Codes require all electrical control boards to be dead front. Early makers of LIVE FRONT switchboards were casually careless about such precautions until they learned the true dangers of dealing with such potential disasters.

DEAD HUNG (deaded off). Tied off to the grid and therefore not part of the working fly system. On occasion, it becomes advisable to dead hang certain lighting equipment to make certain its position will not be disturbed during the show or to free a set of lines for other purposes.

DEAD SPOT. Improperly lighted acting area that is not as bright as other areas. Refocus key lights on that area or check equipment for alignment that may have been altered during relamping. See ALIGNING INSTRUMENTS.

DECK. The stage floor. A term owing its origin to early days of theatre when unemployed sailors helped with the rigging of theatres and left a rich legacy of techniques as well as language.

DELAY. Holding or stopping a cue in progress for a prescribed effect. This process often involves the use of SPLIT FADERS. See also under COMPUTER LIGHT BOARD TERMINOLOGY.

DESIGN FOR LIGHTING. Designing lights for the theatre is as much a part of the production as designing scenery; indeed, many scene designers insist on designing their own lights and costumes, in order to establish unity in the overall production. The lighting designer becomes part of a team working to produce an integrated whole, following outlines predetermined at PRODUCTION CONFERENCES. Among professionals, academicians, and semiprofessionals, there are many differences of opinion in the approach to both design and lighting problems. WASH AND KEY, McCandless, Watson, and 90° FORMULA methods work reasonably well at the university level or for the semiprofessional. The professional often scoffs at such simplistic methods and prefers a more inventive approach, more tailored to the given production. Sometimes the journeyman is contemptuous of the apprentice. Design is a process in which the professional, semiprofessional, and academician can dictate their own methods and organizational approaches. What they must have in common is a knowledge of FUNCTIONS OF LIGHTING and LIGHTING PRACTICE.

Challenge is a necessary concept to the designer, either for the first design or for the four hundred and first design. The designer must be committed to making the best possible design within the limitations of budget, equipment, time, and knowledge.

Analyze the information to ensure both the realistic appraisal of the problems likely to be encountered and practical solutions to those problems. Discussions with the director and other design team participants are an absolute requisite and should come early and often in the lighting designer's involvement with the production so that facts shaping essential concepts and ideas will be clear.

Script/book study. Read the script for the first time through for the story. This will give feelings for characters, emotion, and plot. During the second read-through of the script, jot down notes on some of the particulars. At this time it is necessary to check the progress of the set design so that the setting concept will be firmly in mind for the third reading. If music is involved in the production, playing the recordings during the study and drafting periods may help provide mood and atmosphere. During the third reading look for specifics necessary to the lighting plan in relation to the confines of the set. Look for motivated cues and gimmick lighting, and start thinking of color, angles, hanging positions, and the need for light versus dark. There should be a systematic analysis of the play with a page by page listing of pertinent information such as the scene, location, time of day, time of year, action, light cues, emphasis cues, and special effects. This information should be discussed with the director in production conferences. All of this information should be shared with the director and other team members so that the concepts may be kept within the limitations of the budget, allotted time, and expertise.

Research and knowledge are the keys to problem solving. A constant mental review of questions and answers is necessary for clear understanding. Be aware of your personal limitations and try to expand beyond them. Historical research includes locale, time period, and ambience of the period. In some cases the researcher may look at past productions but this can be fraught with pitfalls because, not only do directors have different script interpretations, but most shows are designed for specific theatres with particular idiosyncrasies. In conjunction with the production team, look for appropriate color, line, form, sets, costumes, and goals. Think also of the impact that other aspects of the play might have on lighting: special movement, dance, music. Decide on color. The true test of good lighting is not the repeated use of one formula but rather the use of light best suited to the production.

Time for thought is necessary to allow ideas, concepts, and research to gel. This is actually an ongoing process with all phases of the design development. Often a difficult problem can be solved by "sleeping on it." Always keep paper and pencil available because ideas and solutions come at strange times.

Presentation allows the designer to give the proposed results of the previous five steps to the production and design team. The presentation can be formal or informal. It is often advisable to show preliminary sketches and concepts in an informal environment before the formal presentation. Because of distance, many professional designers have telephone conferences before flying to the formal presentation. Communicating by phone has its difficulties, however. After approval, the design is ready for the full list and schedule development.

The light plot. The light plot may be defined as the lighting designer's scaled plan of the stage and set showing types of instruments, positioning, circuiting, color media, wattage, areas to be covered, plus the myriad related material concerning the lighting scheme. This material may be presented in scaled PLANS, scaled SECTION DRAWINGS, written schedules, or, most often, in all three forms.

Begin with doodling. Drawings can begin with pencil scratches. First, lay out the rough acting areas from the proscenium line upstage and then areas requiring additional lighting. Using PHOTOMETRIC CHARTS or personal knowledge, figure the probable lighting instruments, sizes, configurations, and positions beginning with the major acting areas.

Drafting the plot. Convert the rough sketches to scale drawings from the scene designer's approved designs. This lighting designer's floor plan will contain most of the necessary information for sections, areas, angles, instruments, mounting positions, circuits, dimmers, focus, and color. Next draw the LAYERING (additional lighting for color, time, or mood shifts). Sections showing trim heights and elevation sightlines, although giving less information than the plans, are nonetheless essential. These drawings must be clear enough for the director to understand and the crew to use for hanging the show. In training for either university or professional work, the use of USITT GRAPHIC STANDARDS is a requisite. These standards cover such things as lettering, title block, symbols, legends, instrument notations, templates, line weights, and drafting protocols. Even with the protocols, there are individual alternatives, such as two ways of drawing boom lights and pipe lights. Both are used professionally and there seems to be no clear-cut preference.

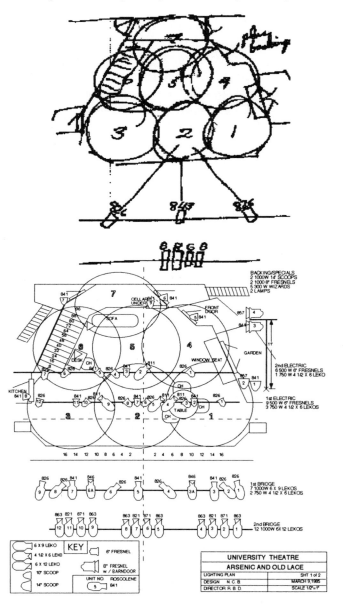

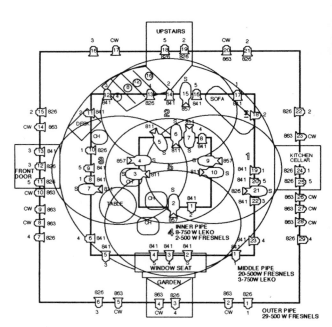

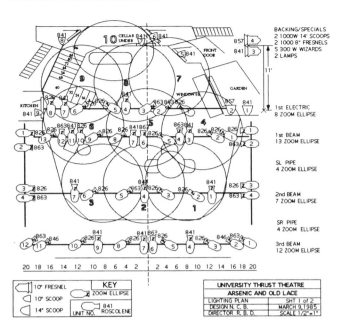

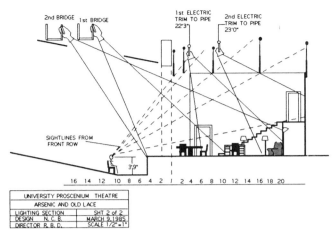

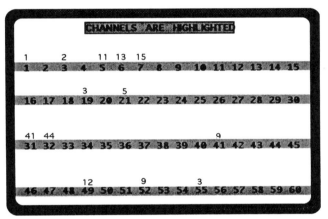

KEY	UNIVERSITY THRUST THEATRE

TYPICAL OF A SCREEN READOUT FROM A COMPUTER SOFTPATCH

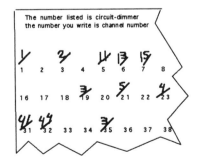

CHECKOFF SHEET FOR A HARD PATCH

Making up schedules and lists. University and professional designers deal with dozens of instruments, large numbers of circuits, and vast numbers of dimmers as well as set-ins, rehearsals, and per-

formances. The professional also deals with shop lists and rentals. Both designers prepare individual "cheat sheets," or schedules, to help keep everything straight. The cheat sheet has a totally different meaning for each lighting designer, and there are no apparent standards at this time for naming these schedules. It does not help at all that the terms "cheat sheet" and "magic sheet" can be interchangeable, though cheat sheets and schedules tend to be more alike whereas magic sheet and color and lighting keys more often than not are the same. This can be a very confusing subject for the lighting student and usually they do what their instructors do. The method providing the most instant access to information for each individual is the system to adopt. The light plot is based on information gathered and recorded under the following categories:

Patch sheets. Since the computer has invaded the lighting field, these sheets must now be separated into two distinct types: (1) **Hard patching**—Traditional listings of circuits being plugged into dimmers. (2) **Soft patching**—On computer dimmer boards using the DIMMER PER CIRCUIT system, the keypad can patch instruments to channels and the CRT shows what is electronically connected.

Cheat sheets. The name given to lists or schedules the lighting designer makes to provide rapid access to information for rehearsals. (1) **Instrument schedules** are lists with unit number, instrument type, wattage, size, mounting position, area of focus, circuit and dimmer plugged into, color, etc. (2) **Hookup sheets** (switchboard hookup) list the dimmer (switch) number, unit

1	X AREA 1	FL. PINK		36	L06	BACKINGS	FRONT DOOR
2	X 2			37	L07		CELLAR
3	X 3			38	L08		UP LEFT
4	X 4			39	L09		UR RIGHT
5	X 5			40	L10	FRONT COLOR WASH	RED
6	X 6			41	L11	" " "	BLUE
7	X 7			42	L12	" " "	GREEN
8	X8			43	L13	" " "	BLUE
9	X	CURTAIN WARMERS		44	L14		
10	X0			45	L15	GARDEN	SCOOP BLUE
11	X AREA X	60 LAV		46	X	"	LAV

CONTROL CHANNEL SHEET

POSITION	1ST	BRIDGE	
#	COLOR	SIZE	COMPLETE
6	826	7½ x 7½	AB
2	846	6½ x 6½	AB
3	841	7½ x 7½	AB
	2ND	BRIDGE	
6	863	7½ x 7½	OK...
3	821		all...

COLOR MEDIA CUT LIST

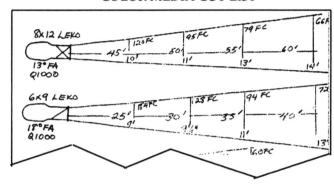

INSTRUMENT DATA SHEET

Number On Hand	Inventory Number	Size	Use
	12	3 3/4 x 3 3/4	3" FRESNELS
	36	4" x 4	3 1/2 x 4 LEKO
(5)	48	6 1/2 x 6 1/2	6 x 6 LEKO
(9)	36	7 1/2 x 7 1/2	6 x 9 LEKO
(15)	60	6 1/2 x 6 1/2	6" FRESNEL
	12	6 1/2 x 6 1/2	

COLOR FRAME LIST

FOCUS SHEET	J.C. SUPERSTAR	COLOR
Switch/Unit	No. 1 TORM LEFT	
12/1	COOL X WASH LEFT TO RIGHT	863
	MASK OUT OF PIT/OFF TEASER LIT LIGHT IN 1	
39/2	WARM X LEFT TO RIGHT	826
	MASK OUT OF PIT/OFF TEASER SLIT IN 1	
43/3	COOL SLASH RIM LIGHT	851
	US TO O SL TO 12 OFF #1 BORDER & LEG	
14/4	COOL SLASH SIDELIGHT	851
	US TO 4 SL TO 12 OFF #1 BORDER & LEG	
17/		

FOCUS SHEET

TYPICAL EXAMPLES OF CHEAT SHEETS

number, mounting position, usage or focus, colors, and instrument type. (3) **Checkoff sheets** are used to keep track of equipment used such as instruments, cables, etc. Keep clutter to a minimum.

Focus charts or sheets. A precise record of the focus and the area covered by each lighting instrument in a production. The focus chart is crucial to the success of any production that changes theatres or is scheduled to tour, but it is also essential that a record be kept for relamping and in case refocusing is required after an accidental bumping during the show. The form used for the focus chart is variable and largely determined by the lighting designer. Historically this sheet provides the switch number, instrument number, detailed focus notes including hard or soft focus, and color. When used with a ROAD SHOW, this information is often supplemented by a FOCUSING CLOTH and a BATTEN TAPE.

Magic sheets. Designers seem to have their favorite formats for getting fast information to help them set cues. Graphics are more easily read than lists, especially in the semidarkness of auditoriums during rehearsals. (1) **Lighting key**—Narrow and wide felt tip pens in colors similar to those used in the instruments and a simplified floor plan with the colored arrows showing the direction from which the light is coming offer the potential for instant recognition. Usually the graphics will show added information such as color manufacturer, color number, channel number, and any other information the designer thinks helpful. (2) **Color key**—A diagram of one or more areas indicating the designer's chosen colors and the directions from which each color will come. Colors will be indicated by the manufacturers' code numbers and directions will be shown by arrows and named locations (1st pipe, balcony rail, 2d beam, etc.). A simple color scheme such as the basic

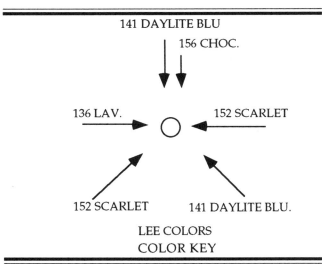

LEE COLORS
COLOR KEY

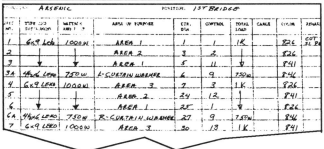

INSTRUMENT SCHEDULE

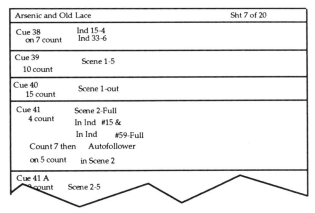

CUE SHEET

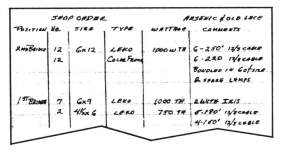

SHOP ORDER

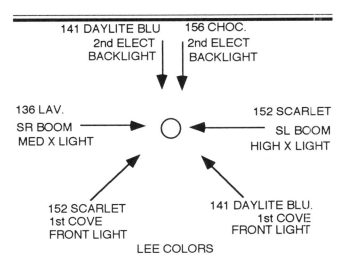

LEE COLORS
LIGHTING KEY

McCandless method certainly will not need a color key chart, but as plots become more complicated and have more layering, the chart will not only explain the scheme to those involved but will also serve as a reference for the designer.

Cue sheet. Before dress rehearsals, the lighting designer, stage manager, and director will get together to rough out cues. To do this they will sometimes use what is known in the movie industry as "storyboarding," which shows lighting changes with thumbnail sketches. Preliminary cues will be used until rehearsal, at which time actual cues will be recorded. The manner in which rehearsals are run is variable and depends on the producer, director, type of show, the organization, the theatre, or the most dominant personality.

Shop order. A list of equipment used for the rental agency, broken down by mounting positions and including all instruments, hardware, lamps, colors, cable, and accessories for the entire show. If the designer is lucky, a staff master electrician will do the shop order based on the light plot; otherwise it is the designer's job. Not applicable for theatres with their own equipment. See ARENA STAGE LIGHTING; BALLET LIGHTING; CONCERT LIGHTING; DANCE THEATRE LIGHTING; FORMULA; ICE SHOW LIGHTING; LIGHTING PRACTICE; MUSICAL LIGHTING; OPERA LIGHTING; PROSCENIUM STAGE LIGHTING; THRUST STAGE LIGHTING.

DEUCE. A professional colloquialism for a 2,000-watt spotlight.

DIAZO (blackline, blueline, ammonia process). A method of reproducing drawings by passing UV light through a drawing on a translucent sheet to photosensitive paper that is then developed by ammonia fumes.

DICHROIC FILTER. A mirror coated with alternate layers of materials of high and low refractive index, designed to reflect only desired wavelengths of light. A cold mirror reflects only visible rays of the spectrum, allowing heat rays (infrared) to pass through the glass. Conversely, hot mirrors allow visible rays to pass through the glass and reflect only the heat rays. By selectively stripping out wavelengths, dichroic filtration can produce pure color with a higher transmission factor than conventional color media. Theatre use of dichroics is gaining acceptance but because of high costs they were largely confined to heat filtration for certain projection lamps and other high-intensity lamps.

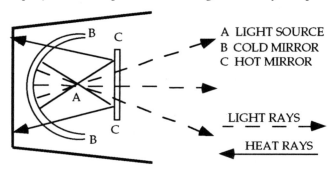

A LIGHT SOURCE
B COLD MIRROR
C HOT MIRROR

LIGHT RAYS

HEAT RAYS

DICHROIC FILTER

DIELECTRIC. A nonconducting material or insulator.

DIELECTRIC STRENGTH. A measure of a nonconductor's ability to withstand the passage of electricity as expressed in VOLTS or kilovolts per unit of thickness. It represents the maximum voltage that may be applied to an insulating material before a breakdown occurs.

DIFFUSED LIGHT. Light spread over a wide area. Shadowless or nearly shadowless light such as that produced by footlights, border lights, floods, or by frost color media, frosted glass, or other media used to disperse concentrations of light. Frost color media are used in spotlights and floodlights to provide a more even coverage with softer, less intense light. See also **Star frost** under FROST.

DIFFUSION FILTER. A filter designed to soften, diffuse, or scatter light rays from an INSTRUMENT. Usually this type of COLOR MEDIA is placed in the COLOR FRAME slot. FROST gel is one example of a diffusion filter. Several manufacturers of color media have a large number of different filters offering various degrees of diffusion.

DIGITAL-TO-ANALOG CONNECTOR. A plug on a computer light board that allows a digital signal in the computer to control analog dimmers.

DILUTE PRIMARIES. Light red, light green, and light blue are often used as toning colors in preference to the more saturated PRIMARY COLORS. By mixing and varying the intensities of both the primary and dilute primary colors, a large variety of toning colors can be produced. Since dilute primaries are less saturated than the primaries and allow much more light to reach the stage, many lighting designers prefer to use dilutes.

DILUTES. See TINT.

DIM (noun). A lighting setup of low intensity.

DIM (dim up, dim down, dim out) (command verb). To increase or decrease intensity of stage lights by means of a DIMMER.

DIMENSIONS ON DRAWINGS. Any drawings pertaining to locations and positioning of lighting instruments should be drawn to scale and sufficiently detailed to ensure proper fitting and positioning before and during the set-in. See DESIGN FOR LIGHTING.

DIMMERS. Any of a number of devices controlling intensities of stage lights. The most widely used electrical theatre dimmers were the resistance dimmers in the late nineteenth century, the autotransformers in the middle of the twentieth century, and progressing through a series of thyratron tube and saturable core dimmers to the present silicon controlled rectifiers. Following is a listing of common classifications; see under individual headings.

AUTOTRANSFORMER. A single-core, single-coil variable-voltage transformer.

INDUCTANCE DIMMER. Obsolete. A rotor stator dimmer.

INSULATED-GATE BIPOLAR TRANSISTOR DIMMER. A digital processing dimmer using reverse phase control.

MAGNETIC AMPLIFIER. Obsolete. A saturable core dimmer.

REACTANCE DIMMER. Obsolete. A dimmer consisting of transformer-type windings placed in series with the lamp and equipped with a movable, laminated core.

RESISTANCE DIMMER. Obsolete. A dimmer that introduced a controlled amount of resistance to the circuit.

SALTWATER DIMMER. Obsolete. A crude, "controlled classroom experiment" substitute for a resistance dimmer.

SATURABLE CORE DIMMER. Obsolete. Primary and secondary coils with a control coil in the center.

SILICON CONTROLLED RECTIFIER (SCR). A dimmer controlled by back-to-back rectifiers.

THYRATRON TUBE DIMMER. Obsolete. A "tube"-type dimmer.

DIMMERS, MASTER. Any of a number of devices used to GANG a group of dimmers to a single control.

Group master (submaster). Controls a grouping of dimmers, switches, or controllers.

Bank master. Controls a BANK.

Scene master. Controls a preset scene.

Grand master. Controls all individual dimmers or switches on the board.

Electrical master. Either a high-capacity dimmer (AUTOTRANSFORMER or electronic) placed in series with the individual dimmers on the board as a direct control of the load, or a smaller autotransformer placed in series with the low-voltage control of electronic dimmers. The latter is preferred because of compactness and versatility. With electrical mastering, individual dimmers should be provided with three-way switches for off, independent, and master positions so that any dimmer can be switched to the master control at any time. Because of the variable load demand placed on the master dimmer, resistance dimmers cannot be used as masters. When lights are dimmed up or down with the electrical master, the same intensity ratio of all stage lights is maintained in what is called PROPORTIONAL DIMMING.

Mechanical master. A large single lever controlling many dimmers that may be locked into a slotted shaft or may use a slip-clutch. This conventional method of mechanically mastering switchboards mounts all dimmer handles on a single slotted shaft. Individual dimmer handles can then be released to engage in the shaft slot as it is rotated into position by a controlling lever or geared wheel. Some boards are equipped with a grand master that will interlock all **Bank masters.** In any case, dimmers in the "full up" position start the dim-out first, and other dimmers "snap in" the slot as it reaches their individual readings on the way down to "out." The initial balance of light intensities is completely destroyed during this dimming process. Electric or electronic mastering provides the proportional dimming necessary to maintain intensity balance.

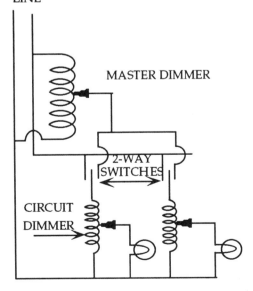

ELECTRICAL MASTER

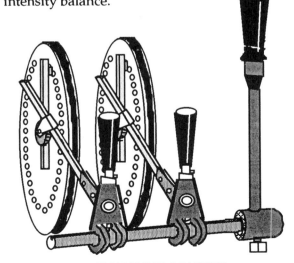

MECHANICAL MASTER

DIMMER CURVE. Calibration of a dimmer by light intensity rather than by voltage or by an arbitrary 1 to 10 scale. See also LAW OF SQUARES.

DIMMER PER CIRCUIT. Each stage lighting circuit is wired directly into a dimmer. Thanks to the computer-assisted lighting controls available today, this system is probably the most efficient distribution system available. However, before modern electronic controls, the dimmer per circuit concept was an unwieldy, inefficient system requiring several electricians and a master mind to assign dimmers to the vast number of locations involved.

DIMMING, PROPORTIONAL. See PROPORTIONAL DIMMING; see also **Electrical master** under DIMMERS, MASTER.

DIP, COLOR (colorine, lamp dip). A lacquer used to color low-wattage lamps. See LAMP DIP.

DIP IN INTENSITY. Involuntary lowering of intensity of stage lights. Many electronic dimmers show a slight dip in intensity or dimming while fading from one scene to another. The cause can be either in the fader itself or in the POTENTIOMETERS (pots) controlling individual dimmers. Mass-produced pots are not always perfectly linear and may not match, resulting in a dip in intensity on a scene-to-scene fade, even though dimmers are set at the same readings. Mismatches on dimmer intensities seem to be more noticeable on the lower half of the dimming scale.

DIRECT BEAM (DB). See **Direct beam** and **Linnebach projector** under PROJECTORS.

DIRECT CURRENT (abbr. DC). Current that flows in one direction, from positive to negative, in contrast to alternating current (AC), which reverses direction. For information on both AC and DC, see ALTERNATING CURRENT.

DISCONNECT (kill). To throw a breaker or switch in a COMPANY SWITCH or other equipment to the "off" position.

DISK (floppy). See FLOPPY DISK.

DISPLAY. See under COMPUTER LIGHT BOARD TERMINOLOGY.

DOORBELL. See schematic under BELL.

DOUBLE PLANO-CONVEX. Two PC lenses placed convex to convex to reduce the focal length. Often used in wide-angle ELLIPSOIDAL REFLECTOR SPOTLIGHTS. See under LENSES.

DOUBLE POLE SWITCH. See **Toggle switch** under SWITCHES.

DOUBLE THROW SWITCH. See **Toggle switch** under SWITCHES.

DOUBLING (double hung). The practice of hanging two instruments with different GELS in close proximity to cover the same area onstage. This allows color shifts or other different effects. See also TRIPLING.

DOUSER (chopper, fader). A cutoff device in a followspot placed between the light source and lens so passage of light may be controlled for a BLACKOUT or FADEOUT. See FOLLOWSPOT.

DOWN. The time of day or evening when a production will end. Usually expressed as "The show will be down at 10:40."

DOWNLIGHT. An instrument focused straight down to form a POOL. It is often used with SATURATED COLORS in DANCE THEATRE LIGHTING.

DOWNSTAGE. Toward the front of the stage. Term derived from early theatres, in which the stage was sloped (raked), and downstage was literally lower than upstage. See also STAGE DIRECTIONS; AREAS.

DRAWING PROGRAMS. Computer programs that facilitate the drawing and/or drafting procedures necessary for PLOTS. See also COMPUTER-ASSISTED DESIGN.

DRAWINGS. The scene designer should provide the following drawings for the technical staff:

   Color samples. Swatches showing colors to be used for the setting, draperies, furniture, etc., to help the lighting and costume designer choose colors that will complement or enhance the design.

   Cross sections. Drawings made at right angles to the main axis of a three-dimensional object showing recesses, overhangs, and any details that might cast shadows or present lighting problems.

   Detailed drawings. Usually the concern of the construction crew but occasionally revealing possible locations for lighting instruments needed for hard-to-light areas.

   Floor plans. Scaled drawings indicating the exact outline of settings on the floor and defining acting areas to be lighted as well as offstage areas where lights may be placed.

Front elevations. Scaled drawings showing a front view, single plain wall or elements of scenery with no perspective. Not usually of much concern to lighting personnel.

Painter's elevations. Color renditions of front elevations that again help the lighting designer choose lighting colors.

Rear elevations. Construction details for the construction crew of some interest to the lighting people when lights must be mounted on the back of the set.

Sketches. Rough perspective drawings indicating the scale with respect to the stage, actors, furniture, etc. Sketches help to establish the mood or the statement the scene designer is trying to make.

From these scaled drawings, the lighting designer determines acting areas needed, locations available for instruments, THROW for the various instruments (and therefore the type of instrument), MOTIVATED LIGHT, and special effects. With this information and after PRODUCTION CONFERENCES have been held, the lighting designer may proceed with the light plot. As indicated under DESIGN FOR LIGHTING, the light plot will consist of many different drawings, lists of equipment, equipment positions, acting area numbers, hookups, color charts, dimmer, readings, cues, etc. See also COMPUTER-ASSISTED DESIGN; DESIGN FOR LIGHTING; SYMBOLS.

DRESS PARADE. Onstage check of all costumes. It is essential for the lighting designer to be ready with focused lights and intended GELS or COLOR MEDIA at this time to determine the effect of colored lights on colored costumes. This is the moment of truth when color choices are proved right or wrong and their fate is determined by the director and the scene, costume, and lighting designers.

DRIP CUP. In large CARBON ARC FOLLOWSPOTS a small cuplike container is placed under the arc itself to catch the drippings so they do not splatter over the mirror and insides of the instrument.

DROP BOX. An electrical plug-in or J BOX (junction box) containing several circuits lowered from overhead via a **Spotline** (see under LINE). In some installations drop boxes hang off the end of the ELECTRICS.

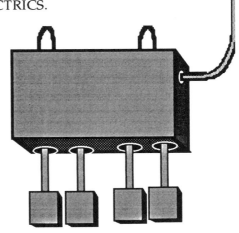

DROP BOX

DUTCHMAN. An objective lens in a PROJECTOR or FOLLOWSPOT.

DYNA-BEAM SPOTLIGHT. Trade name for a high-intensity Kliegl Bros. spotlight of the early 1950s, used for long throws from balcony or booth positions.

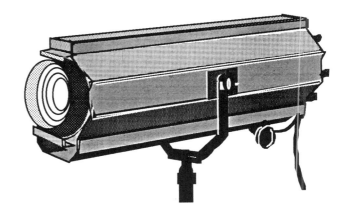

KLIEGL BROS. DYNA-BEAM
(CA. 1949)

E

EARTHING (ground). British expression for grounding an electrical circuit.

EDKOTRON. Obsolete. Century Lighting trade name for a portable SILICON CONTROLLED RECTIFIER dimmer board. The Edkotron appeared in the late 1960s and was one of the first compact portable dimmer boards.

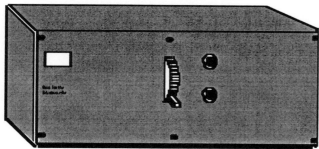

EDKOTRON MASTER CONTROL OR FADER

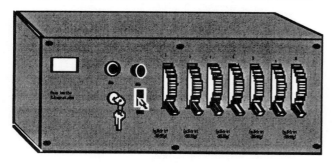

SIX DIMMERS AND A MASTER EDKOTRON

EFFECTS. Special lighting devices used to simulate natural phenomena such as RAINBOWS. They may also include such special effect units as **Chaser, Spinner, Sweeper,** and **Strobe;** see under SPECIAL EFFECTS.

EFFECTS HEAD. The motor-operated unit that gives movement to a SPECIAL EFFECTS machine.

EFFICIENCY (instrument efficiency). A term used to indicate the amount of power emitted from an instrument as light. The higher the efficiency of an instrument, the more light from the instrument and the less power lost as heat.

ELECTRICIAN (juicer, lights, electrics). The individual who operates the control board in a theatre. See also OPERATOR.

ELECTRICIAN'S PLOT. That portion of the designer's light plot the electrician will need to hang and circuit the instruments for a show. See **Drafting the plot** under DESIGN FOR LIGHTING.

ELECTRICITY. Electricity is described as the flow of electrons through a conductor. The subject of electricity is infinitely complex but theatre electricians need not be electrical engineers to light a show. However, they do need to know basic terminology and a few equations. Comparing water with electricity is a familiar method of clarifying terminology. Water pressure is measured in pounds per square inch (psi). The pressure of electricity is measured in volts (units of electromotive force, EMF). A water meter measures flow of water in cubic feet per minute. An ammeter measures flow of electricity in amperes (amps) per second. A waterwheel or turbine converts flow of water to power, and an electric motor converts flow of electricity to power. The resulting power in both cases is measured in horsepower, but in the case of electricity, it is further subdivided into watts, 745.7 watts being equal to 1 horsepower. Even as a given waterwheel may require 100 psi and a flow of 50 cubic feet of water per minute to make it operate, so may a given motor require a 120-volt pressure and a flow of 5 amps per second to make it operate, and a lamp may require 120 volts and a flow of 8.3

amps per second to cause it to operate and produce approximately 1,000 watts (1 kilowatt) of power. Varying sizes of pipe will offer varying resistances to the flow of water, and varying sizes (and kinds) of wire will offer varying resistances to the flow of electricity.

Ohm's law. Direct current flowing in an electric circuit is proportional to the voltage applied to the circuit. The unit measure of resistance of a circuit is stated in ohms. Electrical terms and symbols are defined as follows: E = electromotive force (EMF, pressure, or volts), I = intensity (amps), R = resistance (ohms), P = power (watts). The German physicist Georg Simon Ohm (1787–1854) expressed the relationship of these terms in the following equations:

$$E = IR; \quad I = E/R; \quad R = E/I;$$
$$E = P/I; \quad I = P/E; \quad P = IE.$$

West Virginia formula. One primary concern of stage electricians is to avoid overloading dimmers and circuits. Since lamps are rated in watts, and fuses and breakers protecting dimmers and circuits are rated in amps, one must determine the fuse and breaker size required to handle the cumulative wattage on a given circuit. The above equations are easier to remember if the letters are changed to W for watts, V for volts, and A for amps (called the West Virginia formula for mnemonic purposes).

$$W = VA; \quad A = W/V.$$

Rule of thumb. Rapid calculation with a 15%–20% margin of safety (depending on voltage supply) can be made by moving the decimal point two places to the left when determining amps from watts; thus, a 100-watt lamp requires a flow of approximately 1 amp, and a 500-watt lamp needs 5 amps. See also CIRCUITS.

ELECTRICS

Pipe battens on which lighting instruments are hung. Usually numbered consecutively from proscenium to upstage: first electric, second electric, etc. See BATTEN, LIGHT; PROSCENIUM STAGE LIGHTING.

In professional theatre, a name synonymous with electrical department.

ELECTRODE. Either pole or terminal of an electrical apparatus.

ELECTROMOTIVE FORCE (EMF). The formal name for VOLT, a unit measurement of electrical pressure.

ELLIPSOIDAL REFLECTOR. A reflector designed in the shape of an ellipsoid with primary and secondary focal points. See under REFLECTORS.

ELLIPSOIDAL REFLECTOR FLOODLIGHT (ERF). Although there are several designs of ERF, the scoop is the predominant instrument available in this category. The **Focusing scoop** (see under SCOOP) is designed for the TUNGSTEN-HALOGEN LAMP and its focusing characteristics make it either a floodlight or a directional light. See also FLOODLIGHT.

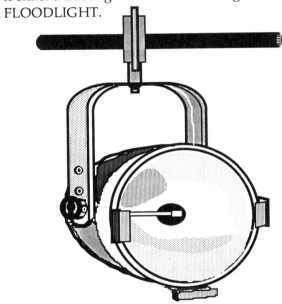

ELLIPSOIDAL REFLECTOR FLOOD

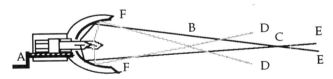

AXIAL MOUNT
ELLIPSOIDAL REFLECTOR FLOODLIGHT
(FOCUSING SCOOP)

 A FOCUSING SCREW
 B SECONDARY FOCAL POINT
   WIDE BEAM
 C SECONDARY FOCAL POINT
   NARROW BEAM
 D WIDE FLOOD
 E NARROW FLOOD
 F ELLIPSOIDAL REFLECTOR

ELLIPSOIDAL REFLECTOR SPOTLIGHT (ERS, Leko, ellips, profile spot [British usage]). A spotlight with an ellipsoidal reflector that directs the light rays to a conjugate focal point, where adjustable shutters are located. The lens system, consisting of two plano-convex lenses or one step lens, focuses on the focal point (and the shutters), producing a hard-edged light, shaped by the internal shutters to the selected pattern. Because of this control feature, ellipsoidal spotlights are particularly valuable as front of the house instruments, where beams must be cut to the proscenium edge and spill light must be kept minimal. Due to the conjugate focal system the light reverses itself, and because of this, the top shutter controls the bottom of the beam of light and the bottom shutter controls the top beam of light. In the United Kingdom two sets of four shutters are available in PROFILE SPOTS, one set in HARD FOCUS, the other set in SOFT FOCUS. Most ellipsoidal spots may be ordered with pattern slots located next to the framing shutters. Metal cutouts, called GOBOS or cookies, may be placed in these slots, making the ellipsoidal spotlight an effective projector. Ellipsoidal spotlights are available in many sizes, designed for lamps ranging from 300 to 3,000 watts, with a variety of lens sizes ranging from 4-1/2" to 12" diameter. Older ellipsoidal spotlights required tubular-shaped incandescent lamps which, because of filament positioning, were designed to be burned base up. Thus, a portion of the reflector had to be cut away to allow proper filament alignment in the reflector (see illustration). Retrofited TUNGSTEN-HALOGEN LAMPS of greater efficiency are available for these older designs but the light field is still uneven because of the missing section of reflector. Later model spotlights designed for the smaller tungsten-halogen lamps are AXIAL MOUNTED, as illustrated. This horizontal positioning of the lamp utilizes the full reflector, thus providing an even field of light and greater efficiency. Variable-focus ellipsoidals, commonly referred to as ZOOM ELLIPSES, are among the most versatile spotlights on the market.

EMBRYO SPOT. See INKY.

EMERGENCY LIGHTS. Battery-powered house lights that turn on automatically in case of power failure. Required installations in auditoriums, above exits, and in lobbies. See also FIRE CODE.

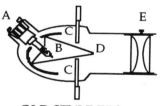

OLD-STYLE ERS

A ADJUSTMENT SCREW
B PRIMARY FOCAL POINT
C ELLIPSOIDAL REFLECTOR
D SECONDARY FOCAL POINT
E LENSES

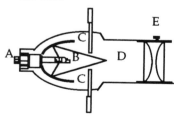

AXIAL-MOUNT ERS

A ADJUSTMENT SCREW
B PRIMARY FOCAL POINT
C ELLIPSOIDAL REFLECTOR
D SECONDARY FOCAL POINT
E LENSES

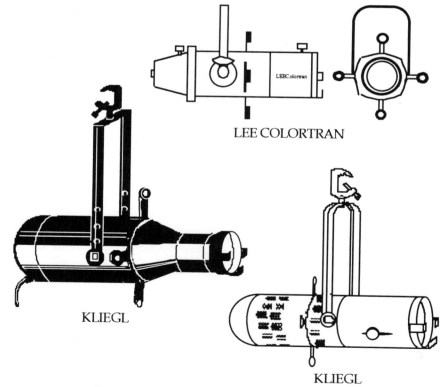

LEE COLORTRAN

KLIEGL

KLIEGL

ELIPSOIDAL REFLECTOR SPOTLIGHTS

EMERY CLOTH. Emery-coated cloth sometimes used as an abrasive to clean electrical contacts. However, it is too coarse and ROUGE CLOTH should be used instead.

EMF. Acronym for ELECTROMOTIVE FORCE.

EMPHASIS. Concentration of attention or interest on a given actor, area, or object. Technical aids used for emphasis include concentration of light; changes in color of light; use of elevations or platforms; use of color or line in settings and costuming; positions of doors, stairs, and points of entrance or exit. See FOCUS OF ATTENTION.

EMT. Acronym for electrician's metal tubing. Conduit used to enclose electrical wiring.

ENCAPSULATED ARC LAMP. See **Light sources** under LAMPS. See also HMI; XENON LAMP.

ENVELOPE (bottle). Professional term for the glass portion of a LAMP.

ERF. An acronym for ELLIPSOIDAL REFLECTOR FLOODLIGHT; see also SCOOP.

ERS. An acronym for ELLIPSOIDAL REFLECTOR SPOTLIGHT; see also LEKO.

EXECUTE (command verb). A command to carry out the cue. "GO" is more often used than "execute." See CUE.

EXIT LIGHTS (exits). Red lights in the shape of the word "exit." Red lighted arrows indicate the fastest way out of a room or building.

EXTENDED APRON STAGE. Stage with an apron that extends from 8' to 12' in front of the proscenium line. Not as large as a thrust stage but similar, although the audience does not sit on the sides of the extension. See THRUST STAGE LIGHTING.

EXTENSION LADDER. Two straight ladders designed to telescope together providing a variable height. Use is limited to positions where the ladder can lean against a wall.

EXTERIOR. Setting for a scene requiring an outside location. Adaptations of WING AND DROP stagings are often used for exteriors. In wing and drop staging and in most exteriors, the lighting designer should take full advantage of sidelighting opportunities. Not only is the effect more dramatic than frontlighting, but if a cyclorama is used, frontlighting will very often cast shadows or BOUNCE on the cyc, ruining the illusion of sky. See also PROJECTED SCENERY.

F

FADE IN (sneak in, steal in) (command verb). Gradual dim up of lights or sound.

FADE OUT (sneak out, steal out) (command verb). Gradual dim down of lights or sound.

FADER

A device that fades intensity of any dimmer assigned to it, up or down.

A device that fades from one scene or preset to another. See also **Cross-fader** under COMPUTER LIGHT BOARD TERMINOLOGY.

FALSE BEAM. An L-shaped beam attached to the ceiling of an auditorium or of a set for the purpose of concealing lighting instruments.

FEEDER (feed line). An electrical line used to power dimmers, control boards, etc. See **Feeders** under CABLE.

FEED LINE (line). The power source. The conductor bringing electricity to the LOAD.

FEMALE BREAKOUT. Professional expression for a grouping of line connectors coming off an ELECTRIC or CROSSOVER PIPE that power lights on the side of the stage opposite the light board on a ROAD SHOW.

FEMALE PLUG (body). The plug connector attached to the FEED LINE (or line) delivering electricity to the LOAD. See PLUGS.

FIELD ANGLE. The part of the cone of light from a spotlight in which intensity ranges from 10% to 49% maximum. The rest of the cone of light, ranging from 50% to maximum intensity, is known as the BEAM ANGLE. In catalogues, these angles are expressed in degrees. These angles are important when focusing spotlights on adjacent areas onstage. If the beam angles of each light touch and the field angles overlap, a good blend of light will result. These angles are not obvious to the eye, but if they are given in the catalogue, a reasonable

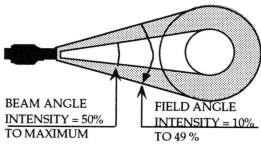

BEAM ANGLE
INTENSITY = 50%
TO MAXIMUM

FIELD ANGLE
INTENSITY = 10%
TO 49 %

BEAM AND FIELD ANGLES

guess can be made as to the overlap needed. See BLENDING; FIELD DIAMETER.

FIELD DIAMETER. The actual diameter of the FIELD ANGLE at a given distance from the spotlight. Some PHOTOMETRIC CHARTS give the field diameter at various distances in addition to the field angle. If circles are used by the lighting designer for the light plot, the circle size should represent the field diameter. See DESIGN FOR LIGHTING.

FIELD INTENSITY. Refers to the footcandle readings within the FIELD ANGLE at a given distance. See PHOTOMETRIC CHART and illustration under FIELD ANGLE.

FILAMENT. A resistance wire in a lamp (usually tungsten) that provides the source of light when it is heated to incandescence by a current. See **Filaments** under LAMPS.

FILAMENT IMAGE. A projection of the filament from the lens of a spotlight. Correct by widening the focus of the spotlight or by aligning the instrument. Some older instruments are not designed correctly, and the image cannot be removed; in such cases the use of frost COLOR MEDIA may be the only solution.

FILL LIGHT. A light designed to reduce shadows or blend areas. Instruments used for fill light may be

FLOODLIGHTS, SCOOPS, BORDER LIGHTS, FOOTLIGHTS, or SPOTLIGHTS. In television, fill light is the other half of KEY LIGHT and goes on top of the BASE LIGHT, the latter being the minimum CANDLEPOWER required for a picture.

FILTER. A term used for COLOR MEDIA or DIFFUSION media. See also STRAINER.

FIRECHIEF. Fiberglass cloth used instead of ASBESTOS CLOTH to protect fabric in the flies from hot lighting INSTRUMENTS. See also ZETEX.

FIRE CLASSIFICATION/FIRE EXTINGUISHERS

Class A: wood, paper, cloth, mattresses, furniture, drapes, etc. Use pressurized water; for very small, not deep-seated fires, use dry chemical.

Class B: paint, gas, oil products, chemicals. Use foam, fog, CO_2, or, for relatively small fires, dry chemical.

Class C: electrical, not microchip. Use CO_2 or dry chemical. For a microchip component electrical fire, use Halon.

FIRE CODE. Laws set up nationally and locally for protection of people in public buildings and places of amusement. Local fire departments will gladly provide desired information for the vicinity. See also NATIONAL ELECTRICAL CODE; NATIONAL UNDERWRITERS CODE. Following are some of the regulations for proscenium theatres:

Aisles. Not less than 5' wide, and wider for large-capacity theatres or those with Continental seating.

Emergency lights. Auxiliary house lights and exit lights that turn on automatically in case of power failure must be provided. Emergency lights are powered from a separate source or by batteries or sometimes both. Exit signs usually are on a separate BREAKER from the main house lights and often receive power from a second source. Some states have stringent laws governing emergency lights. Fire or safety inspectors in a given locale will cooperate in explaining laws.

Exits. Draperies, curtains, or anything that could block exits are not allowed. No false indicators of doors are allowed, and all exits must be clearly marked with lighted signs. Panic bars and hardware must be installed on all doors; no chains are allowed for locking doors.

Fire safety equipment. Fire axes, extinguishers, and hoses must be available at various locations in the auditorium, lobby, foyer, onstage, and at the various levels of the stage and house. Usually the switchboard, sound board, and dimmer space must have CO_2, dry chemical, or Halon extinguishers. Dressing rooms, halls, and rehearsal space must have extinguishers, usually pressurized water and dry chemical. Shops must have extinguishers of the correct types for the hazards found in those areas. All mechanical rooms (rooms containing heating or air-conditioning equipment, fans, blowers, etc.) must also be fully equipped. See also FIRE CLASSIFICATION/FIRE EXTINGUISHERS.

FIREPLACE EFFECTS. Equipment used to simulate fire in a fireplace. Wildly flickering lights, leaping flames of silk, and other such attempts often result in either distracting or worrying the audience. A simple, rotating, transparent cylinder operating from the heat of a lamp or a spotlight beam reflecting off crushed aluminum foil slowly revolving on a phonograph turntable will usually provide an adequate flicker. Coal grates filled with wadded gelatine of all colors, painted broken lenses, or melted glass lighted from below are most effective. A small floodlight or baby spot with medium amber gelatine is sometimes used through fireplace openings to supplement the effect.

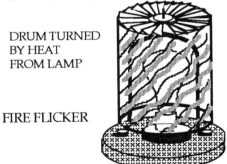

DRUM TURNED
BY HEAT
FROM LAMP

FIRE FLICKER

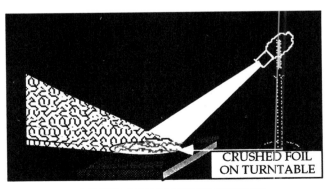

CRUSHED FOIL
ON TURNTABLE

FIREPLACE FLICKER EFFECT

FIREPLACE LOGS. Simulated logs that glow when lighted. Use chicken wire frames covered with flameproofed cheesecloth or scrim grained to resemble logs. Two or three lamps and a rotating cylinder built inside the logs complete the effect. Assembled log units are also available through window display stores, mail order houses, and some supply houses.

FIREPLACE LOGS

FIRST BORDER (concert border). The first border lights upstage of the act curtain. Concert border is an older term for the same thing. See also BORDER LIGHTS.

FIRST STAND. The initial production of a professional show that is expected to be scheduled for performance in other theatres.

FLASH BOX (flash pot). An electrical detonator for flash powder. The flash box consists of two terminals attached to a LINE activated at the switchboard. A strand or two of wire from a piece of ZIP CORD is attached to the two terminals. When the circuit is closed, the wire blows and sparks, igniting the flash powder. The wire cage guards against accidental contact with costumes, draperies, or other flammables. See also SMOKE EFFECTS.

FLASH POWDER. Used for smoke and flash effects where legal. Available in theatrical supply houses in slow, medium, and fast speeds. Check with local fire department.

FLAT FIELD. The British expression for a smooth, evenly spread light across the beam.

FLATTED ELLIPSOIDAL REFLECTOR. A series of small plane reflectors arranged within the ellipsoidal shape. This helps smooth out light from larger filament sources.

FLICKER CANDLE. A portable candle, operating on a 9-volt battery. Manufactured by Rosco Laboratories.

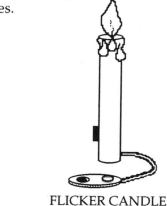

FLICKER CANDLE
WITH SWITCH AND
BATTERY CONNECTION

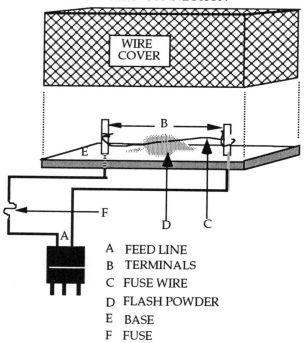

A FEED LINE
B TERMINALS
C FUSE WIRE
D FLASH POWDER
E BASE
F FUSE

FLASH BOX CIRCUIT

FLOAT (footlight). British expression for FOOT-LIGHT. The name came from floating wicks burning in oil.

FLOODLIGHT (bunch light, olivette, scoop). Flood-lights were originally used to light cycloramas and backings or to provide highlights from the side of the stage. Floodlights on standards are rarely called for in present-day light plots. More efficient instruments such as SCOOPS or PARcans offer greater intensity, less bulk, lower wattage, and, when equipped with BARNDOORS, LIGHT SPILL CONTROL as well. HANGING FLOODS or floor-mounted floods for cyclorama lighting are still used occasionally, but again, the improved designs of scoops and cyc strips offer greater efficiency at lower wattage and better control. See CYC LIGHTS; SCOOPS.

HANGING FLOODLIGHT CA 1920s

FLOORCLOTH. See GROUND CLOTH.

FLOOR PLAN (ground plan). A working drawing indicating the exact outline of a setting on the floor. See also DRAWINGS; SIGHTLINE.

FLOOR PLUG (stage plug). Obsolete. See under PLUGS.

FLOOR POCKET. An electrical receptacle recessed in the stage floor and protected with a metal cover. See also PLUGS.

FLOOR STRIP. FOOTLIGHT-type unit for bottom CYCLORAMA lighting.

FLOPPY DISK (floppy). Electromechanical information storage device. Two common sizes are 5 1/4" and 3 1/2". See under COMPUTER LIGHT BOARD TERMINOLOGY. Some boards use magnetic tape or RAM chips instead of floppies.

FLUORESCENT PAINT. See under ULTRAVIOLET LIGHT.

FLUX. A measure of light in units of LUMENS.

KLIEGL BROS. FLOODLIGHTS
OF THE LATE TWENTIES

FLUX, SOLDER. A greasy substance used to prevent oxidizing during the soldering process, to aid in the flow and bonding of solder. Since acid fluxes tend to corrode, paste and stick fluxes are generally considered superior for electrical work. Use only rosin core solder for electronic work. See also SOLDER.

f-NUMBER. The ratio between diameter and focal length of a camera lens. See under LENSES.

FOCAL LENGTH. Distance from the center of a lens or reflector to its focal point. See LENSES; REFLECTORS.

FLOOR POCKET WITH PIN CONNECTORS

FOCAL PLANE. An area in space where an image is in sharp focus. Highly dependent upon the lens used or, in the case of lensless projectors, the placement of the image relative to the filament.

FOCAL POINT (nodal point). The point at which rays of light passing through a lens or reflecting from a reflector converge. See also LENSES; REFLECTORS.

FOCUS

(command verb). To aim lights toward a given AREA or space.

The use of light to direct audience attention to the action or stage location as needed. See also FOCUS OF ATTENTION.

FOCUS CHART. See **Focus charts or sheets** under DESIGN FOR LIGHTING.

FOCUSING CLOTH. Cloth used in ROAD SHOWS to precisely focus lights. A ground cloth or T-shaped cloth that is usually placed with one edge on the PROSCENIUM LINE and aligned to the CENTERLINE. The cloth is marked in feet left and right of center and upstage from the proscenium line. The HOT SPOT of the light is given a location such as 8 R (8' right stage) and 6 up (6' upstage) with 6' diameter.

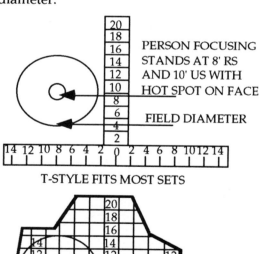

T-STYLE FITS MOST SETS

FULL STYLE CUT TO FIT SET

FOCUSING CLOTHS

FOCUS LIGHTS (verb)

To set positions of spotlights and other lighting equipment.

To aim the lighting instruments to cover given objects or areas.

To adjust the distance between lamp and lens or adjust shutters, thereby changing the size or shape of the area covered by light.

FOCUS NOTES. See **Focus charts or sheets** under DESIGN FOR LIGHTING.

FOCUS OF ATTENTION (prime focus). Lighting can play an important role in giving major emphasis to people or objects onstage. Lights can also deemphasize areas if dark colors or shadows are used.

FOG EFFECT. See under SCRIM.

FOH. See FRONT OF THE HOUSE.

FOLLOW

(command verb). To keep a FOLLOWSPOT focused on performers as they move about the stage.

To increase and decrease light intensity on stage areas, synchronized with the movement of the performer. Most effective if subtly done.

FOLLOWER. An automatic part of a cue that follows the main cue.

FOLLOWSPOT. A spotlight mounted on a swivel so the light may be used to follow a performer. The first effective followspot for the stage was the LIMELIGHT, used in the middle 1860s until superseded by CARBON ARCS early in the 1900s. As the name implies, the light source for the carbon arc is derived from the spark between two electrodes. Early carbon arc lights were monstrous spots, using carbon rods up to 3/4" in diameter and requiring as much as 125 amps of DIRECT CURRENT to operate. An attendant was required at all times to "feed and TRIM the carbons" (maintain the correct distance between rods and replace them as they burned away) and to follow the action on the stage. Improved ARC LIGHTS such as the Strong Followspot incorporated pencil-sized carbon rods and then were adapted to newer ENCAPSULATED ARC LAMPS. The light source is backed by a highly efficient REFLECTOR (metal or glass), which directs light through a control gate containing a DOUSER and IRIS, on through an OBJECTIVE LENS system, and finally out through the color BOOMERANG. The shape of the beam of the followspot can be changed with either the iris or the douser; the focus is changed with the TROMBONE, and the color is changed with the boomerang. Arc lights have the disadvantage of not being able to be dimmed electrically; however, mechanical methods of decreasing intensity may be substituted. Several high-intensity tungsten-halogen followspots are available and are usually more than adequate for the average theatre. As a matter of fact, followspots are seldom used for the average theatrical production. However, they are often necessary for musicals, ballets, vaudeville, operas, extravaganzas, and ice shows, where attention needs to be focused on one or more performers in a group. By reducing the intensity of all stage lights except a followspot on the principals, one is assured of having the attention of the audience wherever the spot is focused. Only larger theatres with a required throw of 200'–400' ever really need the larger, expensive arc light.

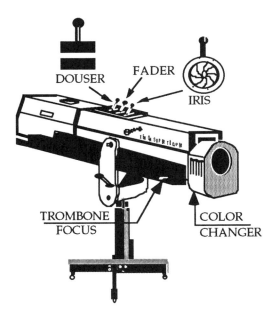

FOLLOWSPOT

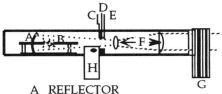

A   REFLECTOR
B   CARBON ELECTRODE
C   DOUSER
D   FADER
E   IRIS
F   OBJECTIVE LENS SYSTEM
G   COLOR BOOMERANG
H   ADJUSTABLE STAND

SECTION OF ARC FOLLOWSPOT

FOOTCANDLE. See also ILLUMINATION; LUMEN. A unit of illumination equal to 1 lumen per square foot. One lumen of light evenly applied to 1 square foot produces 1 footcandle. If the CANDLEPOWER (luminous intensity) of a given lamp is known, footcandles at a given distance can be computed from the following equation:

    footcandles = candlepower/distance in feet, squared.

    For example, illumination at a distance of 10' from a 150-candlepower lamp:

    FC = 150/10 x 10 = 150/100 = 1.5 footcandles.

FOOTLAMBERT. A unit of luminance equal to $1/\pi$ CANDELA.

FOOTLIGHT (foots, floats [British usage]). A trough of lights on the floor or embedded in the floor immediately in front of the curtain and at the edge of the apron. Footlights probably represent the most persistent link with nineteenth-century theatre that exists today. Not only do they seem to resist all efforts at banishment, recently they have even been upgraded to use TUNGSTEN-HALOGEN LAMPS. In the days of low-intensity candle and gas light, the primary position for lights was on the floor between actors and audience, simply because it was as close to the actors as source light

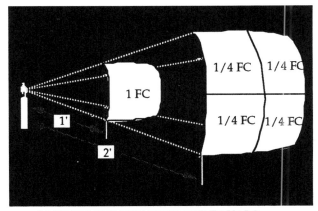

1 LUMEN PER SQUARE FOOT EQUALS
AMOUNT OF ILLUMINATION FROM
1 CANDELA 1 FOOT FROM THE SURFACE.

FOOTCANDLES

could be placed. Light used sparingly from this position may still serve to wash out facial wrinkles and shadows under the eyes, but for the most part, such low-angle lights should be saved for horror scenes, bonfires, or, more usefully, period melodramas and dance. As shown in the illustrations, footlights consist of continuous strips of lights in a wide variety of sizes and shapes of troughs and compartments. Like BORDER LIGHTS, they are conventionally wired in three or four circuits and add control for each of the primary colors, red, green, and blue, plus white, if a fourth circuit is provided. Most footlights are designed for low-wattage lamps placed on 4"–6" centers. Open trough and compartmentalized footlights are usually made for 40- to 100-watt lamps, and roundels are designed for 100- to 200-watt lamps. Tungsten-halogen footlights, more often found on large stages, are always compartmentalized with 300- to 500-watt lamps and use glass strip color filters (the only COLOR MEDIA able to withstand the heat generated by these lamps). Intensity readings on footlights should never be set high enough to cast multiple shadows of the actors on the backwall. For the period melodrama, footlights are often improvised from large fruit cans, cut to resemble the candle reflectors of the nineteenth century, as shown in the illustration. Porcelain sockets are fastened in the reflectors and wired in parallel in a single circuit. Low-wattage, frosted lamps are used.

FOOTSPOT. Small spotlight mounted in the footlight position.

FORESTAGE. See under APRON.

FORMULA. A theory, type, or style of lighting; a method or means of lighting a stage show. A number of different techniques, different types of lights, different locations, and different colors may be used to light productions, and these are grouped into classifications we call formulas. The advantage of teaching formulas is that the student learning such methods rote will be able to light a show reasonably well using these preset methods. The formulas are especially applicable for elementary and high schools and community theatre, where it is normal to have limited equipment.

Formulas for the arena and thrust stage. Two systems are common for lighting arena and thrust stages, with markedly different modeling results.

 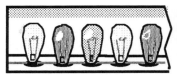

TROUGH REFLECTOR FOOTLIGHTS
RED, BLUE, AND WHITE CIRCUITS - DIPPED LAMPS
FOOTLIGHTS CA 1900s

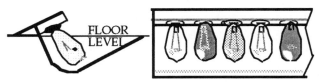

TROUGH REFLECTOR FOOTLIGHTS
RED, BLUE, AND WHITE CIRCUITS OF
DIPPED LAMPS
FOOTLIGHTS CA 1900s

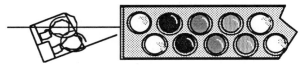

DOUBLE ROW, FOUR CIRCUIT, RECESSED
ROUNDEL FOOTLIGHTS
FOOTLIGHTS CA LATE 1920s

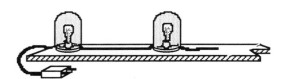

MELODRAMA FOOTLIGHTS

If possible, use the 90° method. See **120° lighting** and **90° lighting** under ARENA STAGE LIGHTING; THRUST STAGE LIGHTING.

Formulas for the proscenium stage. Many formulas use warm tints from one side of the stage and cool tints from the other. In addition, it is advisable to provide overall toning with special COLOR WASHES. See **McCandless formula, Wash formula, Double-reverse McCandless, Watson formula, Combination formula, Wash and key,** all under PROSCENIUM STAGE LIGHTING.

FRAME, COLOR (gel frame). See COLOR FRAME.

FRAMING SHUTTER (paddles). Metal device in the ELLIPSOIDAL REFLECTOR SPOTLIGHT that shapes the beam of light to precise areas. Usually there are four shutters, and because of the lens reversal of the rays the bottom shutter masks the top ray of light, the left shutter masks the right side of the light, and vice-versa. The British PROFILE SPOT has eight shutters, four in HARD FOCUS and four in SOFT FOCUS.

FREEZE ON-OFF. A phenomenon occurring with SILICON CONTROLLED RECTIFIER dimmers in which a malfunction causes a light to stay on or off depending on the gate position. In some early dimmers, disconnecting the instrument from the dimmer was the only solution. The best solution is replacement of the SCRs in the dimmer.

FRESNEL LENS. A lens invented by Augustin-Jean Fresnel, 1788-1827 (pronounced Frā nel´), originally designed for lighthouses and intended to reduce glass thickness. See LENSES.

FRESNEL LIGHT (fresnels, fresnel spotlight). A spotlight providing a soft, diffused light. The fresnel lens was adapted to stage use because its design makes possible a short focal length in a thin, heat-resistant, lightweight lens. The short focal length allows shorter, lighter weight spotlights that are easier to handle, more efficient because the lens is closer to the lamp (capturing more of the light), and require less hanging space. Because the fresnel lens gives a soft-edged, diffused light, its use is confined to behind the proscenium. See also **Fresnel lens** under LENSES.

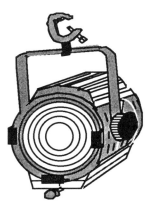

FRESNEL SPOTLIGHT

FRONT OF THE HOUSE (FOH). The auditorium. Loosely construed to mean any part of the theatre in front of the curtain. See also ANTEPROSCENIUM.

FROST. Translucent color media used to diffuse light. Useful in blending area lights and softening harsh lines of a beam.

STAR FROST

Star frost. Frost COLOR MEDIA with the center cut out in an irregular pattern, often star-shaped, used to maintain concentration of light in the center but soften the edges by diffusion. Munroe Pevear of the Pevear Color Specialty Company conceived this idea in the first quarter of the twentieth century when he ground the periphery of plano-convex lenses to make a soft, diffused edge of light for a better blend with other lights. The same effect can be achieved by smearing a drop of oil on the rough side of frost GELATINE, causing the oiled portion to become transparent. (Oil will not work on plastic media.)

FROSTED LAMP. A lamp with a translucent bulb giving a diffused light. All lamps used in spotlights and PROJECTORS must have clear bulbs.

FULL. Refers to maximum intensity of lighting instruments or sound equipment.

FULL UP. A light or grouping of lights at maximum intensity.

FUNCTIONS OF LIGHTING. 1. Selective visibility, controlling audience attention. 2. Showing form, emphasizing the structure. 3. Establishing mood. 4. Illusion of nature, establishing realism. 5. Composition. See **Aesthetics** under LIGHTING PRACTICE.

FUNNEL. See under LIGHT SPILL CONTROL.

FUSE. An electrical conductor in a circuit that melts with heat and breaks circuit if a current greater than rated load is introduced. Fuse boxes requiring screw-type fuses are no longer legal to install and should be replaced with CIRCUIT BREAKERS. However, screw-type fuses (up to 30-amp capacities) are still available. Ferrule-tipped cartridge fuses come in sizes ranging in capacity from fractions of an amp (automotive types) to 60 amps.

Larger capacities, beginning at 100 amps, are provided by knife-blade cartridge fuses. All electrical circuits should be protected by some kind of fuse of a capacity no greater than the intended load. Using fuses larger than specified may cause dimmers or expensive equipment to burn out or, worse, could lead to serious electrical fires. Fuses are wired in series with the load. See **Short Circuit** under CIRCUITS.

FUSESTATS. An adaptor that can be inserted in a plug fuse receptacle to permit only a certain size of fuse to be used.

PLUG FUSE

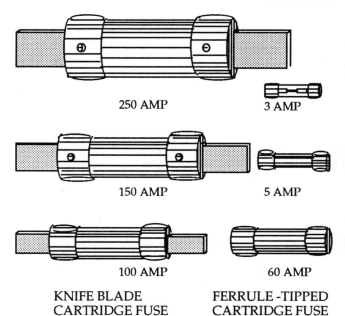

250 AMP   3 AMP

150 AMP   5 AMP

100 AMP   60 AMP

KNIFE BLADE   FERRULE -TIPPED
CARTRIDGE FUSE   CARTRIDGE FUSE

G

GAFFER. Professional term for stage crew department head or foreman.

GALLERY REFLECTOR. Obsolete. A carbon arc floodlight invented ca. 1905 using a nickel-plated parabolic reflector and directional spill rings. A precursor of the incandescent CALIBAN FLOOD of 1916 and the BEAM PROJECTOR of the 1930s.

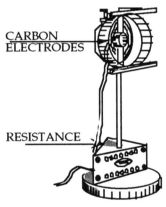

CARBON ELECTRODES

RESISTANCE

GALLERY REFLECTOR

GANG

To hook together two or more electrical units on one circuit.

To operate together two or more dimmers or channels on LIGHTING CONTROL.

GAP. The space between the positive and negative CARBONS in a FOLLOWSPOT. Since carbons burn to mere stubs in 60–90 minutes, motor-driven mechanisms are used to try to maintain the optimum gap for maximum light.

GATE. The aperture between the lamp and the lens on an ELLIPSOIDAL REFLECTOR SPOTLIGHT.

GATING. Power flowing from a dimmer to a lamp by an on-off action. See SILICON CONTROLLED RECTIFIER.

TWO CYCLES OF ALTERNATING CURRENT

SILICON CONTROLLED RECTIFIER

INSULATED-GATE BIPOLAR TRANSISTOR

GATING

GATOR. Abbreviation for ALLIGATOR CLIP. One of several types of spring clips used for temporary electrical connections.

GAUGE, WIRE. Size of wire expressed in numbers referring to the capacity of the wire in terms of AMPERES. See CABLE.

GAUZE, THEATRICAL. A lightweight cloth that can be changed from an opaque drop to a transparent drop by the use of light. See SCRIM.

GEL (noun). See GELATINE.

GEL (verb). To equip a lighting instrument with color media.

GELATINE (gel). Thin, transparent sheets made of animal or grain jelly and dye and used as color media for stage lights. Gelatine comes in sheets approximately 20" x 24" and in nearly 100 different shades and tints. All gelatines will fade with continuous use in a lighting instrument, sometimes within a few hours. In the case of high-intensity instruments, including the tungsten-halogen lights, gelatine may last only a few minutes. See COLOR MEDIA; DICHROIC FILTER.

GELLED. A lighting instrument fitted with color media is referred to as being "gelled." See COLOR MEDIA.

GENERAL ILLUMINATION. Better referred to as BASE LIGHT, it is intended for general coverage as opposed to KEY LIGHT and FILL LIGHT or specific-area coverage such as expected from focused spotlights. General illumination is often, but not always, provided by instruments falling into the broad classification of BORDER LIGHTS; FLOODLIGHTS; FOOTLIGHTS; STRIPLIGHTS.

GENERAL LIGHTS. BORDER LIGHTS, FLOODLIGHTS, FOOTLIGHTS, and STRIPLIGHTS used for toning, blending, and establishing basic color mood for a play. See under separate classifications.

GENERIC TERMS. GEL = COLOR MEDIA; LEKO = ELLIPSOIDAL REFLECTOR SPOTLIGHT; ERF = ELLIPSOIDAL REFLECTOR FLOODLIGHT; ERS = ELLIPSOIDAL REFLECTOR SPOTLIGHT; LIGHT BOARD = most light control units. The dictionary definition of KLIEGLIGHT is a high-intensity arc light; in the theatre, the term is used for any spotlight manufactured by Kliegl Bros.

GENIE LIFT. A trade name for a telescoping pneumatic or hydraulic lift used in place of a ladder to assist in hanging and focusing lighting equipment or aiding in other technical chores that normally require ladders. The genie lift may also serve as a **Tower** (see under LIGHT MOUNTING DEVICES) or BOOM. See also TELESCOPTER.

GHOST LIGHT (night light, work light). A portable, light bulb usually about 200 watts, mounted in a wire cage on a light standard, placed center stage after rehearsals and performances, and used as a safety light to help prevent accidents. See WORK LIGHT.

GHOST LOAD (phantom load). A system of matching a dimmer load with a dimmer capacity. A lamp or a resistance is placed in an unseen, often remote place beneath the stage and connected in parallel with a stage light to load the dimmer for complete dimouts. Usually only resistance dimmers need ghost loads, and they need them only if the load assigned is less than the rated minimum load of the dimmer. On occasion early SILICON CONTROLLED RECTIFIER dimmers assigned low-wattage flame or flicker lamps needed to be ghost loaded also. The problem in that case was not insufficient resistance but rather the inability of the SCR to detect a load at all. See also RESISTANCE DIMMER.

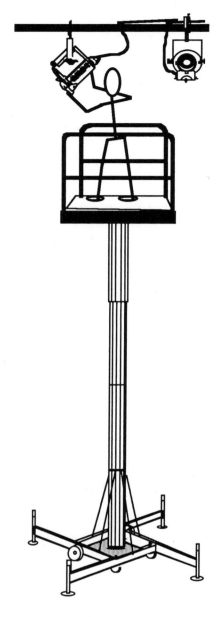

GENIE LIFT

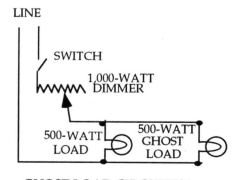

GHOST LOAD CIRCUITRY

GIMMICK LIGHT. Light for lighting's sake. See RANDOM LIGHT.

G LAMP. Globular-shaped lamp. See LAMPS.

GLARE (bounce light). A light reflection too bright for comfortable vision. Glare is caused by too light a background or too bright a contrast of color in the background. Keep all possible light off backgrounds offending in this way.

GLITCH (surge). See COMPUTER LIGHT BOARD TERMINOLOGY.

GO (command verb). Do the cue now. The word "go" is generally preferred to all others as a final cue. Stage managers give warnings 10–30 seconds before saying "go." See CUE.

GOBO (pattern, cookie, mat). A metal cutout that fits into a slot or special holder located next to the SHUTTERS of an ELLIPSOIDAL REFLECTOR SPOTLIGHT. Some spotlights do not have slots and the gobo must be wedged in the aperture. With the gobo in position, the spotlight projects the image on the scenery, floor, CYC, or screen, often giving texture. Literally hundreds of patterns are available from theatre supply houses. The lighting designer should be aware of these patterns and their effectiveness.

VENETIAN BLIND   SKYLINE   VENETIAN WINDOW

GOBOS

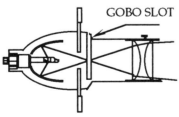

GOBO SLOT

ELLIPSOIDAL SPOTLIGHT WITH GOBO SLOT

GOBO HOLDER. A special carrier which holds the gobo and is then put into the holding slot.

GOBO SLOT. A slot into which the gobo is slid near the shutter (GATE) position (the focal point) in an ELLIPSOIDAL REFLECTOR SPOTLIGHT that is designed to receive a pattern slide for a background projection. *Caution:* This is the hottest part of the spotlight and any gobo designed for this position must be capable of withstanding great heat.

GOBO ROTATOR. A variable-speed, electrical gobo rotating mechanism used for "moving effects."

GRAND DRAPE. The house curtain separating the stage from the auditorium. See CURTAINS.

GRAND MASTER. One large dimmer or dimmer handle controlling all circuits on the switchboard or light board. See DIMMER, MASTER.

GRAND VALANCE (teaser). Older term for what is now usually called the teaser. The first drapery border in front of the GRAND DRAPE, generally made of the same material and often used to vary the height of the proscenium arch and to mask the flies from audience view. The trim height of the grand valance will help to determine the working height of lights on the first border as well as the setting of lights to be used in FRONT OF THE HOUSE positions. This trim height is of great importance to the lighting designer.

GRAPHIC STANDARDS. Certain requirements need to be met when drawing lighting plots. See USITT GRAPHIC STANDARDS.

GRAPHITE. A soft carbon from which carbon electrodes are made for arc lights.

GRATING. A newer product in the light filter category. A plastic film using holographic and optical technology that produces special effects when illuminated. The materials are available at supply companies for experimentation.

GREEN. A primary color. A very unflattering color for the complexion.

GREENFIELD. A flexible armored steel conduit into which electrical wires are pulled.

GREEN ROOM. Traditional waiting room or reception room of a theatre, located near the stage and serving as a meeting place for guests or a place where actors can spend free moments between cues.

GRID (gridiron). Structural framework of parallel beams located near the top of the stage house and designed to support sheaves, loft blocks, headblocks, cable, and rope necessary for flying scenery and lights.

GROUND (earthing [British usage])

A conductor connected to a water pipe or other suitable contact in the earth.

The third wire in an electrical conductor (often uninsulated), which connects to ground in an outlet and in the panel.

GROUND CLOTH (floorcloth). A heavy cloth or canvas cover for the floor that may be painted as part of the design for the setting. The color of the ground cloth becomes an important part of the lighting designer's consideration. It may be used to reflect light to compensate for steep-angle lighting. On the other hand, reflected light from a ground cloth may ruin the attempted isolation of areas needed for **Split staging** (see under STAGING STYLES). The type of show, the staging, and the lighting designer's approach should all be taken into consideration when choosing the color and design of the ground cloth.

GROUND PLAN. See FLOOR PLAN.

GROUNDROW (profile piece). A low silhouette or painted cutout representing hills, mountains, bushes, distant horizons, etc., and designed to stand independently in the background. The groundrow is the masking piece for HORIZON LIGHTS used to light the CYC. Lighting designers will want to check the height of groundrows to make sure they are tall enough to mask their chosen horizon lights.

GROUP. A method of gathering various components under one control such as color groups, area groups, etc. Group mastering is a common concept in LIGHT BOARD control.

GROUP MASTER. Control of one group or many groups by a SUBMASTER.

GUTTER (raceway, wireway). A U-shaped, covered metal trough designed to hold and protect a number of wires or cables.

GUY WIRE. A wire fastened to a high light standard or BOOM for purposes of strengthening and supporting. BOX BOOMS are often guyed for safety.

H

HALATION. A halo of light around a spotlight's main beam. Frequently caused by a dirty or dusty lens. See also ABERRATIONS.

HALF HOUR. A half hour before scheduled curtain. In professional theatre half hour is the time for the house to open and therefore the designated time for all departments to be present and finished with FOH checking. If the production is an open-set show with no curtain, all departments required to work onstage or in the house before the show must have completed their assignments.

HALF PLUG. Obsolete. A plug half the thickness of a stage plug designed so two plugs would fit into a single receptacle. See **Stage plug** under PLUGS.

HANG (fit-up [British usage]) (command verb). To fasten an instrument or accessory to a pipe for use in lighting a production.

HANG (noun). A term for the set-in of a show, which is referred to as "the hang."

HANGER. The pipe or YOKE mounting for a lighting instrument.

HANGING CREW. A special crew, often used in university theatre, to hang, circuit, focus, and gel instruments.

HANGING FLOOD. Obsolete. FLOODLIGHT designed to hang from a pipe as opposed to an OLIVETTE mounted on a floor standard. Hanging floods have been superseded by SCOOPS and CYC STRIPLIGHTS, which are much more efficient.

HANGING FLOODS

HANGING THE SHOW. Setting scenery and lighting for a production. The expression stems from the days of WING AND DROP shows, where most scenery was suspended from the grid. See also SET-IN.

HARD COPY. A document from a computer printer. Computer lighting programs can print out notations and details of the COMPUTER BOARD screen.

HARD-EDGE (hard focus). A light with a clearly defined hard line such as found in an ELLIPSOIDAL REFLECTOR SPOTLIGHT or FOLLOWSPOT.

HARD FOCUS (hard-edge). See HARD-EDGE; STEAK KNIFE; see also SOFT FOCUS.

HARD LIGHT. A hard-edged light beam that produces sharp shadows from a step or plano-convex lens in a spotlight. SOFT LIGHT is diffused. See also LENSES.

HARLEQUIN. A brand name for a roll-type, portable DANCE FLOOR.

HAZARDOUS WASTE. Most chemicals, solvents, cleaning fluids, thinners, dyes, coolants, petroleum products, etc., are considered hazardous materials, and although it is unusual for a theatre to generate great quantities of these wastes, increasing use of plastics and solvents creates a potential problem. The Environmental Protection Agency has developed rules concerning storage and disposal of such waste, and shop management should learn proper care. From time to time, directories are published by the State Offices for Hazardous Waste Management listing regional locations of agencies accepting hazardous materials. Updated information may be had by calling the office of the EPA in your district. (See the blue pages of the phone directory under U.S. Government.) In many cases, state laws governing hazardous waste are more stringent than those of the federal government, so be advised to check locally first. Materials from the electrical department would probably include cleaning solvents and plastics and solvents and dyes used in conjunction with projection slides.

HAZE EFFECT. See SCRIM.

HEAD (gaffer). A department head.

HEADSPOT. A small spot illuminating the head of a performer. Term often used in FOLLOWSPOT directions.

HEAT RESISTING. Any lens, plastic media, or paint made to withstand high temperatures. See THERMOGARD.

HEAT UP (heat-up time). The dimmer reading taken when the lamp in a lighting instrument begins to glow. This is a leading problem with some control units, particularly when cues require a slow dim-up. The board operator must be aware of the idiosyncrasies of the dimmers and compensate for shortcomings. For example, if a dimmer is calibrated on a 0–10 scale, and the lamp does not start to glow until the dimmer reads 4, the electrician must begin the cue with the dimmer set at 4 and then start the count to reach full intensity in the allotted time. In this case the heat-up time is 4 on the particular dimmer. The problem is compounded when you have a number of dimmers all with different heat-up times. This was a common problem with many PRESET BOARDS.

HEAVY COLORS. Saturated, pure colors, usually PRIMARY or SECONDARY COLORS as opposed to TINTS.

HEAVY LIGHT SHOW. Show or production requiring exceptional numbers of lighting instruments or many light cues or both.

HIGH HAT. See **Top hat** under LIGHT SPILL CONTROL.

HIGHLIGHTING (reverse video). See **Reverse video** under COMPUTER LIGHT BOARD TERMINOLOGY.

HIRE COMPANY. British expression for a RENTAL COMPANY.

HIT (command verb). The order given to the FOLLOWSPOT operator instead of the word "GO." It means to take the CUE now.

HMI. Acronym for hydrargyrum-medium iodide. A tungsten short-arc lamp, burning within a high–vapor pressure mercury and argon gas. Other metal iodides are also included in the vapor, pre-

venting blackening of the ENVELOPE and producing the full daylight spectrum. The HMI COLOR TEMPERATURE is 5,600 KELVIN, closely resembling the color of daylight. The HMI lamp is said to be at least 6 times more efficient than common incandescent lamps. 42% of the energy used by HMI lamps is in the visible spectrum as opposed to only 15% of the energy of the standard incandescent lamp. Obviously this is a much brighter lamp with a much lower heat factor, translating into less heat damage to lenses, reflectors, and slides used in projectors. The HMI output of ultraviolet rays is high and although the heat-resistant glass envelope removes a considerable portion of these harmful rays, it is still necessary for operators to exercise great caution in working with these lamps, being careful not to expose eyes and skin to direct rays. HMI lamps require a ballast, an ignition system, and a warm-up period of between half a minute and 3 minutes. HMI lamps are available in the following wattages: 200, 575, 1,200, 2,500, 4,000, 6,000, and 12,000. They are very expensive. Expected lamp life varies between 250 and 750 hours. HMI lamps may be dimmed up to 40% of full brightness but they require DOUSERS or other mechanical dimmers for full BLACKOUTS. Most projectors designed for the HMI lamp are equipped with STRIP GLASS filters that remove the infrared rays, protecting slides from heat which would otherwise destroy them.

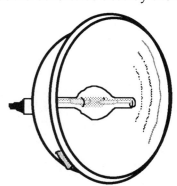

HMI SEALED BEAM

HOLE. Dark space caused by the absence of or lower intensity of light. Normally, stages are lighted with smooth, overall coverage, and light is purposefully dimmed to create darker areas as needed. If unintended dark spaces between areas are found, the problem should be solved by refocusing.

HOLOGRAM. Hologram is the name given to the film on which information about light waves is recorded and from which holographic projections or images may be produced. A holographic projection appears to be a three-dimensional image hanging in free space and can be viewed from several different angles. Expense and complications involved in producing the hologram (obtaining fine-grain, high-quality film large enough to produce holographic images for the stage and the necessary experience of working with laser light sources for the photography) have slowed development of holography for theatrical use. The potential for holographic projection and adaptation to theatre remains tantalizing and needs much more research.

HOLOGRAPHY. The science and art of recording an object wave of something or someone and reconstructing that wave with coherent light (laser) projected on dust, smoke, or a medium such as polyester film.

HOOD

The housing of an older spotlight.

A **Top hat.** See under LIGHT SPILL CONTROL.

HOOK, CABLE. A wire hook on a light STANDARD or GHOST LIGHT, used to hold surplus cable.

HOOKUP. The connecting of cables to instruments, dimmers, and controls.

HOOKUP SHEET. See **Cheat sheets** under DESIGN FOR LIGHTING.

HORIZON. Ground-level sky simulation. Use a GROUNDROW to break line of stage floor and CYC. STRIPLIGHTS or FLOODLIGHTS behind the groundrows will add depth.

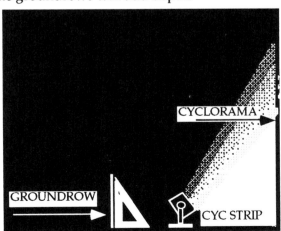

HORIZON LIGHTING

HORIZON LIGHTS. FLOOR STRIPS used for CYC LIGHTING.

HORIZONTAL ANGLE. The angle between two lighting instruments focused on the same area for the purpose of providing plasticity. Optimum results are said to come from approximately 90° horizontal-angle instruments. See **Determining angles** under LIGHTING PRACTICE; also VERTICAL ANGLE.

HORSEPOWER. A unit of power equal to 745.7 watts.

HOT. Designates that an electrical line is activated. Said of a line that is on.

HOT CIRCUIT. An electrical circuit carrying a current.

HOT LINE. An energized electrical line. See under LINE.

HOT PATCH (verb). To interconnect dimmers and lighting instruments on a PATCH PANEL while the circuit is turned on; a dangerous habit that can lead to arcing, burns, and even fire.

HOT SPOT

Stage lighting. A stage area that is brighter, or "hotter," than others because of uneven distribution of light. The problem is solved by refocusing lights.

Rear screen projection. The light from a projector showing through a projection screen of insufficient density is referred to as a hot spot. Either a denser plastic screen is needed or a projector with a lamp of lower intensity.

HOUSE. The auditorium or the audience.

HOUSE BAR. British expression for a permanent batten.

HOUSE BOARD. The built-in control board in a theatre usually used for "in-house shows" only. The house board is a permanently connected panel for lights or sound, controlling only permanent installations within the theatre and seldom used by professional touring shows, which travel with their own controls for lights and sound. The one exception is that the HOUSE LIGHTS usually connected to this board are always used.

HOUSE CURTAIN (grand drape). The permanently installed curtain separating the stage from the house, as opposed to curtains that may be installed for specific productions.

HOUSE LIGHTS. Lights used to illuminate the auditorium. Intensity should be adequate for reading programs, but never glaring. A reading of 10 foot-candles is considered minimum for auditorium illumination.

HOUSING. Outer casing for lighting equipment.

HUE. Technically, distinguishes a color from gray of the same BRIGHTNESS. However, often used loosely for the word "COLOR."

HUM, 60-HERTZ (60-cycle hum). Noise in an audio circuit usually caused by close proximity of 120-volt lines. Sometimes dimmers will cause this problem if audio or microphone lines come too close.

I

ICE SHOW LIGHTING. A show based on the show-manship and talents of ice skaters. Ice shows usually incorporate many specialty numbers; on occasion they use scripted story lines. By the very nature of skating, speed is an integral part of the production. Many of the lighting concepts are based on BALLET and DANCE THEATRE LIGHTING, and the hanging positions are closely associated with ARENA STAGE LIGHTING.

Practice. Basic procedures are outlined in DESIGN FOR LIGHTING and LIGHTING PRACTICE. Since many ice shows are staged in ice arenas not equipped for stage lighting, overhead grids or TRUSSES may have to be suspended from the roof girders to accommodate lighting instruments. Area lighting follows the 90° ARENA LIGHTING formula in pale colors. Two or three more saturated color circuits provide mood and toning variety from the BANGBOARDS and overhead COLOR WASHES. Many colored pools of DOWN-LIGHTS, used for specialty numbers, may also double for ensemble numbers, adding interest, variety, and color. TEXTURE is often achieved by the use of GOBO projections, which may also provide the illusion of scenery. Since ice can act as a reflective surface, the ANGLE OF REFLECTION is of major concern in protecting the audience's eyes from high-intensity FOLLOWSPOTS. The followspot probably is used more in ice shows than in any other type of production. It is not uncommon to find 8–12 followspots providing color, focus, and intensity to star performers. Along with the FOCUS OF ATTENTION used for stars, the BALLYHOO from followspots is often used for accenting ensemble numbers or for curtain calls. CURTAIN CALLS or bows use the BLACKOUT format of arena lighting. Because of the heavy demand on followspots, a special person is often designated to call the followspot cues (see CUE). Special directions are also necessary for followspot operators; the scenic stage wall on one end of the ice surface is "up ice," and the direction away from the scenic wall is "down ice." The lighting designer uses directions for the usual three entrances in the scenic wall: the right, center, and left entrances. The use of the TROMBONE is continuous from the down-ice end of the rink to maintain the size of the spot relative to other spots as the skater gets closer. It is at this time (especially if using a HEADSPOT) that the down-ice followspot operator is very aware that the skater may be traveling 45–50 miles per hour. Unlike in other productions the electricians often perform their own cues without a caller, although the stage manager or lighting designer may call the cues.

Color. Pink, blue, and ambers are the predominant colors for the TINTS in the general or basic lighting. Deeper saturates of these colors are often used as washes, with light red and medium blue also used for mood and toning. An abundance of color is common in the star's specialty numbers;

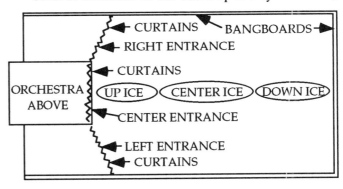

TYPICAL ICE SHOW PLAN

using six different colors from the 10 or 12 followspots is not unusual. White and "frame zero" are used to denote no color in the frame.

Control. Often control is by large-capacity SUBMASTERS, which control banks of colored light from overhead, BANGBOARDS, and color washes. AREA LIGHTS and POOL lights are sometimes GANGED, whereas specials will have individual control. Control equipment can be less sophisticated than needed for many other types of shows since followspots play such an important part in the lighting. ARC LIGHTS in followspots are not electrically dimmed, so they are not connected to the SWITCHBOARD.

ID. Inside diameter of a pipe or tube. The black pipes in fly systems on which scenery and lights are hung are 1 1/4" ID for small- to medium-size stages and 1 1/2" ID for large stages. C-CLAMPS and YOKE CLAMPS will fit either size.

ILLUMINATION. Surface light intensity expressed in FOOTCANDLES. The human eye adjusts to intensities from 1 to 10,000 footcandles, but degrees of brightness above 100 footcandles are not easily discernible. It is therefore seldom necessary to attempt to illuminate any stage with much more than 100 footcandles. A standard light meter may be used to check proper intensity onstage or in the auditorium but few professionals do this.

IN

The set-in of a show as contrasted with the STRIKE or OUT.

Defining stage space. In one: Space from left to right stage between fire curtain and TORMENTOR. **In two:** Space from left to right stage between tormentor and first wing. **In three:** Space from left to right stage between first wing and second wing. See SLIT.

INCANDESCENT LAMP. An electric light with a tungsten filament that heats to incandescence when an electric current is passed through it. Catalogue designations for theatrical lamps not included in ANSI codes carry all pertinent information, including wattage, shape of bulb, maximum diameter, and base type. Catalogue lamp codes are as follows: first numbers indicate wattage; first letter, shape of bulb; second number, size of bulb's

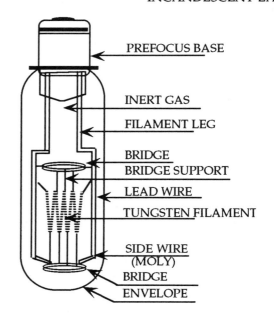

INCANDESCENT LAMP

largest diameter in eighths of an inch. Thus, a T-20 lamp is tubular and 20/8" (2 1/2") in diameter. Numbers immediately following are generally manufacturer code numbers. After code designations, most catalogues list lamp base, volts, filament, approximate hours of life, lumens, etc. Lighting instruments are designed specifically for lamps of a given size, shape, wattage, and base,

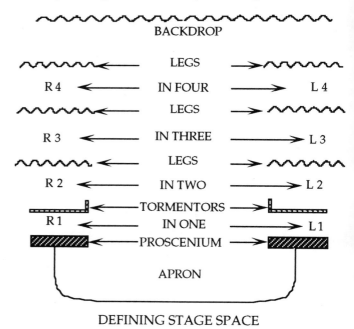

DEFINING STAGE SPACE

although, if so designated, some instruments allow wattages to be interchanged. Buy lamps according to manufacturer specifications and burn lamps according to designated position in order to realize the maximum rated hours of life. See LAMPS.

INDEPENDENT. A dimmer not controlled by a **grand master, group master** (see under DIMMERS, MASTER), preset, or scene master. Independent of all other dimmer controls.

INDUCTANCE DIMMER. Obsolete. An older form of dimmer consisting of a rotor and a stator, in which the rotor is turned through 90°. This type of dimmer was manufactured by the Major Equipment Company during the 1930s and had the advantage of using no brushes or contacts. However, the action of the inductance dimmer was not considered as smooth or efficient as the AUTO-TRANSFORMER and therefore was not widely used in the theatre.

INFINITE PRESET. A preset light board with no limit of available scenes. Computer boards are considered to have infinite preset when limited only by the available memory in the system. See LIGHTING CONTROL.

INKY. A 3" fresnel spotlight designed for a 100- to 125-watt lamp and intended for use in very tight quarters such as a phone booth, under a balcony, etc. Small R-type lamps can also be fitted into tight spaces like the inky but they do not have color or focus capability. See FRESNEL LIGHT.

INNER ABOVE. Acting area on the upper level of the Elizabethan stage separated from the rest of the upper stage by a curtain, which may be drawn to "discover" the action. In Shakespearean stage directions, "above" refers to this upper stage. INKYS work well in these tight quarters, although it is

INKY

common for the acting lights to come from the front or from BOX BOOM positions.

INNER BELOW. Acting area on the lower level of the Elizabethan stage separated from the rest of the lower stage by a curtain, which may be drawn to "discover" the action. In Shakespearean stage directions, "below" refers to this lower stage. Small fresnel spots work well in close confines, where lights are necessarily close to actors; additionally AREA LIGHTS often come from the FOH positions.

INNER PROSCENIUM. A scenic frame set upstage of the curtain to narrow the proscenium width or to facilitate CROSSLIGHTING.

INSERTING. See under COMPUTER LIGHT BOARD TERMINOLOGY.

INSTRUMENT (light, luminaire, unit, lantern [British usage]). The many different types of lights used in stage lighting are called instruments or luminaires. Both terms refer to the complete unit, including HOUSING, LAMP, LENS, REFLECTOR, and any other accoutrements applicable to the unit. See under individual types: BEAM PROJECTOR; BORDER LIGHTS; CYC STRIP; ELLIPSOIDAL REFLECTOR SPOTLIGHT; FLOODLIGHT; FOOTLIGHT; FRESNEL LIGHT; PARcan; PROJECTORS; SCOOP.

INSTRUMENT CHECK. During each preshow check, all lighting instruments are turned on and tested to make sure they work, the focus is correct, and the gel is holding its color.

INSTRUMENT FUSE (board fuse). Small glass cartridge (automotive type) fuse usually rated at very low amperage (e.g., 1/8 A, 1/4 A, 1/2 A) used to protect an electrical circuit associated with control.

INSTRUMENT SCHEDULE. See **Cheat sheets** under DESIGN FOR LIGHTING.

INSULATED-GATE BIPOLAR TRANSISTOR DIMMER (IGBT, IPS™ [Intelligent Power System]). A digital processing dimmer that uses its own microcontroller to control the timing for the gating of the insulated-gate bipolar transistors. This system uses reverse phase control where the dimmer shuts off in a controlled manner during the half cycle rather than at the zero crossing like SCRs. Because of this, the unit is not bothered by most distorted waveforms in the power. No choke is used because of reverse phase control and the controlled turn-off at the half cycle. Since the unit has no choke, noise at the dimmer is negligible, and filament noise in the lamp is subjectively quieter than an SCR. Heat is dissipated via the fins on the dimmer unit and no fan is required. The dimmers are located adjacent to the controlled lights (distributed dimming system) rather than in a central rack. Although the concept of position or batten-mounted dimmers is not new, the use of a front-end processor handling six dimmers with full logic and testing control is. A "focus button" allows the electrician to bring up the dimmer to any intensity

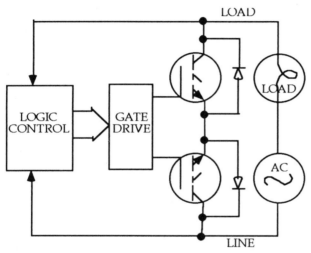

SCHEMATIC DRAWING OF
INSULATED-GATE BIPOLAR
TRANSISTOR DIMMER

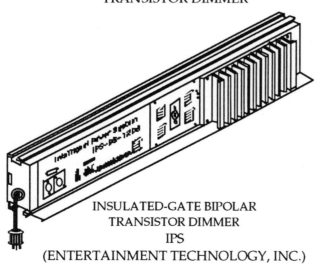

INSULATED-GATE BIPOLAR
TRANSISTOR DIMMER
IPS
(ENTERTAINMENT TECHNOLOGY, INC.)

at the dimmer itself. Virtually "idiot" proof, the dimmer will shut itself down with a dead short or for most other difficulties.

INSULATION, CONDUCTOR. Covering made from nonconducting materials such as fabric, plastic, rubber, used on conductors to prevent short-circuiting and to make them safe to handle. See also CABLE.

INSULATOR. Nonconductor of electricity that acts as a mechanical barrier making electrical equipment safe to handle.

INTENSITY

Color. Degree of purity or saturation of color.

Dimmer. The calibration level or reading.

Light. The amount of light on the stage. Brightness of light on any given area from any given instrument. Light intensity depends on lamp capacity, lens and reflector quality, throw distance, and color media used. Measured in footcandles.

INTERCONNECTING PANELS. See PATCH PANEL.

INTERLOCK

Safety. A safety device on equipment that either kills power when the access door to the electrical box is opened or will not allow the box to be opened until power is turned off.

Mechanical mastering. The ability of individual dimmers to connect (interlock) into mechanical mastering on older switchboards. See **Mechanical master** under DIMMER, MASTER.

INVENTORY. Many theatres and all rental companies keep records of their lighting instruments noting numbers, makes, sizes, and condition of all equipment. Such lists are very helpful to the lighting designer and essential to the guest designer.

INVERSE SQUARE LAW. Illumination decreases by the square of the distance from the light source. If the candlepower of a given lamp is known, footcandles at a given distance can be computed from the following equation: $FC = CP/D^2$, where FC = footcandles, CP = candlepower, D^2 = distance in feet squared.

Example: Illumination at a distance of 10' from a 150-candlepower lamp: Footcandles = 150/10 x 10 = 150/100 = 1.5 footcandles.

IPS. Intelligent Power System is a trademark of Entertainment Technology, Inc., for an INSULATED-GATE BIPOLAR TRANSISTOR DIMMER system.

IRIS. An attachment for a spotlight that varies the diameter of the light beam from closed to wide open. Primary use is to control beam size on an arc light or FOLLOWSPOT.

IZENOUR BOARD. A lighting control board using THYRATRON TUBE DIMMERS, designed and built by George Izenour at Yale University in 1947. Now superseded by computer boards with SILICON CONTROLLED RECTIFIERS.

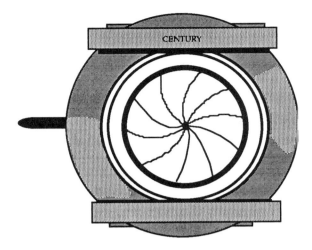

IRIS

J

JACK. A female electrical connector most generally associated with sound systems but sometimes used in telephone PATCH PANELS. The male connector for a jack is a plug.

J BOX (jay box). Short for junction box, used by stage electricians to gang circuits.

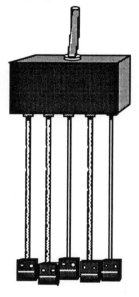

JUNCTION BOX
(J BOX)

JOYSTICK (pan pot). A means of controlling the movement of an automated spotlight or PARcan. Rock, heavy metal, and rap concerts have created a demand for lights that focus, pan, tilt, and change color by remote control. The joystick, a swiveling handle similar to the controls of computer games, has been adapted as the control handle for the movements of some of these lights. Automated PARcans are shows in themselves and have no real function in play production.

Some ELLIPSOIDAL REFLECTOR SPOT-LIGHTS are equipped with joysticks to adjust alignment of the lamp to the reflector and lenses. See ALIGNING INSTRUMENTS.

JUICE. Colloquialism for electricity, power, or the electric department.

JUICER. A colloquial term for the stage electrician who works on the lights.

JUMPER (patchcord, pigtail). A cable with appropriate connectors used for a temporary connection between two circuits. May also serve as a connector in a PATCH PANEL or COMPANY PATCH.

K

KELVIN SCALE. A temperature scale used to designate color of light by the temperature at its source and named after the British physicist and mathematician William Thomson Kelvin (1824–1907). Kelvin units (no degree symbol is used with the Kelvin scale) are the same size as centigrade degrees but the starting point is absolute zero (-273.15° C). Zero degrees centigrade equals 273 K; 100° C equals 373 K. Visible light begins at 600 K. The normal temperature range of gas-filled spotlight lamps is between 2,750 and 3,100 K and the normal range of tungsten-halogen lamps is between 3,000 and 3,400 K. The color of light within this range is compared with the color of sunlight from 40 minutes to 1 hour after sunrise. Warm colors are within the 1,800–3,500 K range. Temperatures ranging from 3,500 to 28,000 K progress in color from the palest blue to the extreme blue of a clear daylight sky. See also COLOR TEMPERATURE.

KEY LIGHT (key). The main source of light for an area, establishing direction of illumination, mood, and atmosphere. FILL LIGHT used in conjunction with key light functions as blending light and may also provide color and atmosphere. Usually BASE LIGHT works as a basic illumination, with several lights flooding an area with, for example, a medium-blue gel. A key light could highlight the actors with a light-straw media, suggesting a full moon, while the fill light in a pale blue could be used to lessen the deep shadow on the far side of the actors' faces. Since spotlights are highly directional, logically they are the preferred instruments to provide key light. See FORMULA; LIGHTING PRACTICE.

KEYPAD. See under COMPUTER LIGHT BOARD TERMINOLOGY.

KEYSTONING. The distortion of a projected image caused by placing a projector in any location other than perpendicular to the screen. When the projector is below the center of the screen, the image appears larger on the top than on the bottom, and conversely, if the projector is above the center of the screen, the image appears larger on the bottom. Placing the projector on either side

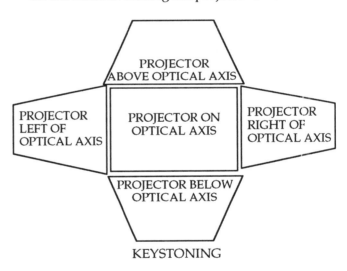

KEYSTONING

of the screen naturally produces similar distortions. With front screen projection, true alignment would place the projector in full view of the audience, possibly obstructing their view. If rear screen projection (projecting on a translucent screen from behind) is possible, the projector may be placed in any position, eliminating the problem. (See PROJECTION SCREEN.) If space or budget will not permit rear screen projection, align the projector and screen as well as possible and compensate by painting an opposite distortion on the slide or by photographing the picture to be projected at the opposite angle the projector is to the screen. With a

91

front overhead projector an easy solution is to pull the bottom of a straight cyc downstage to compensate for the keystoning. See also **Distortion correction** under PROJECTOR, SLIDES.

KICK. Term used to denote that a BREAKER goes off: "the breaker kicked again." It can also be used to order the breaker on: "kick the breaker back in."

KILL (command verb). To turn off lights, remove instruments, cut a cue.

KILOWATT (abbr. kW). A unit of power equal to 1,000 watts. Spotlights are often identified by their kilowatt power; for example, a 1,000-watt spotlight is a 1 kW or an ace, a 1,500-watt spotlight is 1.5 kW or an ace and a half, a 2,000-watt spotlight is a 2 kW or a deuce, a 3,000-watt spotlight is a 3 kW or a tray, etc.

KILOWATT-HOUR (abbr. kWh). Unit of electricity used for pricing. Electricity is sold by the kilowatt-hour, equal to 1,000 watts consumed over a period of 1 hour. Thus a person burning a 100-watt lamp for a period of 10 hours will be billed for 1 kWh.

KLIEGL BROS. A major manufacturing business for almost 100 years. The brothers John and Anton began the company in 1896 as Universal Stage Lighting Company. Since almost everyone used the name Kliegl Brothers, it was officially changed in 1931 to Kliegl Bros. It remained a family-run business for its life.

KLIEGLIGHT

First lighting word to be accepted in general dictionaries as a GENERIC TERM for a high-intensity arc light.

Trade name for any spotlight invented and manufactured by Kliegl Bros.

KLIEGSUN. Obsolete. Trade name for a narrow-beam projector spot manufactured by Kliegl Bros. Originally called the sun-spot.

KLIEGLIGHT 250, 500, OR 750-WATT
CA.1958

KLIEGL 6"-8"
ELLIPSOIDAL
TUNGSTEN-
HALOGEN LAMP

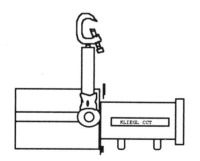

KLIEGL VARIABLE FOCUS ERS

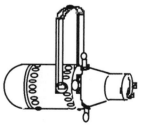

KLIEGL ERS
750, 1,000-WATT

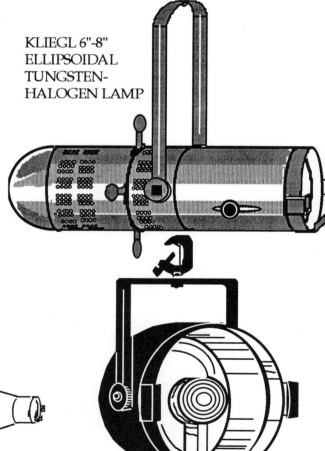

KLIEGSUN

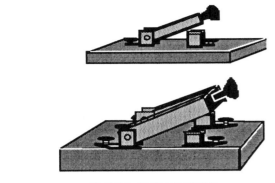

SINGLE AND DOUBLE
KNIFE SWITCHES

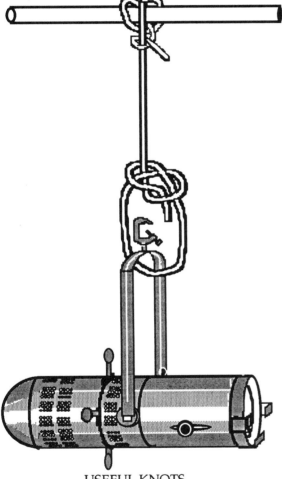

USEFUL KNOTS
CLOVE HITCH ON A PIPE
BOWLINE THROUGH A HANGER
USED TO LIFT LIGHT
TO MOUNTING POSITION

KNIFE SWITCH. Obsolete. A switch in which a blade is hinged to close the circuit between two terminals. Because the knife switch offers no protection to the operator, its use is confined to antennas or equipment requiring very low amperage and voltage.

KNOTS. Useful to the electrician:

Bow. This simple knot used to tie drops to a batten is used to tie cables to pipes.

Bowline. Used whenever a line passes through an eye or ring. The bowline will not slip and is easily untied. Use as a safety line on electrical equipment to prevent equipment from falling and for hoisting instruments into place.

Clove hitch. Used for pipe or wooden battens for supporting electrical pipes from the grid.

Tie-off, pinrail. A figure eight wraparound the belaying pin with a half hitch on top and on the bottom of the pin.

Underwriters knot. A bulky knot tied in flexible two-wire conductors and used to prevent strain on the terminals of plugs not equipped with strain relief devices. However, two-wire conductors are no longer legal.

KODAK CAROUSEL. A lensed projector with a large slide-holding magazine. See under PROJECTORS.

kW. Abbreviation for KILOWATT.

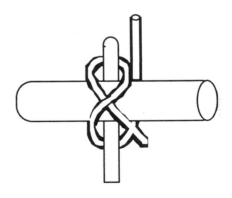

PINRAIL TIE-OFF

L

LADDER. Ladders are essential equipment in every theatre. Wooden ladders are preferred by electricians because they are nonconductors and therefore less dangerous to use while working with electrical circuits. Since ladders are a long-term investment, buy the best and be certain they are rated for at least a 250-pound load. Check bolts and rivets periodically and keep ladders in good repair; a loose or wobbly ladder is a life-threatening hazard.

    A-ladder. A ladder with a vertical extension in the middle of an A-shaped base unit. See A-LADDER.

    Extension ladder. Two straight ladders designed to telescope, providing a variable height. Use of the extension ladder is limited to positions where it can lean against a wall.

    Stepladder. The stepladder is probably the most used ladder in the theatre; they fold up and store easily. Choose only the best and most sturdy. The most useful sizes are 6', 8', 12', and 16'.

    Lighting ladders. See under LIGHT MOUNTING DEVICES.

LAG, TIME. See TIME LAG.

LAMP CARRIAGE. Comprises the lamp holder, lamp, and often the reflector. This assembly moves to and from the lens, changing the focus.

LAMP DIP (colorine). Lacquer used to color light bulbs. Commercial lamp dips are available in many colors for low-wattage lamps that do not burn too hot. To color lamps, dip the lighted bulb in the dye and hang it up to dry. Hand-dipped bulbs are suitable for older striplights and footlights, but heat from lamps of 60 watts or more will cause lacquer to crack, fade, and flake. Boiling caustic soda will remove faded or chipped lamp dip, preparing lamp for recoloring. A better solution is to buy colored lamps, available in most theatrical supply houses in a variety of permanent colors that will not fade or chip.

LAMP HOLDER (socket). The socket in a lighting instrument.

LAMP LIFE. Lamps for theatrical use have an effective life ranging from a few hours to several thousand depending upon their use and their filament designs. Lamp life is part of the data included in ANSI code numbers and is usually listed in catalogues for lamps without ANSI codes.

LAMPLIGHT EFFECT. Although lamplight is actually yellow, it is usually represented onstage by the more flattering color of amber. PRACTICAL lamps used as props should be electrified with a concealed wire if stationary or with batteries if movable. Flashlight batteries and flashlight bulbs are generally sufficient. Practical lamps should be 25–40 watts to avoid distracting intensities. Supplemental light used in conjunction with a cue is provided by spotlights on the same circuit so the lighting operator controls all lights while the actor fakes the cue.

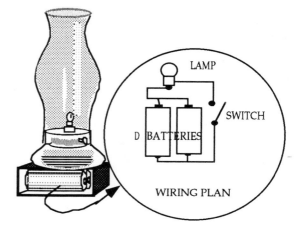

PRACTICAL LAMP TO BE CARRIED

LAMPS (bulbs, globes, lights). Because there are so many lamp sizes, shapes, and types of bases required by theatrical lighting equipment, choosing lamp replacements for instruments used to be a formidable job. Recognizing the dilemma, the ANSI assigned code letters to lamps describing the following characteristics: wattage, voltage, size, life expectancy, base type, bulb shape, lumens, burning position, and color temperature. Now a simple three-letter designation on the order sheet will ensure that the purchaser receives the correct lamp. See ANSI.

The parts and characteristics of most of the more commonly used lamps are described and illustrated below.

Base position. Many lamps are designed so the proper spacing between filament and glass envelope is provided only when the lamp is burned in the correct position. Such lamps are designated burn base up, burn base down to horizontal, etc. Life expectancy of the lamp is greatly reduced if such designations are ignored.

Bases. The metal part of the lamp that fits into the socket. Lighting instruments are designed for miniature, candelabra, medium, and mogul bases.

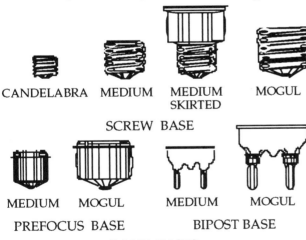

CANDELABRA   MEDIUM   MEDIUM   MOGUL
                      SKIRTED
              SCREW BASE

MEDIUM   MOGUL   MEDIUM   MOGUL
PREFOCUS BASE   BIPOST BASE
          LAMP BASES

Bayonet base. A round base with two pins of different sizes on the topside edge providing positive filament orientation. It is important to specify whether a single-contact (SC bay.) or a double-contact (DC bay.) bayonet base is needed.

Bipost base. Med Bp (medium bipost) and mog Bp (mogul bipost) are the two sizes used with the two-pronged base used in spotlights and pro-

jectors. The bipost base ensures positive orientation of filament with optical system.

Mogul end prong. Mog EP, appears only on larger PAR LAMPS.

Prefocus base. Med Pf (medium prefocus) and mog Pf (mogul prefocus) are used in spotlights and projectors and provide positive orientation of filament to optical system.

RSC base (recessed single contact). Many tungsten-halogen lamps made for spotlights have the RSC base. See ANSI designations.

Screw base. Med Sc (medium screwbase) and mog Sc (mogul screwbase) were used in early spotlights. Stage use of screw bases is now confined to some BORDER LIGHTS, FLOOD-LIGHTS, FOOTLIGHTS, and STRIPLIGHTS.

END PRONG   SCREW TERMINAL   SIDE PRONG
          PAR LAMP BASES

RSC
TUNGSTEN-HALOGEN   DC BAY   SC BAY
          LAMP BASES

Bulb shapes. The bulb is the glass portion of a lamp, housing the filament. Following is a list of the shapes commonly used in theatre equipment.

Arbitrary (A-type). The shape of the common household light bulb. Often used backstage as cue lights, usually 7 1/2 or 15 watts.

Globular (G-type). Generally used in older spotlights, of 100- to 2,000-watt ratings. Most theatre spotlights now require the T-type lamp.

Parabolic reflector (PAR, sealed beam light). PAR is an acronym for parabolic aluminized reflector, which is incorporated in the bulb, providing direction and great efficiency to the light. Originally called birdseye lamps after their inventor, Clarence Birdseye (of frozen food fame), PAR lamps are available in many sizes, PAR 38 (4 3/4" diameter), 46 (5 3/4"), 56 (7"), and 64 (8") being the most popular. Wattages include 150, 200, 300, 500, and 1,000 watts, and beam widths include narrow spot, medium flood, and wide flood. 100-watt

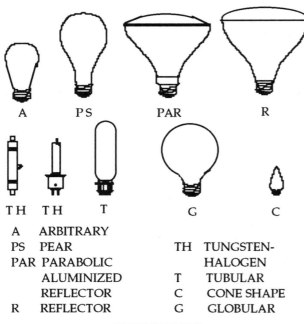

A — PS — PAR — R

TH — TH — T — G — C

A — ARBITRARY
PS — PEAR
PAR — PARABOLIC
    ALUMINIZED
    REFLECTOR
R — REFLECTOR

TH — TUNGSTEN-
    HALOGEN
T — TUBULAR
C — CONE SHAPE
G — GLOBULAR

BULB SHAPES

PAR lamps are available in six standard colors (red, blue, green, yellow, amber, pink) and, occasionally, in daylight white. Housings for PARs (PARcans), which include yokes and color media holders, are available from full-service theatrical supply houses. Special bases for larger sizes require special sockets. See also PARcans.

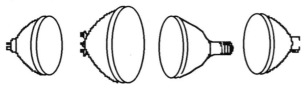

PAR LAMPS

Pear-shaped (PS). Often used in older footlights, striplights, and border lights. OLIVETTES require PS lamps with screw bases, which come in assorted sizes up to 1,000 watts.

Reflector (R-type). Used in some border lights, footlights, and striplights. Similar to PAR lamps but with a diffused, less concentrated beam of light. The most frequently used clear R-lamps in theatre include the R 30 (3 3/4" diameter), 75 and 150 watts; the R 40 (5"), 150, 300, 500 watts; and the R 40, 75-watt color lamp. Colors are limited to red, blue, green, yellow, amber, pink, and sometimes daylight blue.

Filaments. Lighting instruments (particularly spotlights) are designed for a given filament configuration and a specified distance from the base to the center of the filament, LCL (light center length). If lamps with the wrong configurations or measurements are used, the lighting instrument will not function according to specifications. Always relamp according to the manufacturer's designated ANSI code numbers.

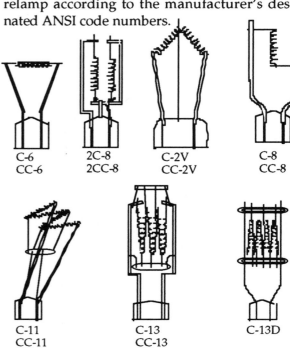

C-6
CC-6

2C-8
2CC-8

C-2V
CC-2V

C-8
CC-8

C-11
CC-11

C-13
CC-13

C-13D

FILAMENT DESIGNATIONS

Light sources

Arc. The now almost obsolete carbon arc used for almost a century as the light source for special effects, projectors, and followspots is now being replaced by encapsulated short-arc lamps.

Short arc. An encapsulated (enclosed in a glass envelope), high-output, short-arc light. Used predominantly for projectors and followspots. See HMI; XENON LAMP.

XENON ARC LAMP

Incandescent. Gas-filled, tungsten filament lamps have been the standard since their introduction in 1914. See INCANDESCENT LAMP.

Tungsten-halogen (TH, quartz iodine, QI). A lamp using a halogen gas around a compact filament. Used in instruments designed specifically for this type of lamp, the TH lamp can also be retrofitted for older instruments. It should be noted that the terms "QI" and "quartz iodine" are misnomers in common usage. See RETROFIT LAMP; TUNGSTEN-HALOGEN LAMP.

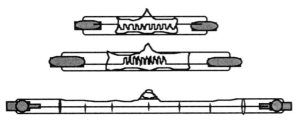

DOUBLE-ENDED TUNGSTEN-HALOGEN LAMPS

LAMPS, ORDERING. Older lamps have a complicated set of specifications for resupplying. In ordering these lamps the following information must be specified: wattage, shape, size, base type, base size, and filament type (e.g., 500-W/T-12/ med prefocus, filament CC-13). The ANSI code is far simpler; just provide the three-letter code (FEL, BTM, EHR, etc).

LAMPS, PRACTICAL. A prop lamp that must light. See LAMPLIGHT EFFECT.

LANTERN. The British term for a lighting instrument.

LASER. Acronym for light amplification by stimulated emission of radiation. Coherent and pure light, meaning it is one color and one wavelength. It is created by passing high voltage through a gas-filled tube in a magnetic field, causing ionization and radiation of light. The magnetic field causes the radiation to oscillate between mirrors in each end of the tube, building velocity. At a given speed, one of the mirrors is designed to allow the radiation to pass through instead of being reflected back. The resulting light is the coherent light of the laser beam, the same light that is used in everything from supermarket checkouts to space probes; eye surgery to weapons; computer printers to transcontinental communications. Such concentrations of light are extremely dangerous. Prolonged exposure to even the low-power lasers (0.001 watt, or 1 milliwatt) can cause eye damage. Laser beams of 0.5-watt power constitute the top limit allowable in the entertainment field. For the safety of operators and viewers alike, only those with training and full knowledge of the safety literature issued by the U.S. Department of Health and Welfare should be allowed to use lasers above 1 milliwatt (mW) in power. Laser power required for HOLOGRAPHY photography is well beyond the safe point.

LAW OF CHARGES. Like charges of electricity (positive and positive) repel and unlike charges of electricity (positive and negative) attract.

LAW OF REFLECTION. The ANGLE OF INCIDENCE equals the ANGLE OF REFLECTION.

LAW OF SQUARES

Light intensity. Intensity of light decreases in inverse proportion to the square of the distance from the source. *Example*: If a light source produces 32 footcandles at a 1' distance, the same source will produce 8 footcandles at a 2' distance (32 FC/2' x 2'); and 2 footcandles at 4' (32 FC/4' x 4').

Dimmer curve. Said to be square law when the specified readings on the control calibrations produce apparent corresponding readings in light intensity. The controller "zero" reading for a standard square law curve is typically about 12.5 volts.

LAYERING

Drawing (overlaying). A drawing made on a transparent sheet of paper or plastic and superimposed on another drawing. For complicated light plots, it is convenient and neater to layer drawings as needed for the light plot on a floor plan, thus clarifying positioning and use of equipment.

Lighting. Special lighting for different scenes or shifts in mood. This can be achieved by DOUBLING or TRIPLING.

LCL (abbr. light center length). Used in lamp catalogues to indicate the distance between the center of the filament and (in a screw base lamp) the bottom base contact point, (in a bipost lamp) the bottom of the bulb, or (in a prefocus lamp) the top of the base.

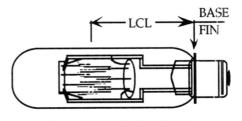

LIGHT CENTER LENGTH
OF PREFOCUS LAMP

LD. An acronym for LIGHTING DESIGNER; sometimes used for lighting director.

LEG. The hot side of the line. A branch or component part of a circuit. One leg of the line can refer to the 110-volt circuit between one of the hot lines and the neutral line. See also CIRCUITS.

LEGS. Narrow drapery panels forming the side wings of a complete set of stage drapes and used for side masking.

LEKO (Lekolight). Trade name of the former Century Lighting Company (now Strand) ellipsoidal spotlight. Often used as a generic name for any brand of ellipsoidal spotlight. The name was derived from the first two letters of the names of the cofounders of the Century Lighting Company, Joseph Levy and Edward Kook.

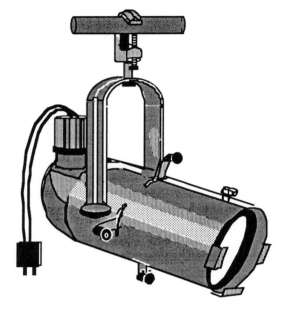

CENTURY LEKOLITE
(250, 500, OR 750 WATTS, CA. 1964)

LENSES. Clear glass or plastic ground or cast to change the direction of light rays passing through. Lenses used in spotlights are generally made of crown glass (low dispersion and low index of refraction), cast and polished but not corrected. Lenses are designated by diameter and focal length; thus, a 6" x 8" lens is 6" in diameter with an 8" focal length. If unknown, the focal length (distance from the center of the lens to the point where rays converge) can be estimated by holding the lens in direct sunlight, adjusting until the sharpest point of light appears on a surface, and measuring the distance from that point to the lens. The thicker the lens, the shorter the focal length. The range of focus in a spotlight falls between the lens and the focal point. Short focal lengths are used for short THROWS and long focal lengths for long throws. The focal length of two lenses used together is figured with the equation: $F = (f_1 \times f_2)/(f_1 + f_2 - D)$, where F = the combined focal length of both lenses, f_1 = focal length of the first lens, f_2 = focal length of the second lens, and D = distance between lenses in inches.

Example: What is the focal length of a 4" lens and a 6" lens placed 2" apart? $(4" \times 6")/(4" + 6" - 2") = 24/8 = 3"$.

Dirty lens. A dirty or dusty lens will disperse light almost as effectively as a FROST gelatine. Theatres are notoriously dirty, dusty places; take the time to wash or at least dust lenses.

CENTURY LEKOLITE
(4 1/2" LENS, 250, 500, OR 750 WATTS, CA. 1948)

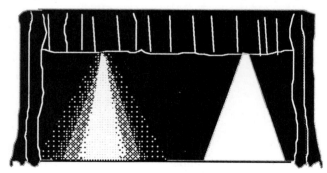

POOLS OF LIGHT: DIRTY LENS AND CLEAN LENS

f-number. In photographic equipment, the amount of light allowed to pass through the lens is a variable controlled by an IRIS. The f-number is the focal length of the lens divided by its effective diameter as determined by the iris setting. Applied to a spotlight, a 6" x 12" lens would then be 12/6, or an f-2 lens, providing no iris or obstruction was allowed to change the diameter of the lens.

Fast lens. A thick lens capable of transmitting a large amount of light. Generally speaking, a short focal length. Note that a shorter focal length lens captures nearly twice as much source light as a longer focal length lens.

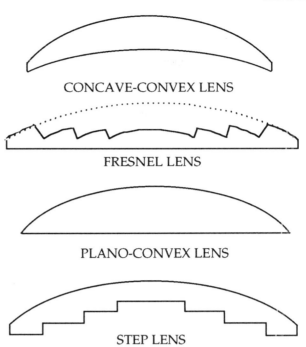

CONCAVE-CONVEX LENS

FRESNEL LENS

PLANO-CONVEX LENS

STEP LENS

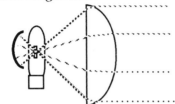

SHORT FOCAL LENGTH

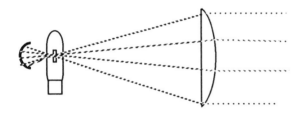

LONG FOCAL LENGTH

Slow lens. A thin lens capable of transmitting a smaller amount of light. Generally speaking, a long focal length.

Lens shapes

Concave-convex lens. Usually used as a part of multilensed components.

Double plano-convex lens. Two plano-convex lenses with the convex sides facing each other shorten the focal length, making wide-angle instruments.

Fresnel lens (pronounced fra nel'). See also FRESNEL LIGHT. A thin lens produced by casting the curvature of the lens in concentric rings, which are then stepped back to the plane surface, thus making possible short focal lengths in thin lenses. Thin lenses have the advantage of reducing weight, offering more tolerance to heat, and thus permitting the use of higher wattage lamps in smaller, more compact instruments. The plane surface of the fresnel lens is given a waffle pattern, which diffuses the light and eliminates any apparent aberration or pattern that might come from the risers of the lens. The resulting soft-edged, diffused light makes for ideal blending of areas on the stage but precludes the use of fresnel spotlights in the auditorium.

Objective lens. The lens or lenses in a projector used to bring a slide into focus on the screen. It usually consists of two plano-convex lenses in a tube in fixed relation to each other but capable of moving together to adjust the focus.

Plano-convex lens (PC lens). Plane on one side and convex on the other, the plano-convex lens gives a sharp-edged light that is ideal for BEAM, BOOTH, or BALCONY mounting positions.

Step lens. The reverse of the fresnel lens, the step lens has risers placed on the plane side of the lens, leaving the convex side with its original curve. Step lenses, available with or without black risers to reduce color ABERRATIONS and spill, are lightweight, heat-resistant, and produce a hard-edged light suitable for BEAM, BALCONY, or BOOTH mounting positions. Many ellipsoidal spotlights are equipped with step lenses, but a sharper focus is obtained with a double plano-convex lens system.

Zoom lens. A system of lenses in which focal lengths may be changed either remotely or manually. The ZOOM ELLIPSE spotlight increases efficiency by adjusting the lenses to serve equally well for a 20' or 40' throw; for example, from either the first ELECTRIC or the BEAM position. The zoom is effected by varying the distance between the lenses or the distance from the light source to the lenses, either by a slide mechanism or fixed slots to receive the lenses.

LENSLESS PROJECTOR. See Direct beam and Linnebach under PROJECTORS.

LEVEL. Intensity of light, expressed either by a percentage or by a calibrated-scale reading.

LIGHT AREA. A three-dimensional space that a spotlight is capable of lighting between the floor and a 7' height. See AREA.

LIGHT BATTEN (electrics, light pipe, light border, bar [British usage]). A pipe, TRUSS, or extruded-aluminum RACEWAY from which lighting instruments may be hung. In permanent installations, cables and multiple circuits are often included in packaged light battens designed especially for hanging and circuiting instruments. If light battens must be made in the theatre, black pipe (1 1/4" diameter for small stages and 1 1/2" diameter for large stages, inside dimension) should be used. Most C-CLAMPS or other instrument-mounting clamps are designed to fit either pipe size.

LIGHT BOARD. A name given to any type of LIGHTING CONTROL system. See CONTROL BOARDS AND CONSOLES.

LIGHT BRIDGE. A narrow metal catwalk placed in the first BORDER or first ELECTRIC position and used for mounting and focusing lighting instruments. Bridges are usually either counterweighted or controlled with an electric motor or a winch. With a light bridge, electricians have the advantage of being able to mount lighting instruments from the floor, raise the bridge to the prescribed height, and focus from the bridge, thereby saving a great deal of ladder work.

LIGHT CUE. Any movement of light or change in light balance from the control board. See also CUE.

LIGHT CURTAIN. (1) A sheet of light from PARcans or spotlights mounted close together in a single line and shining straight down on the stage. This can be a very intense lighting effect. (2) A bank of spotlights mounted onstage and deliberately focused into the eyes of the audience. This effect, used in outdoor theatres without act curtains, blinds the audience to scene changes taking place on the darkened stage. The technique lacks subtlety but works.

LIGHTING ACCESSORIES. See accessory wanted: CLAMPS; LIGHT SPILL CONTROL; LIGHT-MOUNTING DEVICES; PLUGS; etc.

LIGHTING BACKINGS. See BACKING LIGHT; **Backing Light** under LIGHTING PRACTICE.

LIGHTING COLORS. See under COLOR.

LIGHTING CONTROL. Over the years, there have been at least four major categories of control equipment: **Switchboards, Light boards, Control boards,** and **Consoles.** (See under CONTROL BOARDS AND CONSOLES.) Most lighting control has at least two components: the physical area of control (front end) and the dimmer mechanism (back end). They can be referred to by the type of dimmer used; for example, an autotransformer board can mean it is a light board with autotransformer dimmers. The name given can also be based on the type of mechanical control used, such as a player board or an interlock board. "Light

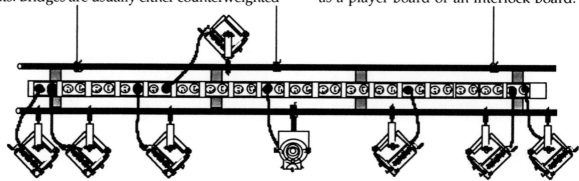

LIGHT BATTEN

100

board" and "board" are generic terms that can describe any type of control. However, the term "control" can refer to both the front end and the back end.

Front ends. These are the individual or groups of handles, switches, buttons, keys, and other controls the ELECTRICIAN'S hands touch to operate the lights for a show. For example, switchboard, light board, control board, player board, preset board, computer board, interlock board, console, autotransformer board, piano board, resistance board, switchboard.

Back ends. These are the dimmers which actual dim the light onstage and as such are a part of the control. The three most common types in use over the years are resistance dimmer, autotransformer dimmer, and silicon controlled rectifier dimmer. See AUTOTRANSFORMER; MICROPROCESSOR; PIANO BOARD; PRESET; RESISTANCE DIMMER; SILICON CONTROLLED RECTIFIER; SWITCHBOARD. See also DIMMERS.

LIGHTING CONTROL LOCATIONS. The ideal location is nonexistent. Various locations and their advantages and disadvantages are as follows:

Downstage on control side of stage at floor level (where the curtain control is located; usually stage right). This is the oldest location and allows close contact with the command center but interferes with scene changes, stage manager's duties, entrances, and offers virtually no visibility of the stage.

Downstage above floor level on control side of stage. Close contact with command control, out of the way, better visibility of stage except for box sets with ceilings.

Downcenter stage in conductor's pit. Out of the way, good visibility of stage, but too close to perceive subtle changes and removed from command control.

Control room in back of theatre. Out of the way, excellent visibility, best if stage manager is in same space, otherwise requires reliable intercom system. Generally the preferred location.

LIGHTING DESIGNER (LD). A person who conceives, researches, designs, drafts, and oversees the implementation of the lighting for a production. See DESIGN FOR LIGHTING.

LIGHTING INSTRUMENTS. See under individual classifications: BEAM PROJECTOR; BOR-DER LIGHT; FLOODLIGHT; FOOTLIGHT; PARcan; PAR LIGHT; SCOOP; SPOTLIGHT; STRIPLIGHT.

LIGHTING LAYOUT. British expression for area separation.

LIGHTING POSITIONS. See **Instrument positions** under LIGHTING PRACTICE.

LIGHTING PRACTICE

Aesthetics

Ambience (mood). Light supports the mood of the play through its color, intensity, focus, or angle. For example, comedy generally calls for lighter colors, higher intensities, uniform coverage, and "normal" angles, whereas tragedy is better served by darker, more foreboding colors, lower intensities, shadowy areas, and more dramatic angles of light. Shining moonlight through a window and creating menacing shadows can reinforce the action and mood of a play.

Complementing design (composition). Using light to enhance the design or composition of the stage setting. Examples are projections of shadows of leaves on a window, venetian blinds on a wall, clouds on a sky cyc.

Modeling (revealing form). Emphasizing facial features and three dimensional effects through the use of two or more lights with different colors from different sources, sidelighting, backlighting, or whatever kind of lighting the designer thinks appropriate.

Naturalizing light (illusion of nature). Making artificial light look more like natural light. This involves paying careful attention to the choice of colors to fit the occasion and placing lighting sources at angles approximating the normal angle of natural light to be simulated.

Selective visibility. The use of light to focus audience attention on a particular person or object. This may vary from the obvious, a single PINSPOT focused on the chosen subject, to the subliminal, a slight increase of intensity on a given area.

Properties of light

Color. Color choice will be determined by a number of factors, including specifics of the play, preferences of the director and designers, costume colors, color media chosen.

Distribution. Distribution of light falls between the extremes of flooding an area with a wash of light or confining it to a point as with a PINSPOT.

This again will be governed by the playwright, director, scene designer, and lighting designer.

Quantity. The intensity of light. This obviously involves the initial choice of instruments, size of lamps, and color to be used as well as spotlight positioning and the final choice of dimmer reading.

Classifications

Area lighting. Acting areas of between 8' and 10' in diameter located within the confines of the set or sets, individually lighted and individually controlled. Instruments chosen for area lighting will usually be ELLIPSOIDAL REFLECTOR SPOTLIGHTS for FRONT OF THE HOUSE lights and FRESNEL LIGHTS for stage lights, but ZOOM ELLIPSES may be used in either or both positions.

Backing lights (offstage lighting). These are lights designed to illuminate areas behind doors, windows, or hallways, namely, those areas that are not major acting areas. Lighting backings is an important part of lighting the realistic play. Entrances and exits should never be left in the dark unless specifically mentioned in the script. Small floods, spotlights, or PAR units are sufficient for most backings, but larger spots or beam projectors are necessary when an intense light is needed to flood through an opening onto the stage. Lighting from overhead sometimes uses floodlights or scoops, but spotlights that can be focused through the opening onto the stage are preferred because of better control. Be careful of skimming the backing flats with a parallel beam of light, which will exaggerate any irregularities and imperfections on the flat surface. Use colors as dictated by motivation or as a continuation of colors chosen for area lights.

Backlight. Spotlights mounted above and slightly behind the acting area and used to provide a highlight or glow of light on the head and shoulders of the performer. This highlight is also useful as a separation light to help keep the actor from blending into the background. See also BACK-LIGHTING.

Color washes. Washes may originate from any position although they are most often located in the FOH. However, if border lights are part of the existing equipment, they are used to provide a color wash from overhead. Washes are usually used to provide mood, color, locale, and ambience.

They are also useful for blending areas and for toning the scene. Since color washes generally use saturated colors with lower light transmission, instruments chosen for the FOH washes should be high-wattage ellipsoidal spotlights of sufficient intensity to compensate for the reduced light transmission. See also COLOR WASHES; PHOTOMETRIC CHARTS.

Cyc lights. Used to provide background light for groundrows, cycloramas, skies, and drops. These instruments are usually in the nonspecific or general lights category and are intended to flood large areas. They are located on standards in the wings, on the floor in front of the cyclorama, or hung from pipes high in the flies. They may be in the form of BORDER LIGHTS; CYC STRIPS; FLOODLIGHTS; SCOOPS; or STRIPLIGHTS. Colors will be determined by script requirements and the discretion of the lighting designer and director. See **Cyclorama lighting** under COLOR SCHEMES.

Key and fill light. Terms originating in film and television lighting but universally accepted now. Key light is brighter, more concentrated light, providing modeling. Fill light literally fills around the key (similar to the TV base light) with a lower intensity, wider focus light, supplementing and smoothing the coverage from a different angle. Instruments used for area lights of this type are usually ellipsoidal spotlights, but the fill lights may be fresnel lights if spill is not a concern.

Motivated light. Light appearing to originate from a specific source such as the sun, a fire, a lamp, etc. Realistic plays should have realistic light sources; thus an interior night scene may appear to be lighted from a lamp, overhead fixture, fireplace, or moonlight through a window. The apparent source may be the key light such as strong sunlight through a window, or it may be part of the atmosphere such as a source suggested by a projected venetian blind on the wall.

The lighting color scheme should relate to the motivational light (the apparent light source). If, for example, a PRACTICAL fireplace is stage left, warm colors would be placed in spotlights focused from the stage left position and cool colors in spotlights focused from the stage right position. The lighting of the stage left area might be higher in intensity than that for the other areas and be further strengthened by a small spotlight, floodlight, or effects light placed inside the fireplace. Crosslighting of this nature is highly desirable and should be planned for windows, doors, wings, and TORMENTOR positions. Artistry in lighting is attained through the lighting designer's choices of motivated sources, colors in spotlights, intensities for the various stage areas, angles of lighting, random or gimmick light, and use of color washes. Instruments chosen for motivational light will be determined in part by the motivational source: firelight, special effects; lamplight, softness of the fresnel; sunlight, intensity of the BEAM PROJECTOR, FOLLOWSPOT, or ellipsoidal spotlight.

AUXILIARY SUPPORT FOR
PRACTICAL LAMP

MOTIVATED LIGHT SOURCE

Random light (gimmick light). Light for lighting's sake. Random light is basically for effect only and is nonmotivational, although it may enhance a motivated effect. Many episodic or nonrealistic plays do not need motivated light, and in such cases, gimmick lights may be used according to the lighting designer's judgment to provide dramatic value, emphasis, mood, etc. Any type of instrument may be used for gimmick lighting as long as it provides the necessary effect and control and does not spill into unwanted areas. The lighting designer should be warned not to be too "cute" with gimmick lighting; lighting that calls too much attention to itself may very well be stealing that attention from the play, where it belongs.

Sidelighting. See CROSSLIGHTING. Generally refers to any light located on the side of the stage: in the wing, tormentor, or proscenium positions. Sidelights are most valuable in providing modeling effects. Instruments chosen for sidelighting will depend upon effect desired. If the source simulated is the sun or moon, a high-intensity ellipsoidal spotlight or beam projector placed as far away as possible will be needed to produce the effect of single-source, parallel rays of light. If the source is to be artificial light, the chosen instrument could be a fresnel light mounted closer to the motivational source. If a flood of light is the object with no apparent motivation, SCOOPS or a BANK of lights of the PARcan variety might be preferred.

Objectives of stage lighting. Summing up the aesthetics, the properties, and the classifications of lighting, they all contribute to the success of a production in the following ways:

Lighting actors in a smooth, even light.

Providing modeling that will reveal facial features and help keep the actors from fading into the background.

Providing intensity control for all acting areas onstage so attention may be focused wherever and whenever needed.

Providing color variations that will suggest moods, locations, times of day, seasons, etc.

Providing atmosphere; leaf patterns, grill patterns, shadows, flickering fires, etc.

Providing or suggesting motivated light sources when appropriate: floor lamps, chandeliers, wall brackets, fireplaces, sunlight or moonlight through windows, streetlights, etc.

Preparations. The problem of coordinating the light design with the time available to execute the design is seldom dealt with in texts and is probably one of the most important lessons of all. All too often good lighting concepts are never realized because the light plot is too complicated to be completed in the available set-in time. All the aesthetics in the world are worthless if time does not permit proper execution. As with most things, lighting is a balancing act, and time is a very serious consideration. Keep the lighting concept simple enough to fit the limited time frame of the set-in.

Before thinking about lighting a show or putting a light plot on paper, a thorough study of the theatre must be made to determine all possible locations for lighting equipment. Every theatre will have its idiosyncrasies, but most proscenium theatres will include some of the facilities shown in the diagrams. Most thrust stages will have equivalent positions, or possibly improvised equivalents. To determine distances (THROWS) between light sources and areas to be lighted and the angles at which the lights will strike the stage, it is necessary to either draw or locate a scaled plan and elevation of the stage and auditorium. Information provided from these drawings will help determine choices of lighting instruments as well as their locations.

Instrument positions

Front of the house positions (FOH). This designation refers to any position on the audience side of a proscenium arch or, in the absence of an arch, the audience side of the theatre. Only instruments providing hard-edge light (such as ELLIP-SOIDAL REFLECTOR SPOTLIGHTS) should be used in the FOH position. The soft-edge light of a FRESNEL LIGHT or the use of frost color media should be avoided in the FOH position because of the uncontrolled, diffused spill of light into the audience.

Balcony (rail). In a theatre with a balcony, this location refers to spotlights positioned on the balcony railing or on special hangers in front of and below the railing. Since lights hung from this position are at such a low angle to the stage, their use is best confined to either COLOR WASHES or FILL LIGHT. *Caution:* A pan or shelf is required under such installations to protect the audience below; check with the fire department or safety inspector.

Booth. In reference to lighting in the traditional proscenium theatre, the booth is located slightly above the audience in the rear of the auditorium and generally is the location for followspots, projection equipment, and large hard-edge, high-intensity spotlights. The term

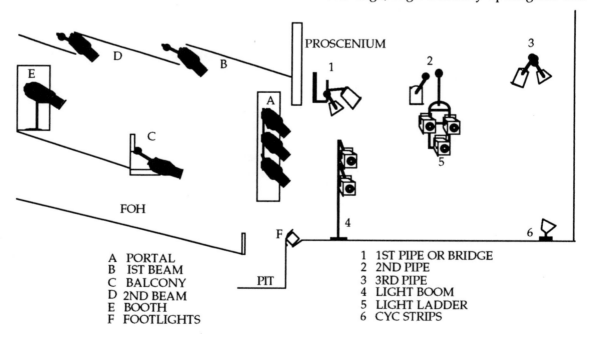

A PORTAL	1 1ST PIPE OR BRIDGE
B IST BEAM	2 2ND PIPE
C BALCONY	3 3RD PIPE
D 2ND BEAM	4 LIGHT BOOM
E BOOTH	5 LIGHT LADDER
F FOOTLIGHTS	6 CYC STRIPS

THEATRE SECTION

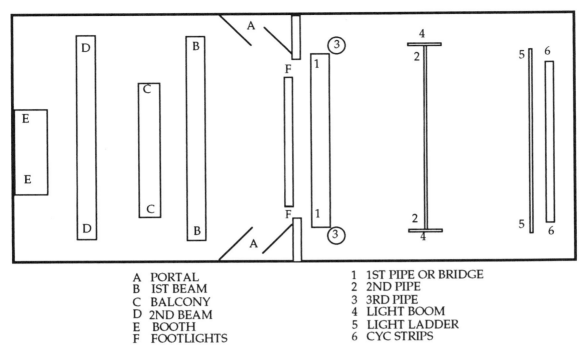

A PORTAL	1 1ST PIPE OR BRIDGE
B IST BEAM	2 2ND PIPE
C BALCONY	3 3RD PIPE
D 2ND BEAM	4 LIGHT BOOM
E BOOTH	5 LIGHT LADDER
F FOOTLIGHTS	6 CYC STRIPS

THEATRE PLAN

may also refer to any enclosed area, such as a sound booth or a stage manager booth associated with the operation of a show but not generally used as a lighting position.

Ceiling positions (beams, slots, catwalks, bridges). Positions in or near the auditorium ceiling, designed to accommodate hard-edge spotlights that will provide both AREA LIGHTS and color washes for the downstage areas. If a second opening (second beam) exists, it will accommodate specials and washes.

Sidewall (portal, proscenium, coves). Slots may be cut into the wall or pipes may be mounted on the sidewalls of the auditorium near the stage on each side of the proscenium. They represent extensions of the wing lighting positions onstage and provide sidelighting in front of the proscenium arch.

Onstage positions for lighting

Footlights. If any provision has been made in the original building for FOOTLIGHTS, the accommodation is usually built into the floor at the downstage edge of the stage and provides space for low-angle lighting. The use of footlights is not universally accepted and is largely up to the discretion of the director and designers. Some stages have allowed space in front of the apron to place lighting instruments for special effects such as campfires or cauldrons.

Overhead pipes (borders, light pipes, electrics). Ideally, the angle of these pipes to the acting areas serviced should match the overhead FOH angles. (See determining lighting angles below.) The first pipe is the prime position for instruments used to light the second tier of areas onstage and it is highly desirable to have this angle match the angle of the FOH prime position to provide a smooth blend of light between these adjacent areas. The number of light pipes needed will depend on the depth of the stage and the height of the pipes from the floor. Usually, the distance between pipes will vary from 8' to 12'. Pipes are numbered from the downstage proscenium to the upstage backwall, and the numbering usually coincides with the wing position for sidelights hung from suspended light ladders or TREES. Thus, beginning with the first ELECTRIC behind the act curtain, there would be 1st, 2d, 3d, etc., pipes and 1st, 2d, and 3d, etc., wing lights or spot pipes.

Light bridge. A narrow, metal catwalk sometimes placed in the first border or first electric position and used for mounting and focusing lighting instruments. Bridges are usually counterweighted and controlled by either motor or winch. With a light bridge, electricians have the advantage of being able to mount instruments from the floor, raise the bridge to the prescribed height, and focus from the bridge, thereby eliminating much ladder work.

Determining angles

Vertical angles. The vertical angle is determined from the SECTION DRAWING by drawing a line between the spotlight and the floor area to be covered and measuring the angle formed by that line and the floor. This angle will vary between a vertical 90°, which may create a dramatic effect but will leave the face in complete shadow, and a flat 0°, which will light the face so completely all features will be lost in the washout and all attention diverted to the shadow on the backwall. It becomes apparent that "normal lighting" will fall somewhere in between these extremes. Maximum "normalcy" has been established at 37.5°, but from a practical point of view, vertical angles between 35° and 50° are satisfactory. It should be added that unless dealing with a pinpoint of light, there will be considerable angle variation between the downstage and upstage of any designated acting area.

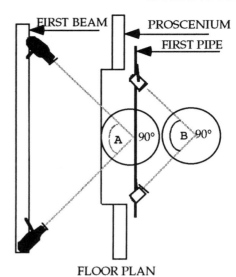

FLOOR PLAN

A - BEAM HORIZONTAL ANGLE
B - 1ST PIPE HORIZONTAL ANGLE
DETERMINING HORIZONTAL ANGLES

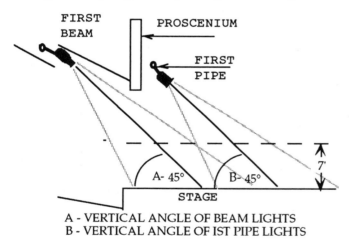

A - VERTICAL ANGLE OF BEAM LIGHTS
B - VERTICAL ANGLE OF IST PIPE LIGHTS

DETERMINING VERTICAL ANGLES

Horizontal angles. Horizontal angles are determined from the floor plan of the theatre or from the light plot. In most light plots, at least two spotlights will be assigned to cover each area. Horizontal angles are measured on the floor plan between the lines drawn from each of the two spotlights and the center of the area they will cover. For optimum modeling of the face and body, this angle should double the vertical angle. For example, if the vertical angle is 35°–45°, the horizontal angle should be 70°–90°. In practice, however,

both angles will be modified by the confines of the building, and the designer is fortunate to settle for about 40°–45° for both vertical and horizontal angles.

Dramatic angles. Positioning lights at either very high or very low angles will produce dramatic results. These extremes are useful for effects such as the macabre, weird, strange, or unearthly. The results may be enhanced with color. Do not overdo. Lighting designers should augment the production, not create one of their own.

Determining areas. Lighting AREAS are designated acting areas averaging 8'- 12' in diameter, located within the confines of the set or sets, individually lighted and individually controlled. To facilitate the learning process, areas are often drawn as circles, representing the circle of light reaching the stage from a particular size and focal length spotlight. The number and location of areas will be determined by the blocking of the show, and the lighting designer must work in close harmony with the director to determine these areas and any special considerations. When the director's wishes are known, areas are placed on the light plot (see DESIGN FOR LIGHTING) and numbered sequentially. Numbering varies with the lighting designer, but in the nonprofessional or academic theatre, it often begins with downstage right and proceeds across stage. There will be as many areas as needed to accommodate the stage size and setting of the production. *Note:* Although it is often helpful to draw circles representing areas to begin with as a help in choosing spotlights, the finished product is apt to be messy and cluttered. Circles are often omitted in the finished light plot.

Script requirements. Script considerations include those written instructions or suggestions made by the playwright. Often these suggest MOTIVATED LIGHT. An example of this would be a description of the setting for the play: "cool moonlight streams through the french windows and a warm fire crackles in the fireplace." Occasionally, a director will choose to ignore the playwright's stage directions altogether, sometimes transplanting the play to different locations or different periods. Such transplants require extensive discussions with all involved personnel far ahead of schedule so there will be no surprises at the first dress rehearsal. Other considerations outside the confines of the script are often added by the director to heighten the effects to be created. More often than not, these additions are simple and uncomplicated, such as adding a special downlight to heighten dramatic value of a fireplace effect or requesting a wall bracket to provide motivation for increased light intensity in an obscure corner. See also ARENA STAGE LIGHTING; BALLET LIGHTING; CONCERT LIGHTING; DANCE THEATRE LIGHTING; ICE SHOW LIGHTING; MUSICAL LIGHTING; OPERA LIGHTING; PROSCENIUM STAGE LIGHTING; REPERTORY THEATRE LIGHTING; ROAD SHOW LIGHTING; THRUST STAGE LIGHTING.

LIGHT MOUNTING DEVICES. Great confusion can exist with some of the following terminology because all of the devices can be mounted on the floor, hung from overhead, or flown from the rigging system.

Batten (electrics, light pipe, light border, bar [British usage]). The primary onstage hanging device for lighting instruments. See LIGHT BATTEN.

Boom (light standard, boomerang, light tower). A weighted base with a pipe upright on which side arms are mounted and lighting instruments hung. May be located almost anywhere and usually in any wing.

Ladder. Two vertical pipes with rungs between, suspended from the grid or hung from a pipe. Allow clearance under the lowest spotlight for passageway.

Tower (light tower, torm towers, teaser tower). A three-dimensional pipe unit used to hang lights on "in 1" (see IN). See TOWER.

Trees. Vertical pipes with side arms, suspended from the grid or hung from a pipe.

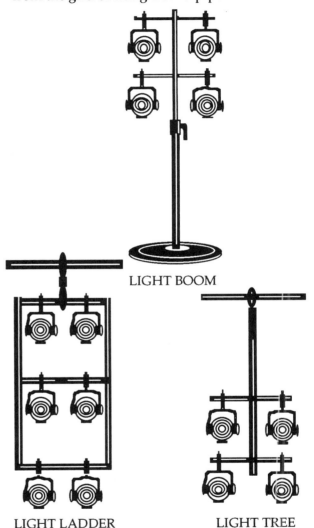

LIGHT BOOM

LIGHT LADDER   LIGHT TREE

LIGHTNING EFFECT. Photographic flashbulbs are ideal for single, intense flashes. High-intensity photographic lamps with a 4- to 6-hour life are adequate for repeated flashes. CYC STRIPS with 500-watt tungsten-halogen lamps give good distant or heat lightning effects. The TIME LAG involved in heating and cooling filaments of high-wattage lamps is generally undesirable for lightning effects. A jagged streak of lightning can be projected on the sky cyc with a fabricated projector patterned after a **Linnebach** (see under PROJECTORS) only substituting a photographic flash lamp as a light source. The streak is cut in a piece of cardboard large enough to cover the opening of the projector. The greater the distance between lamp and cutout, the sharper the lines of the streak. A quick flick of the switch produces a lingering streak across the cyc; a photographic bulb used as the light source for the Linnebach will produce a flash. *Caution:* An obsolete method of creating lightning by wiring a carbon rod and a large rasp and dragging one across the other is fraught with danger from both the flash and the potential shock. This is definitely not recommended.

LIGHT PALETTE. Trade name for top-of-the-line Strand computer board, the next smaller board is the Mini Palette.

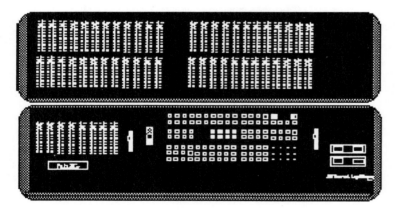

LIGHT PALETTE 90
STRAND

LIGHT PLOT. See under DESIGN FOR LIGHTING.
LIGHT, SIGNAL. See CUE LIGHTS.
LIGHT SPILL. Light straying from the main beam of an instrument, falling on parts of the stage where it is not wanted. Causes are numerous but could include reflection from color frame, another light, prop, piece of scenery, etc.; cracked lens; poorly designed ventilation holes; diffusion from dirty lens. Once the problem is identified, the solution is usually obvious.

LIGHT SPILL CONTROL. The devices illustrated are designed to control the beam spread of light, to frame given areas, and to keep light from spilling onstage into areas where it is not wanted. Designed to be used on spotlights. See also MASKING; WRAP.

Barndoor (blinder, shutter). A commercial product made of metal shutters (flaps) that shape the light either with two shutters (two-way) or with four shutters (four-way).

Funnel. A conical metal device that contracts the beam of light.

Louvre (spill ring). A series of concentric metal rings or parallel slats.

Top hat (hood, Ted Lewis, snoot). Sheet-metal shield resembling (and sometimes made of) stovepipe, painted black.

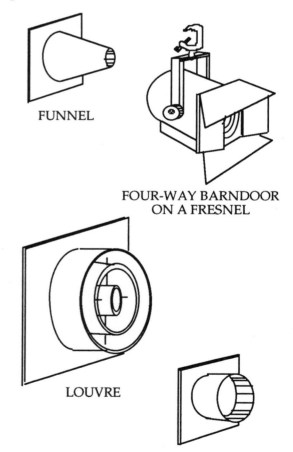

FUNNEL

FOUR-WAY BARNDOOR
ON A FRESNEL

LOUVRE

TOP HAT

LIMELIGHT (calcium light, Drummond light). A bright white light, a precursor of the arc light, once popular for stage use. The light source was created by directing an oxyhydrogen flame against lime. The limelight was first developed for geodesic purposes in Scotland in 1825 and named after its inventor, Captain T. Drummond (1797–1840), a British engineer. The first recorded use on the stage was in London in 1837 but it was not until the mid-1860s that it found its way to the United States. The point source of light resulting from the flame on lime made possible the use of a lens and gave the theatre its first practical spotlight. Early supplies of oxygen and hydrogen were contained in India rubber bags, and the lighting man (called the "gas man" during this period) had his problems trying to keep a balance of oxygen and hydrogen going to the burner. Despite inconveniences, bulky equipment, and frequent unscheduled blackouts, the limelight persisted in the theatre for many years because of its uncontested brilliance at the time.

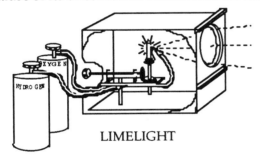

LIMELIGHT

LINE

Electrical. Source of power; the "line" side of a circuit, as opposed to the "load" side. See also CIRCUITS.

Feed line. Conductor delivering power to equipment.

Hot line (leg, live line, live wire). An electrical circuit carrying a potential and usually terminating in a receptacle or panel. A LEG of a line as opposed to the ground or neutral wire.

Spot line. A single rope line from the GRID placed in an exact location for the purpose of flying a special effect or a special piece of equipment. A spot line is also sometimes needed as a cable pickup or a safety line attached to the top of a BOOM.

LINNEBACH PROJECTOR. See under PROJECTORS.

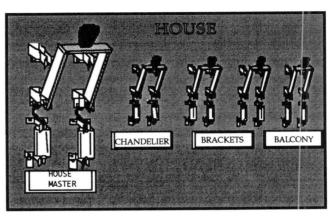

LIVE FRONT HOUSE LIGHT CIRCUITS
EARLY TWENTIETH CENTURY

LIVE FRONT. Obsolete. On early SWITCH-BOARDS wires were not always enclosed, and an entire group of live KNIFE SWITCHES was often open to the operator's touch when working. This type of switchboard was called a live front.

LOAD. Any electrical equipment using power. The current or amperage used in a circuit. Electrical plugs are often marked "load" (male plug) and "line" (female plug). See also CIRCUITS.

LOAD-IN. Transfer of scenery or lighting equipment from trucking vehicle to the scene dock or stage where production is scheduled.

LOBSTERSCOPE. A disk attachment for a spotlight, once used to produce a flicker of light. The disk was irregularly perforated and revolved in front of a spotlight. Control was originally by hand or by a clock mechanism, but if any have survived, they would now be upgraded to a variable-speed electric motor. The attachment was used for flickering fires and a slow-motion effect. These effects are now often accomplished by the STROBE LIGHT.

LOGS, FIREPLACE. See FIREPLACE LOGS.

LONG FOCUS. A spotlight with a long space between lamp and lens, making it a LONG-THROW SPOTLIGHT. A 6" x 12" (6"-diameter lens with a 12" focal length) is considered a long-focus unit. See also SHORT FOCUS.

LONG-THROW SPOTLIGHT. A spotlight with a lens system designed for a throw of 40' or more.

LOUVRE. See under LIGHT SPILL CONTROL.

LOW-VOLTAGE LAMPS. Usually very intense lights operating from 12 to 24 volts. Often these lights are equipped with built-in reflectors. They are considered very efficient lamps. The MR 16, in particular, has become a popular light source. It has a dichroic reflector and operates on 12 volts. Available in 5°–40° spreads, the MR 16 can be bought in a minature PARcan instrument. Aircraft landing lights with 24-volt requirements give a harsh light similar to the lower voltage units and are extremely intense. As soon as these small point source filaments become available, they will be adapted to show business needs.

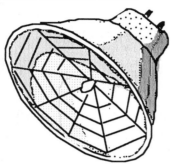

MR 16
LOW VOLTAGE LAMP

LUG. A device that attaches an electrical wire to a terminal or bus bar bolt. Some of these devices must be soldered onto the wire; others are solderless. See also BURNDY.

LUMEN. A standard unit of measurement of the rate of flow of light energy. One lumen equals the flow of light through 1 square foot of a sphere having a radius of 1 foot and a light source in the center of 1 CANDELA. For many years a special candle made to specific dimensions with special wax and wick was used as the standard measurement of intensity. Later, special incandescent lamps were manufactured under controlled circumstances to pro-

vide the standard for illumination. In 1948, the glow of platinum at 2,045 Kelvin (the temperature of its solidification) was adopted as the basic standard of luminous intensity. The candela, adopted in 1979 as the international standard of luminous intensity, now supersedes all other standards for intensity measurement. One lumen of light evenly applied to 1 square foot produces 1 footcandle. Expressed in equation form: footcandle = lumen/ area (in square feet). See also FOOTCANDLE.

LUMINAIRE (instrument, unit, light, lantern [British usage]). Technical term describing a complete lighting instrument: lamp, socket, housing, reflector, lenses, mounting device, and plug. The term is gaining universal acceptance.

LUMINESCENCE. Ability of some materials to give off light when stimulated by an outside source such as ULTRAVIOLET LIGHT.

LUXTROL. Autotransformer dimmer, manufactured by Superior Electric Company of Bristol, Connecticut. Available in either individual dimmers, non-interlocking dimmers, motor-driven dimmers, or in packages of three, four, or six interlocking dimmers. Used for permanent or portable control systems of the 1950s and 1960s.

LUXTROL SIX-PACK
WITH MASTER

M

MAGAZINE. A British term for a color BOOMER-ANG.

MAGAZINE BATTEN. British term for BORDER LIGHT.

MAGENTA. A secondary color in lighting. Complement of green. See COLOR MIXING.

MAGIC SHEET. See **Magic sheets** under DESIGN FOR LIGHTING.

MAGNETIC AMPLIFIER. Obsolete. An older form of dimmer based on the saturable core principle of using a small current and low voltage varied by means of a POTENTIOMETER or AUTOTRANS-FORMER to control voltage output of a large coil. No tubes were involved in this system and the only moving parts were relays and potentiometers. Magnetic amplifiers were manufactured in 3,000- to 10,000-watt sizes and were available in two, three, four, five, and infinite preset. Infinite preset control was set up on cards similar to the punch cards in early IBM systems, and the electrician simply used the preset fader to fade from one card setup to another. The magnetic amplifier seemed destined to control the dimmer market in the 1950s, but its bulk, weight, and cost gave way to the silicon controlled rectifiers that followed in the 1960s. See REACTANCE DIMMER.

MAIN. The main or primary DISCONNECT. The phrase "pull the main" means to turn off the power at the power source by turning off the switch.

MAJOR EQUIPMENT COMPANY. Defunct. A Chicago-based instrument and accessory manufacturing business.

MALE PLUG. An electrical connector, used on the load side of the line. See under PLUGS.

MANUAL CONTROL. A light board without any electronic memory devices. Each handle is controlled by hand.

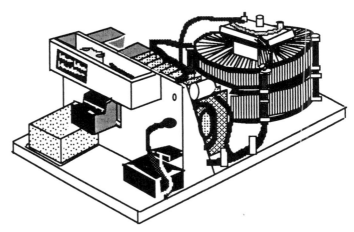

MAGNETIC AMPLIFIER

MANUFACTURERS. Defunct firms are listed in the text of this book, active businesses are listed in the back of the book under Selected List of Manufacturers and Distributors. The stage lighting business is notorious for the turnover in firms.

MARK IT (command verb). To write down dimmer readings of light intensity. For a shorthand group of symbols used for light board cue sheets see **Symbols** under COMPUTER LIGHT BOARD TERMINOLOGY.

MAROONS. British expression for electrically detonated material used to make explosions.

MASKING. It is necessary at times to block unwanted light spill from an instrument. Black aluminium foil (WRAP) is ideal for this purpose. STAND-OFFS (devices used to create heat-absorbing space between a light and its color frame) require masking to prevent spill, and WRAP serves this purpose well. Light leaks appearing where scenery is joined, between GROUND-ROWS and the floor, and between backings and scenery can be fixed with black cloth strips. See BACKING LIGHT.

MASTER BOARD. On early ROAD SHOWS the main SWITCHBOARDS, usually large PIANO BOARDS, were called master boards. Smaller AUXILIARY BOARDS were added to handle special and last-minute add-ons.

MASTER DIMMER. See under DIMMERS, MASTER.

MASTER ELECTRICIAN. See under STAGE CREW.

MAT. A device used to change the beam shape of a spotlight. See GOBO.

MATRIX PATCHING. Any combination of dimmers may be patched into any controller.

McCANDLESS. Refers to Stanley McCandless, who wrote *A Method of Lighting the Stage,* and the lighting formula named after him. See under FORMULAS; PROSCENIUM STAGE LIGHTING.

MECHANICAL INTERLOCK. See **Mechanical master** under DIMMERS, MASTER.

MEDIA, COLOR. Translucent colored glass, plastic, or gelatine used to color stage lights. See COLOR MEDIA.

MEDIUM-BASE LAMP. See **Bases** under LAMPS.

MEDIUM FOCUS. A 6" x 6'" lens is in this category, halfway between a SHORT-FOCUS and a LONG-FOCUS instrument.

MEMORY AVAILABLE. See under COMPUTER LIGHT BOARD TERMINOLOGY.

MEMORY LIMIT. See under COMPUTER LIGHT BOARD TERMINOLOGY.

MERCURY SWITCH. A silent toggle switch using mercury as the contact between two terminals. Must be mounted in near-upright position. See under SWITCHES.

MERCURY VAPOR LAMP. In this kind of lamp, ultraviolet radiation is produced by passing an electrical current through vaporized mercury and then filtering out the visible light. This is a very efficient source of UV light, far better than carbon arc sources. However, there are disadvantages: A warm-up period of several minutes is required before use, and when it is turned off, the light must be allowed to cool before it will reignite.

MICROPROCESSOR (computer board, board). A computer lighting control unit with a microprocessor as its heart. These compact devices can be added to most electronic dimmers with an interface. Usually they consist of keypads, assorted faders, submasters, masters, and readouts or a CRT (cathode ray tube screen), and, most important, memory. The ability to create cues, record and save cues, play back cues, and be assigned to a variety of control makes the microprocessor a truly flexible device. The many accessories available include printers for hard copy, designer remotes, electrician's remote, self-diagnostic tests, special effects units, etc. Available as control boards or consoles.

The Scene Master by LEEColortran features: (1) Channel and/or submaster controllers. Arranged in banks of controllers, each controller may be set up to control either a channel or a submaster. Individual channel handles are more common on preset boards. (2) Override keys. Used to override timed fades and to take over manual control. (3) Faders. Usually several, often between one and three with an added split fader; on some boards some may be assigned various functions. (4) Grand master controller. (5) Next/Last keys. Used for recording cues. "Next" saves current cue and records next. "Last" permits edit or change of previous cue. (6) Screen keys. "Soft function keys." Function is assigned to each key and displayed on a screen. (7) Display keys. Give access to screen displays such as Stage, Preview, Submaster, Effect, Patch, Setup. (8) Record keys. Record Cue, Submaster. (9) Control keys. Used to create a cue sheet. Cue, time, effect, delay, full, clear, etc. (10) Playback keys. Start, stop, move to particular cue, or change timing. (11) Wheel. Used to set channels with finger-tip control. Also used to adjust levels proportionally. (12) Blackout. Takes all channels to zero.

MINI-BRUTE. A low-voltage, modern-day bunch light. See BRUTE.

MINI-STRIP. A low-voltage CYC STRIP first developed by Lighting and Electronics, Inc. It is made in 6' sections with a double row of MR 16, 75-watt, 12-volt lamps designed to cover a height of 24' when placed within 18" of the cyc. There are 10 lamps in each row, one row equipped with the flood lamp and the other with the spot lamp. Each group of 10 is wired in series, thus eliminating the need for a transformer. The mini-strip is a very useful, highly efficient STRIPLIGHT.

MIRROR (hot and cold). See DICHROIC FILTER.

MODE. See under COMPUTER LIGHT BOARD TERMINOLOGY.

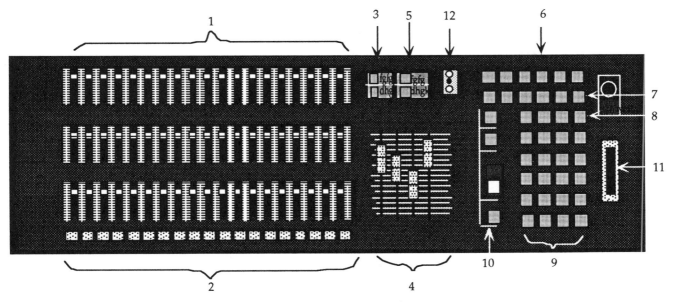

LEE COLORTRAN SCENE MASTER

MODELING. Achieving a three-dimensional effect through use of lights of two different colors or different intensities coming from two different sources. See **Aesthetics** under LIGHTING PRACTICE.

MOGUL BASE. Largest of the lamp base sizes. See **Bases** under LAMPS.

MOL (maximum overall length). Abbreviation used in lighting catalogues indicating total length of LAMP from base to tip (base to base in double-ended lamps). See also LCL (light center length).

MONOCHROMATIC. Consisting of one color (HUE), although intensity may vary (CHROMA).

MOOD. An emotional quality or attitude established by the playwright and/or director and reinforced by the lighting designer through angle of light, intensity, color, etc. See **Ambience** under **Aesthetics,** LIGHTING PRACTICE.

MOON BOX. A bright light housed in an opaque cone with FROST gelatine covering the large end. Mounted behind a translucent scrim or reflector sheet, the "moon" can be raised or lowered according to dictates of the script.

MOONLIGHT EFFECT. Moonlight scenes are usually lighted with a FILL LIGHT of blue or blue-green overall coverage (see COLOR MEDIA) and a white or light-straw KEY LIGHT highlighting the acting area. Sometimes a perforated metal plate (STRAINER) is made to fit a spotlight frame and is used in place of color as a filter to reduce light intensity but maintain brilliancy for highlighting areas. Always check costume and makeup colors under blue or green light before making final decisions; results are sometimes startling and it is cheaper to change color media than costumes.

MOTIVATED LIGHT. Light originating from a logical source. See **Motivated light** under LIGHTING PRACTICE.

MOTOR-DRIVEN DIMMER. An older system of remote control in which electric motors were connected to RESISTANCE and AUTOTRANSFORMER DIMMERS.

MOUNTING EQUIPMENT. All the assorted equipment used to HANG lights for a production. This includes the pipe in various POSITIONS as well as HANGERS, CLAMPS, etc. In lighting professional theatre where equipment is rented, meticulous lists must be made because items not ordered are never delivered.

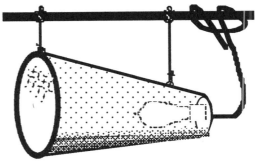

MOON BOX
Ca.1900s

MOVEMENT. A controllable quality of light. See also **Properties of light** under LIGHTING PRACTICE.

MOVING PROJECTION. See PROJECTED SCENERY.

MULTIMETER. A multipurpose testing device, usually showing AC and DC volts, continuity, and OHMS. See also VOM; WIGGY.

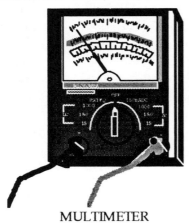

MULTIMETER

MULTIPLE PIN CONNECTOR (spider, three-fer, three-way tap). A three-way plug for pin connectors. See PLUGS.

MULTIPLEXING. The ability to send multiple signals over a pair of wires. Used extensively for dimmer control on microprocessor light boards.

MULTISLIDE DIMMER. An AUTOTRANSFORMER dimmer with several sliders for separate dimmer control working on a common, large core. See DAVIS BOARD.

MUSHROOM (mush). Obsolete. Generic term for a PAR or R-type lamp.

MUSICAL LIGHTING. Basically the musical since the middle of the 1940s is a play with music and dance fully integrated into it. The older style musical was a play with music and dance added to it, even to the point of not advancing the little plot there was. Because most musicals involve three forms of stage lighting—dramatic, operatic, and dance—the lighting designer must determine a method of combining these forms into one plot. The large-scale, fluid nature of musicals makes area lighting very important and with the computer light board can be GANGED into complex scenes. CROSSLIGHTING is needed for the dance sequences; instant control of toning lights or color washes will be required for the fast changes from day scenes to night scenes and mood shifts; solos or duets will need toning colors highlighted with FOLLOWSPOTS on the principals. The details involved in modern musical lighting can be overwhelming.

Practice. The staging of most large-scale musicals involves small scenes in the downstage areas known as "in one"; medium-sized scenes take place up to "in two," and full-stage scenes "in three" or "in four" (see IN). While one scene is being played "in one" (the shallow set), the next scene is being set UPSTAGE, and scenes are alternated thus through the show. Full stage is used for dance numbers involving most of the cast. The lighting designer must therefore plan the lights in what are referred to as ganged "zones," consisting of individual areas ganged to correspond with wing positions. Basically, musicals are mounted in the equivalent of what once was known as WING AND DROP staging, which made full use of crosslighting. Crosslighting is still one of the most effective means of lighting dance numbers and serves for dramatic numbers as well. If hanging space is available, spotlights used for crosslighting should be hung from LADDERS on ELECTRICS to free the floor for entrances, scenery movement, props, etc. Because of the many scenes involved in most musicals, the stage is almost always cluttered with scenery, both at stage level and in the flies. Since space can be at a premium, the lighting designer must plan to get full value from each instrument hung, using each one in as many scenes as possible. Double-check to make certain that any lighting instruments to be hung will not interfere with planned scene changes. The use of FOLLOWSPOTS is almost mandatory for musicals. In so many instances there is literally no other means of separating principals from cast or chorus, particularly in the musical numbers where a chorus accompanies the soloist. Improvements in followspot and lamp design make it possible to use a SOFT-EDGED light that may sneak into a scene and ease into a HEAD SPOT in a subtle way that will not jar the audience. Learning to make smooth transitions from STRIPPING the stage with a band of light to following the actor with a tight spot takes practice on the part of the operator and patience on the part of the lighting designer and director alike. Since musicals are usually larger, lighter, and brighter than other theatrical forms, they generally need more instruments, larger instruments, and higher wattage lamps. ELLIPSOIDAL REFLECTOR SPOTLIGHTS are always the chosen lights for front of the house use, and the current trend seems to call for their use backstage as well. FRESNEL LIGHTS, however, will also work well onstage and indeed, because of the diffusing effect of the lens, may be easier for the inexperienced to focus and blend than the ellipsoidal spotlight. For full-stage scenes, the designer should try to get as many overhead spotlights mounted as is practical and take advantage of all available space in the wings as well. Sufficient equipment is required both overhead and in the wings to provide a minimum of two color circuits (one day and one night); three color circuits will provide subtle varieties and greater color choices. If BORDER LIGHTS are available and spotlights are not, they can be made to serve as toning lights, although they will not provide the intensity that can be expected from spotlights. BACKLIGHTING as separation light and/or toning auxiliary is most useful in all forms of stage lighting, particularly the musical and dance. On a medium-sized stage, either the 1,000-watt ellipsoidal or 1,000-watt fresnel light will work well for backlighting. If a sky cyclorama is planned for the production, provision for overhead lighting and floor lighting (horizon lights) must be made as well. See COLORS; CYC LIGHTING; CYCLORAMA. Follow-spots, usually two or more, should have sufficient intensity to cut through the regular stage lighting with a 6' or 8' beam. Typically, the 3,000-watt or 5,000-watt DYNA-BEAM, capable of being dimmed and producing a soft-edge beam, is ideally suited for the musical production in a medium-sized theatre. The TROMBONE-type focus provides easy transition from tight focus to stripping. It may be found that the followspots carry the load of SPECIALS for musicals.

Color. As with lighting dance, lighting musicals calls for the use of more saturated colors, both PRIMARY and SECONDARY, and greater control over these colors to produce the variations in the scenes a musical demands. Very often, it may be found that if color washes are properly set and GELLED, they, with the help of the followspots, provide much of the lighting needed for some of the scenes.

Control. Maximum control is desirable for lighting the musical, but as with dance, blocks of individual areas are involved and therefore it may be possible to group many more lights either by area or color. Whenever followspots are used, it is necessary to have a stage manager or lighting director "call the show" in order to coordinate followspot and switchboard operators. The person calling lights, usually the stage manager, must be located in a position where all action can be viewed and must have an infallible means of communicating with all followspot operators plus the electrician on the control board. The stage manager works from a cue sheet or "book" with all cues clearly marked, including a one half to one minute warning for each cue followed by the GO cue (see CUE). For FOH followspot operators, directions are sometimes given according to the operator's left and right, not necessarily stage left and stage right. A smooth lighting operation takes time and lots of rehearsal. See also **Lights for musicians** under ORCHESTRA PIT.

N

NANOMETER. Unit measurement of light waves equal to one billionth of a meter; used to identify a color's place on the COLOR SPECTRUM.

NATIONAL ELECTRICAL CODE (NEC, code). Regulations governing wiring practices. Produced by the National Fire Protection Association. Copies may be obtained from local inspection departments.

NATIONAL UNDERWRITERS CODE (fire code). Produced by the National Fire Protection Association. The National Underwriters Code often forms the model for fire laws and regulations in local communities.

NEC. Abbreviation for NATIONAL ELECTRICAL CODE.

NEON. An inert gaseous element used in electric light bulbs or tubes in place of a filament. Discovered in 1898 by the English chemist Sir William Ramsey, neon was first made into a patented light by a Frenchman, George Claude, prior to World War I. The first neon sign used in the United States appeared in Los Angeles in 1921. Because it offfered a continuous line of light, the neon tube was once considered a potentially ideal lamp for CYC STRIPS, FOOTLIGHTS, and BORDER LIGHTS. However, because it could not be dimmed at the time, it was never really developed for those uses. New techniques have made it possible to dim neon within 3% of its total voltage, but lighting designers and electricians tend to favor the more familiar lighting instruments with their greater intensity and focus control.

NEON CIRCUIT TESTER. A small tester to determine if a circuit is hot or not. The tiny neon light source will respond to voltages from 110 to 220. Always test a circuit before working on it.

NETTING. See SCRIM.

NEUTRAL BUS. A copper bar enclosed in a steel electrical cabinet or panel. Neutral wires from all circuits are attached to the neutral bus, and it in turn is attached directly to a ground connection.

NEUTRAL WIRE (common, ground). The common wire in a three- or four-wire circuit. See CIRCUITS.

NICHROME WIRE. High-resistance wire used in resistance dimmers, electric heaters, stove elements, etc.

NICOPRESS. A crimping hand tool used with a sleeve to fasten two like wire cables together forming a loop or a union. This tool provides the electrician with a quick means of applying safety cable to equipment to guard against falls. The cables are inserted in a Nicopress sleeve, which is then crimped by the Nicopress tool; this is a much faster method of fastening cables than the conventional wire rope CLAMPS. Manufactured in several sizes, the Nicopress tool will usually handle two or three sleeve sizes; the most useful to the electrician are 1/16", 1/8", and 3/16". The tool is expensive but it is worth it because of the time saved.

NEON CIRCUIT TESTER

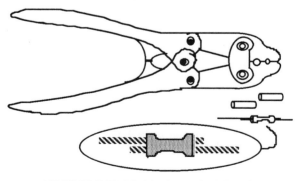

NICOPRESS TOOL AND SLEEVES

NONCONDUCTOR. Any material that will not conduct electricity. The best nonconductors include glass, porcelain, Bakelite, and rubber. Used as insulators and fronts for panel boards for electrical equipment.

NONDIM CIRCUIT (hotline). One or more circuits on the control board supplying electrical power through an "on-off" switch rather than a dimmer. Light control boards should provide several nondim circuits for special effects such as prop appliances, electrically triggered flashes, smoke effects, signal systems, and safety lights onstage.

O

OBJECTIVE LENS (dutchman). The lens or lenses in PROJECTORS used to bring a slide into focus on a screen. See under LENSES.

OD. Outside diameter of a tube or pipe.

OFFSTAGE. Any part of the stage not included within the confines of the setting or acting areas. See also AREAS; STAGE DIRECTIONS.

OHM. A unit of electrical resistance. The German physicist Georg Simon Ohm (1787–1854) discovered the basic rule that in any circuit the electrical current is directly proportional to the voltage and inversely proportional to the resistance. See ELECTRICITY.

OHM'S LAW. See ELECTRICITY.

OLIVETTE. Obsolete. A floodlight on a standard formerly used to light the lower portion of CYCLORAMAS from both sides of the stage or to provide a flood of light through a window or a wing. The olivette consists of a boxlike housing on a pipe standard, painted white inside to provide diffused reflection for the 300-, 500-, or 1,000-watt lamp used as the light source.

OLIVETTE: A FLOODLIGHT
OF THE 1920s

ONSTAGE (noun). Acting area or that portion of the stage visible to the audience.

ONSTAGE (verb). A call to actors and/or crew to report to the stage. See also PLACES.

OP. Acronym for "opposite the prompter." OP generally refers to stage left because prompters are usually positioned stage right, where control of the curtain is usually located. Stage right is known as the prompt side. Prompt side and OP are stage directions found in acting editions of old plays. Present use of these terms tends to be confined to professional theatre. See also STAGE DIRECTIONS.

OPEN BOX ARC. Obsolete. An early twentieth century OLIVETTE using a CARBON ARC as the light source.

OPENING (opening night). First public performance of a production.

OPERA LIGHTING. An opera is simply a dramatic presentation set to music, and therefore, its lighting is an extension of the basics of stage lighting as explained under LIGHTING PRACTICE. Opera is usually on a scale much larger than life. Plots stretch the imagination; characters, emotions, and actions are exaggerated; and the large casts often include choruses. To accommodate these multitudes, opera invariably requires larger stages, which in turn demand larger auditoriums holding more patrons to help defray expenses incurred by the many settings and large numbers involved in cast, chorus, orchestra, and production. All of this is reflected in the lighting designer's need for more and larger spotlights with higher wattage lamps to accommodate longer THROWS to more and larger areas. Opera perhaps more than any other form of Western theatre has always been steeped in tradition, which means that stage settings, stage direction, and stage business are almost as familiar to the subscribers as the plots and scores. Such traditions are slow to change and are best not tampered with by the new lighting designer unless approved or suggested by the conductor and stage director. However, with the more frequent use of English translations, plus radio and television presentations, opera has gained a larger audience and has become less bound by tradition and therefore more willing to accept simplified staging and more dramatic lighting. With less need for expensive drops and traditional scenery and with more emphasis on simple, dramatic lighting and projected scenery, opera budgets are coming within the fiscal realms of many more theatres. Before approaching the lighting problem, the designer must consult with both stage director and musical conductor to become familiar with their interpretations and any possible variations planned. Unlike most theatrical practice, the opera conductor has authority over the stage director and will have the final say. As with other forms of theatre lighting, the lighting designer's approach to opera is to become familiar with the story line and plot, absorbing all clues for light setups and changes. Take note of seasons, times of day, moods, atmosphere, etc. See DESIGN FOR LIGHTING.

Practice. Because of the size of opera stages the basic light plot will require the stage to be divided into 10 or 15 AREAS and because of the many scenes involved, each area will be covered in both warm and cool COLORS. In addition to the FIRST BORDER (first ELECTRIC), larger stages usually require the use of second or third BORDERS for mounting DOWNLIGHTS, area lights, and blending lights for the UPSTAGE areas. CROSSLIGHT-ING or WASH LIGHTS from the PORTALS or BOX BOOM positions in the front of the house (FOH) as well as from TREES, BOOMS, or PIPE LADDERS in the wing positions onstage are essential to opera lighting. Again, these wash lights will provide warm and cool coverage with separate control. The basic light plot will also include individually controlled BACKLIGHTS in each of the designated acting areas. Often a few specials are needed either for hard-to-light areas or as auxiliary lights to supplement or highlight certain scenes. Most directors and many lighting designers rely on at least two or more (often three) FOH FOLLOWSPOTS to complete their lighting plot,

and some even require followspots from a LIGHT BRIDGE upstage of the curtain. Some kind of projection equipment is usually needed as well, ranging from large scenic PROJECTORS capable of filling the cyc or screen with detailed scenes to the simple ELLIPSOIDAL REFLECTOR SPOT-LIGHTS with GOBOS providing atmosphere or mood patterns. Projections are used to provide English subtitles in some opera houses. This can present problems for the lighting designer since the subtitles must be visible from all parts of the auditorium. Remembering the exaggerated scale of opera, it is essential to double-check the throws required of all instruments to be used and choose accordingly. See PHOTOMETRIC CHARTS for tips on lens sizes and focal lengths required for various throws. FOH lights will need to be ellipsoidal reflector spotlights of 1,000- to 2,000-watt capacity (larger for large theatres), and if they are ZOOM LENS spots, they may be adjusted to give optimum performance in any of the FOH positions (see BEAM). Followspots should be capable of being dimmed, preferably electrically but at least mechanically. If followspots have a SOFT FOCUS, their use will be far less conspicuous and the attention of the audience will be correctly focused on the singers, not on the sharp beam of light. Spotlights to be used on the stage proper will be of 1,000- to 1,500-watt capacity and may be either zoom lens ellipsoidals or FRESNEL LIGHTS. Areas are easier to blend with fresnel lights, but if projections are planned, the diffusion from a fresnel may spill onto the cyc, fading the sharpness of the picture, unless a BARNDOOR is used. Ellipsoidal spots are somewhat brighter, and as long as the lenses are clean, they will be less apt to interfere with the projection. FOOTLIGHTS are optional (if there are no projections) or entirely up to the discretion of the director and conductor. However, it is hard to refute the claim that singers can see the conductor better without the glare of footlights. If available, BORDER LIGHTS offering FILL LIGHT and wash light are certainly appropriate for opera; however, in their absence, spotlights as wash lights are perhaps even more effective.

Color. Color plays a very important role in opera because it sets the mood along with the music. HEAVY COLORS are very dominant in many scenes to give the ambience necessary to the story line. PRIMARY and SECONDARY COLORS are used from both the crosslighting positions and the FOH color washes. Even area lights can be of a darker VALUE than in many other types of productions. Color is mood and mood is color in opera, and both are used in profuse amounts.

Control. Individual control over each area is a must for opera, particularly the three center areas DOWNSTAGE, where the majority of solos, duets, trios, and quartets are sung. Individual color control of washes from both FOH and wing positions should also be provided, permitting day and night scenes. Special effects lights will require their own dimmers as will any PROJECTORS. Color circuit control is necessary for border lights and footlights, if used. Smooth CROSS-FADES from scene to scene will provide continuity and keep the show flowing. If fades are made by timer, OVERRIDE CONTROL is essential to ensure synchronization of light and music cues. See also **Lights for musicians** under ORCHESTRA PIT.

OPERATING CHARACTERISTICS. Describes the relationship of dimmer control to the reaction of the dimmer involved.

OPERATING LIGHT (board light). A small colored light, often dimmer controlled, focused precisely on the operator's work area and carefully shielded to prevent spill that might be seen by the audience.

OPERATOR

Theatre. The person responsible for the control of lights, sound, followspots, projectors, or any other equipment associated with a theatre production.

Union. Motion picture projectionists are known as operators, members of IATSE, the technical theatre union.

OPTICAL AXIS. An imaginary line running perpendicular to each of the major components of a lensed instrument; namely, the filament, reflector, and lens of a spotlight. If any one of the major components is out of alignment, HALATION and ABERRATION will occur, and the efficiency of the instrument will be impaired. See ALIGNING INSTRUMENTS.

OPTICAL SYSTEM. The lens, lamp, and reflector of an instrument.

ORCHESTRA. The entire front lower floor of the auditorium. Originally, the orchestra was the circular arena (orkestra) in the Greek theatre in which the chorus performed.

ORCHESTRA PIT (pit). Sunken area immediately in front of the stage intended to accommodate an orchestra. Many larger theatres have hydraulic orchestra lifts in the pit, permitting pit level to be brought up to stage height where it can be used as an apron if an orchestra is not needed. Smaller theatres not anticipating extensive use of orchestras often have covers built for the pit, providing similar extensions of acting areas when needed. It should be noted that for some productions the orchestra is placed above and behind the performer and it is still referred to as the pit. The lighting designer should be reminded that the angle used for any light coming into the pit must be steep, because musicians trying to read music and watch a conductor at the same time are unhappy in the extreme if there are spotlights shining in their eyes as well.

Lights for musicians. Providing sufficient light for musicians in the pit and keeping it off the stage for BLACKOUTS or dimly lit scenes is always a challenge. The problem is lessened if the depth of the orchestra pit is sufficient, but light reflected off 50 (more or less) sheets of music at auditorium level can devastate a blackout. If the conductor is willing and the score allows, the solution can rest in switchboard control of the orchestra lights, which can be programmed into cues. If this is not feasible, the conductor might be persuaded to assume dimming responsibilities and be provided with control of the orchestra lights. Lighting the entire orchestra with shielded downlights from the BEAM instead of music stand lights is another solution that has been tried with varying degrees of success.

OSHA. The Occupational Safety and Health Act of 1970 governs most of the safety rules concerning industry at large and theatre as well. See SAFETY.

OUT

Instrument. Said of a lamp or instrument when it is turned on but no light appears. If the unit is not turned on, it can also be referred to as out or off.

Show (drag out, strike, tear down, derig [British usage]). The disassembly of a show as contrasted with the IN or SET-IN.

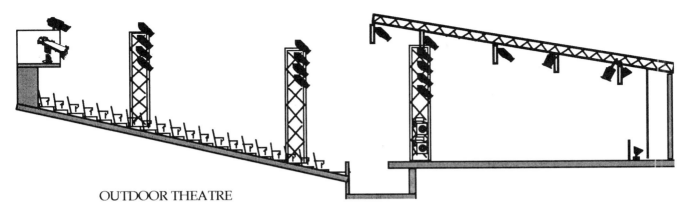

OUTDOOR THEATRE

OUTDOOR THEATRE LIGHTING. In outdoor theatre, sometimes the stage and audience are both open; however, often one or the other is roofed. Amphitheatres, aqua theatres, open-air concerts, and the renowned Santa Fe Opera, all fall into this category. Lighting in this environment makes for interesting problems, not the least of which is keeping the electrical apparatus watertight.

Practice. If a partial roof exists, either over the stage or over the auditorium, there will be positions in the rafters and girders for lighting instruments. These positions will be used as described in LIGHTING PRACTICE for similar positions, using the same kinds of instruments for the same functions. No special treatment should be necessary under these circumstance. However, if no roof is available, prime lighting positions are nonexistent, and TOWER or BOX BOOM positions must be substituted. If weather is a factor to reckon with, it may be necessary to wrap electrical connectors in plastic and provide for some kind of protective tent over lighting instruments whose hot lenses or open lamps would break if rained upon. The use of GELATINE COLOR MEDIA is obviously precluded since even small amounts of water destroy the gelatine's rigidity. Plastic color media are the solution. If BOOMERANGS are to provide the main mounting positions onstage, they should be placed on both sides of the stage in as many wing positions as are available and equipped with PARcans, possibly in BANKS. At least two circuits will be necessary on each boomerang to provide day and night scenes, and three circuits for variations would be better. In certain situations, FOOTLIGHTS may be used to advantage to help with TONING and BLENDING; however, they are likely to be the most vulnerable of all instruments in the case of inclement weather. In most outdoor theatres, provision has been made (or may be improvised) for a lighting gallery at the rear of the "house," and if either spotlights or BEAM PROJECTORS of high enough capacity to cover the usual 100'–200' throw can be made available, this is a possible position for toning lights. Obviously, with that long THROW, saturated colors will be out of the question. The lighting gallery position is also the place for FOLLOWSPOTS, which may provide the bulk of special lighting either by STRIPPING the stage or focusing on the areas of action.

Color. Generally speaking, because of the distances involved and also the lack of darkness, all long-throw units are in TINTS or WHITE. Because dusk can be very bright and the summer hours are long, lights may not be effective until the last half of the show. Footlights and SIDELIGHTS can have COLOR WASHES in both PRIMARY and SECONDARY COLORS because of their shorter throws. Followspots play a leading role in the highlighting of stars or major performers.

Control. Largely due to the mass of light "thrown" at the stage, control does not need to be as sophisticated as in most other types of shows; the exceptions are the specialty opera and musical production stages. Specialty theatres, which are dedicated to only one type of production (such as opera), may require a complex lighting control system. However, in outdoor theatre all controls need to have large current-handling capabilities.

OUTER STAGE. That part of the Elizabethan stage projecting into the court. See STAGES.

OUT FRONT. Auditorium or parts of the theatre given over to the audience.

OUTLET (receptacle). A permanent electrical installation to which electrical equipment may be attached. The outlet is placed on the line, and the load (equipment) is plugged into the outlet. Modern theatres often have a large variety of different types of outlets: CONVENIENCE OUTLETS for 120-volt building applications, JACKS for sound, specialty outlets for television, and pin connectors or twistlocks for stage. See PLUGS.

OVAL BEAM. Obsolete. A FRESNEL spotlight introduced by Kliegl Bros. in 1956 featured a special lens that produced an oval beam. The lens could be rotated to "stretch" the beam in two directions, making it easier to light corners.

OVERALL DIMENSION (OD). Outside dimension; outside diameter.

OVERLOAD (verb). To put a load on a circuit or dimmer in excess of its capacity. Always protect dimmers and circuits from overloads and potentially expensive burnouts by fusing to the correct capacity. Avoid the hazardous temptation to increase the fuse size of a circuit that tends to blow often. Reduce the load. See AMP to determine capacities.

OVERRIDE CONTROL. A special dimmer or a switch on a light board which allows the operator to take over control independent of a PRESET, MASTER, or timer.

KLIEGL OVAL BEAM
FRESNEL

P

PAN (command verb). To move the beam of a FOLLOWSPOT left or right without tilting the instrument.

PAN AND TILT. Automated remote control powerheads designed to hold spotlights that pan (usually 270°) and tilt 90°. These lights may be programmed to work automatically or can be controlled by an operator and are used primarily for rock concerts. Pan and tilt spotlights are very expensive. There is little need for them in conventional theatrical productions.

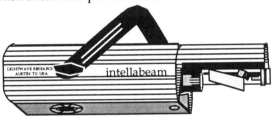

MIRROR REFLECTION
PAN AND TILT

PANEL LIGHT. A small light on a panel, radio, amplifier, dimmer, etc., indicating when equipment is on or off. Replacements are available at radio repair shops and electronics stores. Check proper voltage as written on lamp base.

PANEL, PLUGGING. See PATCH PANEL.

PANIC BUTTON (panic system). An auxiliary houselight switch installed in a stategic location, usually accessible to the electrician, house manager, and stage manager, to be used only in emergency. As a joke, many theatres have a pretend panic button for use when the electrician or stage manager panics. These are amusing but not to be confused with the real panic button, which is **no joke.**

PANI PROJECTOR. Considered to be top-of-the-line scenic projectors, Panis are manufactured by Ludwig Pani of Vienna, Austria. The 4,000-watt projector uses the HMI enclosed arc lamp, which is best able to provide the intensity necessary for ideal theatrical projection. See also PROJECTORS.

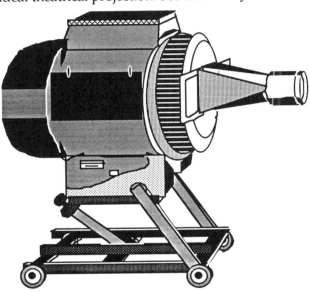

PANI 4,000-WATT PROJECTOR

PARcan. A nonfocusing spotlight in a can-like housing designed for PAR lamps. The PARcan has clips on the front to hold COLOR MEDIA and can be either a flimsy can or a very solid, well-built unit depending upon price and manufacturer. PARcans are often used in rock shows and industrial shows, where they may be chrome plated and

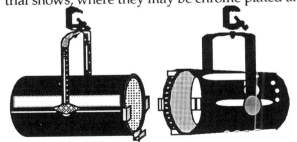

PARcans

equipped with autopanning devices and remote-controlled color changers. These extras add a great deal to their cost but add nothing to their value as theatre lights. Their main function as theatrical lights is as auxiliaries, specials, and lights that may be used in hard-to-reach positions.

PAR LAMPS. Short for parabolic aluminized reflector lamps. The built-in reflectors designed to reflect light from its FOCAL POINT into parallel rays make this lamp highly efficient. It is available in 150-, 200-, 300-, 500-, 600-, and 1,000-watt sizes and makes an inexpensive substitute for spotlights. In addition to individual mounts for PAR lamps, many BORDER LIGHTS and STRIPLIGHTS are designed to use these efficient lamps as well. The potential of PAR lamps may be appreciated when it is realized that the intensity of a PAR 150-watt lamp is almost the equivalent of that of an older 500-watt FRESNEL spotlight. See also LAMPS.

PARABOLIC REFLECTOR. See under REFLECTORS.

PARALLEL CIRCUIT. See under CIRCUITS.

PATCH AT LEVEL. See under COMPUTER LIGHT BOARD TERMINOLOGY.

PATCHCORD (adaptor)

A conductor (part of a patch panel) designed to connect an outlet to a dimmer or a control to a dimmer.

A conductor intended to extend the length of another conductor or to convert from one type of connecting plug to another.

PATCHING. Connecting a given lighting instrument to a given circuit or connecting a given circuit to a given dimmer.

PATCH PANEL (patch, plugging panel, interconnecting panel, cross-connecting panel). Electrical panel designed to allow any DIMMER control to be connected to any load. There are many different patch panel designs, including those that connect dimmers with dimmer controls. Such control is necessary for smooth operation of the complicated light plots common to modern theatre productions. In theatres with limited numbers of dimmers, it is not uncommon to find interchanges occurring during a performance where a dimmer may be assigned to one instrument during one scene and then repatched to serve another spotlight for the next scene. Portable SWITCHBOARDS (PIANO BOARDS, DAVIS BOARDS,

etc.) are equipped with their own outlets and lighting instruments are plugged directly into the desired dimmer. Permanently installed control boards must have the capability of controlling any light or any group of lights with any dimmer. This allows dimmer handles to be grouped for the convenience of the operator.

Interconnecting panel. See **Slider patch** below.

Mini patch (spaghetti patch). Used in many preset consoles the mini patch is a telephone type using miniature plugs on a short 6"-8" wire. Within the 6" x 8" receptacle board, half the holes represent the dimmers, and the other holes are channels of control. The short jumpers go from the dimmer hole to the channel hole. It is easy to visualize that with 96 dimmers and 60 channels it is a mess of crisscrossed wire looking like a mass of wet spaghetti coming out of a pot (hence the nickname). The area is so congested and tiny that often long-nose pliers are required to make or break connections.

Programmable patch (soft patch). Electronic patching featured in certain computer boards allowing various dimmers to be patched to any control channel. This method is as simple as assigning a circuit number to a dimmer via a keypad. See under COMPUTER LIGHT BOARD TERMINOLOGY.

Rotary switch. The Kliegl Bros. rotary switch with cold make and break (DEAD CIRCUIT patching). First introduced in 1951, it is another means of interconnecting dimmers and circuits. It is popular in public schools because of its safety factor. The rotary switch is placed in line between outlets and dimmers. Each dimmer is connected to its individual contact switch. By rotating the selector to a chosen dimmer number, any outlet can be connected with any dimmer. The only problem with this system is the large amount of space it requires.

Slider patch (interconnecting panel, bus bar-type, Quick-Connect). A compact patch panel consisting of a permanent installation of vertical and horizontal bus bars with a sliding pin or interconnecting device, usually on the load BUS BAR. Each vertical bar is wired directly to a dimmer and each horizontal bar is wired directly to a stage outlet or vice versa depending upon the manufacturer. By moving the pin or slider to the desired dimmer bar

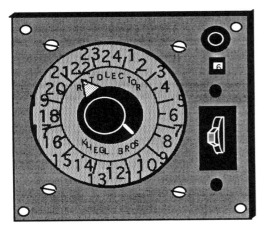

ROTOLECTOR
SELECTS ANY OF 24 CIRCUITS
(KLIEGL BROS. Ca. 1951)

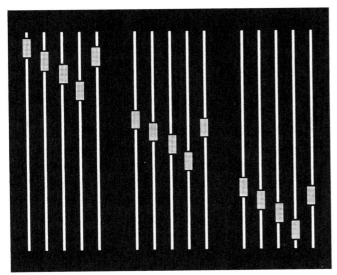

QUICK-CONNECT
CIRCUIT SELECTOR
DAVIS Ca. 1950s

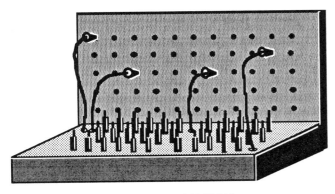

SINGLE-POLE TERMINAL
TELEPHONE-TYPE PATCH PANEL

and plugging it in, any outlet or any number of outlets can be put on any dimmer. Slider-type panels are custom-made for theatres. A common type of slider patch consists of vertical and horizontal bus bars with a sliding pin on each horizontal bar, spring-loaded so that it can be pushed in, slid to desired location, and released. Each slider represents one stage load with a capacity of 20 amps. Each bus bar represents one dimmer or other power source and has a maximum capacity of 40 amps. Although not recommended, patching can be done during play. Since "hot patching" can produce arcs, shortening the life of the equipment, it is advisable to patch cold (power off).

Telephone-type. One of the most common of the older patch panels   resembles an old-fashioned telephone switchboard, with each dimmer connected to a receptacle and each outlet onstage connected to a patchcord. The patchcords are then plugged into any dimmer receptacle, making it possible for any dimmer to control any light.

PATTERN. See GOBO.

PC SPOT. See PLANO-CONVEX SPOTLIGHT.

PERCHES. British term for TOWERS on left and right proscenium used for TORMENTOR spots.

PHANTOM LOAD. See GHOST LOAD.

PHASE. A unit of electrical time based on the rotation of AC generators. In reference to power hookups, theatre in the United States generally uses single-phase or three-phase. See CIRCUITS.

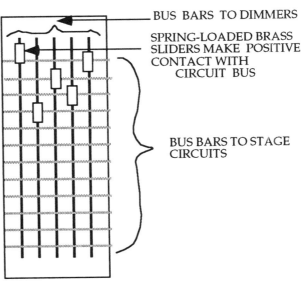

BUS BARS TO DIMMERS

SPRING-LOADED BRASS SLIDERS MAKE POSITIVE CONTACT WITH CIRCUIT BUS

BUS BARS TO STAGE CIRCUITS

QUICK-CONNECT EXPLANATION

PHOSPHORESCENCE. Emission of light without heat from a material that glows for a limited time in the dark after being activated by a light source.

PHOSPHORESCENT PAINT. Paint that glows in the dark for a short time after being exposed to light. Useful in small amounts for SPIKE MARKS or landmarks to guide actors and crew in blackouts. Phosphorescent paints are available or can be ordered from paint stores and art supply houses as well as full-service theatrical supply houses. Not to be confused with ULTRAVIOLET LIGHT.

PHOTOMETER. A meter used to measure light intensity. Sometimes used on the stage for setting lights to discover HOT or cold SPOTS but more often associated with television and photography, where intensity is crucial to accurate color recording.

PHOTOMETRIC CHART. Record of intensity expected from different instruments, lenses, and lamps at various THROWS. Catalogues from reputable lighting manufacturers provide photometric charts explaining light intensities expected of different spotlights at different throws and with different lamps. This is critical information for the technician about to purchase lighting equipment for a theatre or for the designer looking at an inventory of spotlights for the first time and puzzling over which spotlight would be suited for which location. The photometric charts shown here are typical of catalogue charts and will provide samples of instruments and their charted performances to help the prospective user determine their capabilities. More successful lighting is possible if the designer learns how to match the performances of spotlights selected. To illustrate the problem, if AREA 3 is to be lighted from the FOH beam (a 40' throw) and area 6, the adjacent UPSTAGE area, is to be lighted from the border (a 20' throw), it becomes obvious that in the absence of a ZOOM ELLIPSE, two very different instruments must be used to achieve a balance of intensities on these two areas. Of course, balancing intensity may be partially accomplished with DIMMERS, but it must be remembered that as a spot is dimmed, brilliancy decreases and color values change, often drastically. If by working with charts we can approximate an even light distribution across the stage without changing dimmer readings, the result will be an intensity balance plus the bonus of color uniformity.

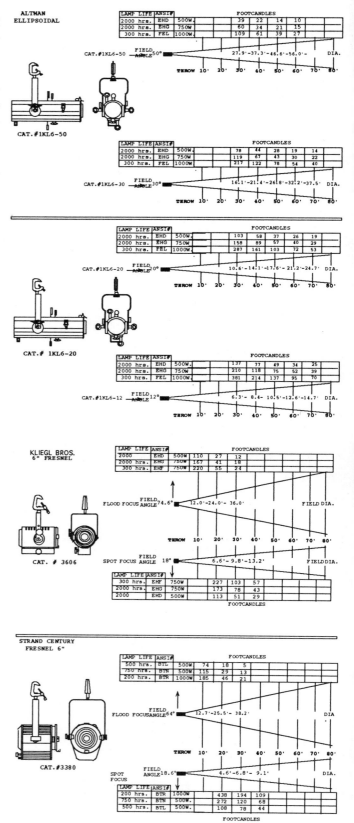

ALTMAN ELLIPSOIDAL

CAT.#1KL6-50 — FIELD ANGLE 50°

LAMP LIFE	ANSI#		FOOTCANDLES			
2000 hrs.	EHD	500W	39	22	14	10
2000 hrs.	EHG	750W	60	34	21	15
300 hrs.	FEL	1000W	109	61	39	27

27.9'–37.3'–46.6'–56.0'– DIA.
THROW 10' 20' 30' 40' 50' 60' 70' 80'

CAT.#1KL6-30 — FIELD ANGLE 30°

LAMP LIFE	ANSI#		FOOTCANDLES				
2000 hrs.	EHD	500W	78	44	28	19	14
2000 hrs.	EHG	750W	119	67	43	30	22
300 hrs.	FEL	1000W	217	122	78	54	40

16.1'–21.4'–26.8'–32.2'–37.5' DIA.
THROW 10' 20' 30' 40' 50' 60' 70' 80'

CAT.#1KL6-20 — FIELD ANGLE 20°

LAMP LIFE	ANSI#		FOOTCANDLES				
2000 hrs.	EHD	500W	103	58	37	26	19
2000 hrs.	EHG	750W	158	89	57	40	29
300 hrs.	FEL	1000W	287	161	103	72	53

10.6'–14.1'–17.6'–21.2'–24.7' DIA.
THROW 10' 20' 30' 40' 50' 60' 70' 80'

CAT.#1KL6-12 — FIELD ANGLE 12°

LAMP LIFE	ANSI#		FOOTCANDLES				
2000 hrs.	EHD	500W	137	77	49	34	25
2000 hrs.	EHG	750W	210	118	75	52	39
300 hrs.	FEL	1000W	381	214	137	95	70

6.3'–8.4'–10.5'–12.6'–14.7' DIA.
THROW 10' 20' 30' 40' 50' 60' 70' 80'

KLIEGL BROS. 6" FRESNEL

CAT.# 3606 — FLOOD FOCUS FIELD ANGLE 74.6°

LAMP LIFE	ANSI#		FOOTCANDLES		
2000	EHD	500W	110	27	12
2000 hrs.	EHG	750W	167	41	18
300 hrs.	EHF	750W	220	55	24

12.0'–24.0'–36.0' FIELD DIA.
THROW 10' 20' 30' 40' 50' 60' 70' 80'

SPOT FOCUS FIELD ANGLE 18°

LAMP LIFE	ANSI#		FOOTCANDLES		
300 hrs.	EHF	750W	227	103	57
2000 hrs.	EHG	750W	173	78	43
2000	EHD	500W	113	51	29

6.6'–9.8'–13.2' FIELD DIA.

STRAND CENTURY FRESNEL 6"

CAT.#3380 — FLOOD FOCUS FIELD ANGLE 64°

LAMP LIFE	ANSI#		FOOTCANDLES		
500 hrs.	BTL	500W	74	18	5
750 hrs.	BTN	500W	115	29	13
200 hrs.	BTR	1000W	185	46	21

12.7'–25.5'–38.2' DIA.
THROW 10' 20' 30' 40' 50' 60' 70' 80'

SPOT FOCUS FIELD ANGLE 18.6°

LAMP LIFE	ANSI#		FOOTCANDLES		
200 hrs.	BTR	1000W	438	194	109
750 hrs.	BTN	500W	272	120	68
500 hrs.	BTL	500W	108	78	44

4.6'–6.8'–9.1' DIA.

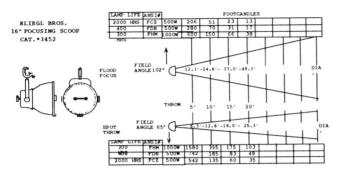

KLIEGL BROS.
16" FOCUSING SCOOP
CAT. #3452

LAMP LIFE	ANSI#		FOOTCANDLES			
2000 HRS	FCZ	500W	206	51	23	13
400	FDN	500W	280	70	31	17
300 HRS	FHM	1000W	600	150	66	38

FLOOD FOCUS — FIELD ANGLE 102° — 12.3'-24.6'-37.0'-49.3' DIA
THROW 5' 10' 15' 20'
SPOT THROW — FIELD ANGLE 65° — 6.3'-12.6'-19.0'-25.3' DIA

LAMP LIFE	ANSI#					
300	FHM	1000W	1580	395	175	103
400	FDN	500W	742	185	83	48
2000 HRS	FCZ	500W	542	135	60	35

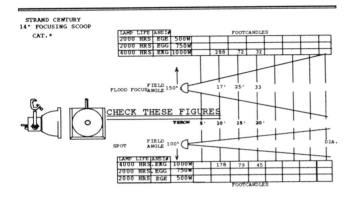

STRAND CENTURY
14" FOCUSING SCOOP
CAT. #

LAMP LIFE	ANSI#		FOOTCANDLES		
2000 HRS	EGE	500W			
2000 HRS	EGG	750W			
4000 HRS	EKG	1000W	288	72	32

FLOOD FOCUS FIELD ANGLE 150° — 17' 25' 33
THROW 5' 10' 15' 20'
SPOT FIELD ANGLE 100° DIA.

CHECK THESE FIGURES

LAMP LIFE	ANSI#				
4000 HRS	EKG	1000W	178	79	45
2000 HRS	EGG	750W			
2000 HRS	EGE	500W			

FOOTCANDLES

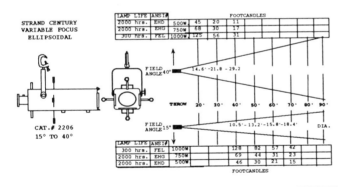

STRAND CENTURY
VARIABLE FOCUS
ELLIPSOIDAL

CAT.# 2206
15° TO 40°

LAMP LIFE	ANSI#		FOOTCANDLES		
2000 hrs.	EHD	500W	45	20	11
2000 hrs.	EHG	750W	68	30	17
300 hrs.	FEL	1000W	125	56	31

FIELD ANGLE 40° — 14.6'-21.8-29.2
THROW 20' 30' 40' 50' 60' 70' 80' 90'
FIELD ANGLE 15° — 10.5'-13.2'-15.8'-18.4' DIA.

LAMP LIFE	ANSI#					
300 hrs.	FEL	1000W	128	82	57	42
2000 hrs.	EHG	750W	69	44	31	23
2000 hrs.	EHD	500W	46	30	21	15

FOOTCANDLES

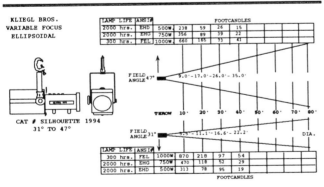

KLIEGL BROS.
VARIABLE FOCUS
ELLIPSOIDAL

CAT # SILHOUETTE 1994
31° TO 47°

LAMP LIFE	ANSI#		FOOTCANDLES			
2000 hrs.	EHD	500W	238	59	26	15
2000 hrs.	EHG	750W	356	89	39	22
300 hrs.	FEL	1000W	660	165	73	41

FIELD ANGLE 47° — 9.0'-17.0'-26.0'-35.0'
THROW 10' 20' 30' 40' 50' 60' 70' 80'
FIELD ANGLE 31° — 5.5'-11.1'-16.6'-22.2' DIA.

LAMP LIFE	ANSI#					
300 hrs.	FEL	1000W	870	218	97	54
2000 hrs.	EHG	750W	470	118	52	29
2000 hrs.	EHD	500W	313	78	35	19

FOOTCANDLES

Different manufacturers have different methods of compiling photometric material. The two charts included here are relatively representative of some well-known spotlights. A close look at the charts will quickly show the striking differences in performances of the eight spotlights and the need for the lighting designer to be aware of available lighting equipment. Drawings of instruments appearing on the left of the charts help to identify equipment; manufacturer catalogue numbers give a positive identification. Varying lens sizes and focal lengths determine the FIELD ANGLE. With lens sizes, the first number equals diameter in inches and the second number indicates focal length in inches. ANSI codes describe the various lamps used.

In these charts the FOOTCANDLE measurements represent maximum illumination taken at the center of the beam of light. Bold numbers in each chart identify the throw in feet. FIELD DIAMETER is the diameter of the beam representing 10%–50% of maximum intensity of light from a given spotlight at a given distance. To find the proper spotlight for your job, use your light plot to determine the throw of the spot to the area and the diameter of the beam needed. From the bold numbers in each series, choose the chart showing the range of throw needed. Within the diagramed light cone, find the diameter closest to required specifications, remembering that these chart figures represent field diameters and will need to be of sufficient size to allow overlapping of adjacent areas. Finally, look at the footcandle and lamp data and try to match intensities for each area on the stage. Because the human eye has difficulty discerning degrees of intensity above 100 FC, it is seldom necessary to plan brighter areas. Footcandles are cumulative. If two spotlights are focused on the same area from the same distance and each delivers 50 FC, the resulting total should measure 100 FC on a light meter.

PIANO BOARD. Obsolete. A portable switchboard consisting of resistance dimmers and using a **Mechanical master** (see under DIMMERS, MASTER), housed in a box resembling an upright piano crate. See also SWITCHBOARDS. See illustration on following page.

PICK UP (command verb). To put the beam of light of a FOLLOWSPOT on a performer.

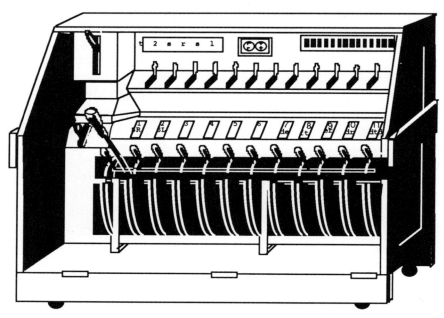

PIANO BOARD

PIE FORMULA. See under AMPERE.

PIGTAIL. A length of stage cable with appropriate connectors. See ADAPTOR.

PILE ON. To override one dimmer control with a second control. It is sometimes necessary to increase the intensity of one or two lights. With light boards using presets, this is accomplished by piling on. This technique cannot be used to decrease intensity below the dimmer reading on the preset.

PILOT LIGHT. A small light used by stage managers or electricians for reading cue sheets. Such lights must be masked from the stage with a shield, and they are sometimes dimmed with blue GELATINE. See also PANEL LIGHT.

PIN CONNECTOR. A heavy-duty electrical plug specially designed for theatre use. See under PLUGS.

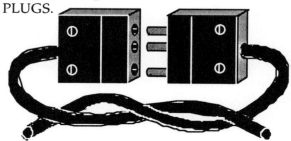

PIN CONNECTORS

PINSPOT. A spotlight either focused or shuttered to a narrow beam. When using ELLIPSOIDAL REFLECTOR SPOTLIGHTS for pinspots, the beam must be centered before shuttering to the proper size; otherwise the intense heat at the center of the beam may warp the shutter. If a FRESNEL LIGHT is used, the focus is closed as tight as possible and a FUNNEL or BARNDOOR is used to further reduce spill. If a FOLLOWSPOT is used, the TROMBONE, the IRIS, or both are needed to form a head-sized pinspot.

PINSPOTS

PIPE. Black iron pipe available at plumbing and hardware stores is usually the only kind of pipe the electrician needs. Standard C-CLAMPS and

128

YOKE CLAMPS made for lighting instruments are threaded for 1/2" pipe and pipe fittings and are designed to clamp onto 1 1/4" or 1 1/2" pipes used as battens in the fly system. Special LADDERS and BOOMS are usually made in the shop with pipes cut and threaded as needed. Pipe is measured by inside diameter (ID) and is usually sold in 21' lengths. See also TAP AND DIE SETS.

PIPE BATTEN (pipe, bars [British usage]). A single pipe on a set of lines, part of the fly system in the theatre. This should not be confused with a LIGHT BATTEN, which is a mounting device for lighting instruments and may consist of a pipe or an elaborate set of pipes and circuits. Most single pipes use 1 1/4" or 1 1/2" ID pipe. The word "batten" can also refer to a wooden batten used with scenery in older theaters.

PIPE CLAMP. The C-clamp and the yoke clamp are the two types of pipe clamps used to fasten lighting instruments to pipes. See under CLAMPS.

PIPE FITTINGS. Attachments for fastening and joining pipe.

  Coupling (sleeve). A short piece of pipe threaded on the inside and used to join two lengths of pipe. At least one of the pipes must be free to rotate in order to use the coupling.

  Elbow. Angles of 45° or 90°, threaded on the inside.

  Flange. A round plate with a threaded hole in the center to receive pipe. Available in standard pipe sizes and used to fasten pipes to the floor, wooden bases, walls, etc.

  Nipple. Short length of pipe threaded at each end and used with couplings or elbows to join two pipes. Nipples vary in length from about 1" (close nipple) to 6" (long nipple).

  Sleeve. See **Coupling** above.

  Tee. A coupling device that joins three pipes in the shape of a T.

  Union. A double coupling with a special fitting in the middle making it possible to join two pipes, neither of which is free to turn. The union consists of a fitting for each pipe and a nut that draws the two fittings together.

PIT. See ORCHESTRA PIT.

PLACES (command verb). Order given by the stage manager or assistant, alerting cast and crew that curtain is going up and that each member is to be in place and ready.

PLAN. Technically a plan view is a floor plan, but loosely, a plan can include all DRAWINGS.

PLANO-CONVEX LENS. A lens that is curved on one side and flat on the other. See under LENSES.

PLANO-CONVEX SPOTLIGHT (PC, PC spot). Obsolete. A spotlight with a plano-convex LENS. Because of their inefficiency, few PCs are in use any more.

PC SPOT MANUFACTURED
BY MAJOR IN LATE 1920s

PLASTER CYC. A permanent backwall of a theatre, plastered, painted white, and used as a sky cyc. Plaster cycs are excellent screens for projections or for sky but they do scratch and chip over time and are difficult to repair. The most satisfactory shape for cycs intended for projections is curved to help maintain equal distances between the projector and cyc, thus maintaining the correct focus and uniform intensity. Sand-floated plaster with a coarse grade of sand is best for plaster cycs. Never allow scenery to be stacked against a plaster cyc; it scars too easily. See also CYC.

PLASTERLINE. See PROSCENIUM LINE.

PLASTICS. Many plastics are made by polymerization, a process that links identical molecules to produce a plastic substance. These plastics are known as polymers. Although most plastics will either burn, melt, release toxic fumes, or all three when subjected to fire, the ease with which they are formed and machined makes them intriguing materials for many theatrical uses, including slides for projectors and color media for lights. Following is a list of some of the kinds of plastics electricians will find useful, a few of the ways they may be used, and some of the fume hazards, combustibility, and ability to self-extinguish.

  Acetate. Transparent sheets of plastic used as slides for low-temperature, DIRECT BEAM projectors. Colored felt-tip pens may be used on either acetate or glass slides. Acetate sheets come in standard sizes of 20" x 50" and vary in thickness from 0.2 mils (0.002") to 125 mils (1/8"). *Warning:* Acetate, being a thermoplastic, starts to distort at temperatures of about 130° F and melts at about 220° F. Moderately easy to ignite; not self-extinguishing. See also SLIDES, PROJECTION.

Acrylic (Acrylite, Lucite, Plexiglas). Available in sheets, tubes, bars, rods, clear, or colored. Clear or translucent plastic sheets used to build furniture, objects of art, etc. For a translucent floor that permits dramatic use of light, a 1/2" thickness will show little weight deflection if joists are on 2' centers. Stock sheet sizes are 4' x 6', but standard sizes are usually available in 4' x 8', 5' x 6', and 5' x 8'. Thicknesses of acrylic sheets include 1/8", 1/4", 3/8", 1/2", 5/8", 3/4", 1", and 1 1/2". Acrylic surfaces scratch easily; lightweight oil or a thin wax will help conceal scratches. Acrylics may be thermoformed and are easily cut with a skip-tooth band saw blade. Finer teeth saws tend to become hot enough to melt the plastic as they cut; sometimes it reseals as fast as the cut is made. Acrylics may also be drilled with metal bits and turned in a lathe. Slow speeds must be used with all power tools to avoid friction heat. Use of sandpaper or emery cloth will result in a frosted or translucent effect and a wet rouge cloth will maintain the clear transparency. Readily ignited; not self-extinguishing.

Mylar. A thin polyester film used as a releasing agent for casting resins, color media, and a variety of reflective surfaces. Mylar is much more heat resistant than acetate and is therefore more suitable as a transparency for slides in certain PROJECTORS. Fumes are moderately harmful; easily ignited; not self-extinguishing.

Phenolics (Bakelite R). Usually used as an insulating material in electrical work. Difficult to ignite; self-extinguishing.

PLATE DIMMER. A name for a RESISTANCE DIMMER shaped like a dinner plate.

PLAYER BOARD. Obsolete. A mechanical slider-type light control board. The slider traveled 12"-18" to give better control. Usually used with resistance dimmers or autotransformers, the dimmer was rotated with a chain or wire cable connected to the slider traveling in a slot on the surface of the board.

PLOT. The common term used for light plot. See DESIGN FOR LIGHTING.

PLOTTER. A computer drawing machine that allows the use of different colored pens and different line width pens as an outputting device for a COMPUTER ASSISTED DESIGN program. The CAD program and plotter may be used to prepare drawings on large sizes of paper as determined by the size of the plotter. Printers may be used instead of a plotter but the paper is legal or letter size and often too small.

PLUG FUSE. See under FUSE.

PLUGGING BOX

A portable box for multiple electrical hookups. Plugging boxes are made to accommodate two or more plugs.

Obsolete. Same as above but specifically designed to accommodate the STAGE PLUG. The stage plug plugging box was a rudimentary form of PATCH PANEL for PIANO BOARDS, which were equipped with stage plug outlets on the top front of the board.

PLUGGING PANEL. See PATCH PANEL.

PLUGGING STRIP. A multiple-outlet device designed to provide power to several lighting instruments. The plugging strip may be a DROP BOX serving only a few lights or it may be a built-in part of a LIGHT BATTEN, providing both power and circuitry for a major portion of the lighting system.

PLUGS. Electrical connectors of various types designed to make temporary connections in an electrical circuit. Most states require three-prong plugs for new installations, the third prong grounding the load. A female plug (body), contains one or more receptacles for prongs and fastens to the LINE (power supply). A male plug (cap) contains one or more prongs and fastens to the LOAD (equipment to be used). Plugs in common use in the theatre (excluding sound equipment) include the following:

Edison plug. Standard household plug not considered durable enough for stage equipment but used for PRACTICAL lamps, appliances, and shop equipment.

Half-plug. Obsolete. A stage plug made half the thickness of a standard stage plug so two could fit

EDISON PLUGS

STAGE PLUG

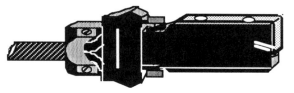

TWO-FER

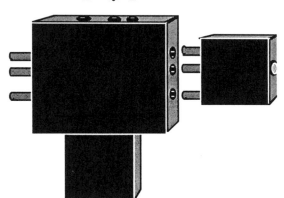

PIN CONNECTOR THREE-FER

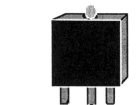

TWISTLOCK PLUGS

into one plugging box receptacle. Like the stage plug, half-plugs have no provision for a ground wire and are therefore illegal.

Multiple pin connector (spider). An electrical connector with three or more female outlets to accommodate more than one male connector.

Pin connector (slip connector). An electrical plug and receptacle particularly suitable to stage use because of the flat, rectangular design (does not roll if stepped on). Available in 20, 30, 60, and 100 amps. Most theatres try to standardize on one size, usually 20 amps, for portable equipment.

Polarized plug. Electrical plugs or receptacles designed to fit together in one way only and often used in switchboard hookups where PATCH PANELS are used. Polarized plugs eliminate the possibility of connecting equipment backward. Most twistlock plugs and all plugs with three or more prongs have polarity; that is to say, they will fit together in one way only.

Stage plug (floor pocket, wall pocket). Obsolete. A large plug made for heavy loads of 20, 30, and 50 amps, designed for recessed pockets, usually in stage floor, wall, or portable plugging boxes. No provision for ground wire, so are illegal.

Two-fer and three-fer (Y). A multiple connector consisting of two or three female outlets attached to one male plug by 2' or 3' lengths of cable. Sometimes a special single appliance is available.

Twistlock plug. Round plugs that lock together when twisted, giving positive connections that cannot be pulled apart accidentally.

POCKET. See FLOOR POCKET.

POLARIZED PLUG. See under PLUGS.

POLE. One of the terminals (positive or negative) supplying electrical energy.

POOL. An area covered by light from overhead spotlights in a near-vertical position. Dramatic lighting, but it completely obliterates facial detail unless compensated by other light from below, the front, or reflected from another surface (floor, table, costume). Pools are often used in BALLET LIGHTING and in DANCE THEATRE LIGHTING.

PORT (portal). An opening in the sidewalls or the ceiling of an auditorium, used as an FOH position for lighting INSTRUMENTS. See BEAM POSITION; PORTAL.

PORTABLE BOARD. Control boards that are lightweight enough to be moved from place to place and used to control lights, sound, hydraulics, curtains, etc. Touring theatres must plan on using their own control boards if there is to be any reliable lighting plan. Most touring COMPANIES carry silicon controlled rectifier dimmers controlled by either PRESET BOARDS or, in larger companies, COMPUTER BOARDS. AUTOTRANSFORMER dimmers are used on occasion as AUXILIARY BOARDS.

PORTABLE WIRING. TEMPORARY WIRING designed with many CABLES running from the DIMMERS to the INSTRUMENTS, which are HUNG and STRUCK for road shows.

PORTAL. In many theatres, portals are built as permanent side entrances to the apron, and if they are carefully designed, they will provide ideal space for mounting instruments for CROSSLIGHTING. Portals designed for lights only are tall, narrow slots, cut in the side of the proscenium or auditorium walls. They should be a minimum of 18"–24" wide, 6' above stage level, and 8' high. More generous allowances make for more versatile use. Portals should include masking shields to conceal spotlights from the audience, and there must be access to the portal from behind for focusing.

PORTAL LIGHTS. Instruments chosen for the portal position should be ellipsoidal spotlights that can be focused to cut the proscenium with a hard-edge of light. Portal lights should be chosen to match the intensities of TORMENTOR LIGHTS (if used), and the designer should follow the procedure covered in CROSSLIGHTING, choosing SHORT-THROW SPOTLIGHTS in the lower position, medium-throw spotlights in the center position, and LONG-THROW SPOTLIGHTS in upper position.

POSITIONS. The places where lighting INSTRUMENTS may be HUNG. See BEAM POSITION; BOOTH LIGHTS; CYC; ELECTRICS; FOOTLIGHTS; PORTAL; SIDELIGHTING; RAIL. See also RACK.

POSITIVE/NEGATIVE

Batteries. Poles on a battery, which have the polarity marked on them.

Carbon arcs. Two different polarities marked on CARBONS for FOLLOWSPOTS.

Electricity. The two lines in a cable may be referred to in this manner, with the HOT LINE being the positive and the NEUTRAL WIRE being the negative.

POT. See POTENTIOMETER.

POTENTIAL. Electrical pressure. The tendency for an electric current to flow. In a small flashlight battery, there is a 1 1/2-volt potential between the two terminals; in a house circuit there is usually a 120-volt potential between the lines. The question, Is there potential? asks whether power is on. See also ELECTRICITY.

POTENTIOMETER (pot). A small variable-resistor, similar to a radio volume control, used with electronic dimmers, sound equipment, etc., to vary the intensity of light or sound.

POWER FORMULA. See under ELECTRICITY.

POWERSTAT. Obsolete. An autotransformer dimmer made from 3 amp to 45 amp output. One of its selling points was its ganging of large dimmers with electric motor controls. Made by the Superior Electric Company of Bristol, Connecticut.

PRACTICAL. Any functional or apparently functional property or piece of scenery, for example, windows and doors that open; fireplaces that appear to contain and be burning logs; lamps that turn on; and switches on walls that look or sound as if they are turning on the lights of the room (they must never be wired to do this).

PREFOCUS BASE. A type of lamp base that keeps the filament in a fixed relationship with the reflector and lens. See **Bases** under LAMPS.

PRESET. A method of setting light intensity on a light board for one or more scenes in advance. When one scene is completed, a fader or master dimmer is used to fade the lights down on one scene and up to preset intensities for the next scene. See also COMPUTER LIGHT BOARD TERMINOLOGY.

PRESET BOARD (console, control board, board). A lighting control system with two or more scenes of dimmers controlling the same lights. The first scene is assigned one set of readings (CUE) and the second scene is assigned another. When the action onstage dictates, the CROSS-FADER dims out the first scene and dims up the next scene. System presets rely on the operator or an assistant to reset the scenes between cues. These boards use faders, split faders, cross-faders, submasters, and masters

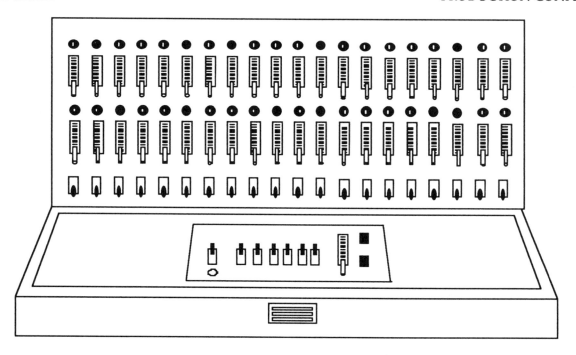

20-DIMMER, 2-SCENE PRESET CONSOLE

to produce flexibility and movement from one scene to another. Some systems are very large; 5 to 10 scene presets are not uncommon. The preset board takes full advantage of the small, low-voltage, inexpensive controls for dimmers that make it economically feasible to assign any number of controls to a dimmer. Originally assembled as consoles, these preset units are now made as small portable 2-scene control boards often incorporating microprocessor features. Small preset boards are popular because they are less expensive than a computer board though a MICROPROCESSOR can be added in some cases. Do not confuse the ability to preset a cue in preset boards with the microprocessor's memory ability.

PRESET SHEET. An additional cue sheet listing only the presetting information for each cue. This specialized sheet is usually reserved for complicated, fast-moving shows, sometimes called set-reset shows.

PREVIEWING LIGHT CUES. Checking other light cues without disturbing the lights of the scene in progress. See under COMPUTER LIGHT BOARD TERMINOLOGY.

PREVIEW PRODUCTION. A special performance of a production prior to OPENING and often one of the final dress rehearsals.

PRIMARY COIL. The windings in a transformer that are connected to the power side. See TRANSFORMER.

PRIMARY COLORS

    Lights. Red, green, and blue. See **Additive method** under COLOR MIXING.

    Paint. Red, yellow, and blue. See **Subtractive method** under COLOR MIXING.

PRIME FOCUS. When the audience's full attention has been directed to a performer or in rare cases an object, that person or object is referred to as having the prime focus. This attention can be forced easily with lights, either through focus, intensity, or color. Other methods of directing audience attention involve set or costume design.

PRODUCTION CONCEPT. The general plan or direction a production will take from inception to completion. This direction is usually supplied by the director, although in some productions, designers may be asked for input.

PRODUCTION CONFERENCE. A conference or series of conferences held well in advance of production dates and involving the director, scene designer, lighting designer, costume designer, stage manager, and other personnel involved in production decision making. Those attending the production conference should have studied the play prior to the conference date and come prepared to discuss interpretation of the script, preliminary set designs, costume suggestions, prop problems, special effects, and color schemes of sets, costumes, lights, etc. The production conference is designed to discuss all phases of the production so there will be no surprises at dress rehearsals.

PROFESSIONAL THEATRE. Generally refers to theatres employing union workers in some or all areas within the organization. See UNIONS.

PROFILE SPOT. A British term for a Strand ELLIPSOIDAL REFLECTOR SPOTLIGHT with two sets of shutters, one producing a SOFT-EDGED light beam and the other a HARD-EDGED light beam.

PROGRAMMABLE PATCH (soft patch). See under COMPUTER LIGHT BOARD TERMINOLOGY

PROJECTED SCENERY. Scenes projected either on a translucent screen from behind (upstage) or on an opaque screen from in front (downstage). There are obvious advantages to projected scenery: fast scene changes in multiple-set shows; reduction of time and money spent building scenery; no storage problems; smaller operating crew. However, there are certain disadvantages that may not be so obvious. Designers and directors should be aware that projected scenery is not always the cheap, easy answer to scenic effects. The initial expense of suitable projection equipment can represent a large portion of an annual lighting budget and replacement of the HMI lamps used in many of the projectors will also prove expensive. A great deal of time, material, and photographic expense can go into making slides. Compensating for distortion (KEYSTONING) caused by the angle at which the projector light hits the screen is often frustrating, trial and error work requiring hours of time (see SLIDES, PROJECTION). Set-up and special technical rehearsals must be allowed for adjusting, experimenting, determining angles, etc.; dark floors, furniture, and even costumes that will absorb ambient light must be agreed upon as well as SIDELIGHTING, BACKLIGHTING, and steep-angle lighting to avoid spill and shadows on the screen. Upstage acting areas that are too close to the screen to be lighted must be sacrificed. Such problems need to be thoroughly understood and trade-offs agreed upon in PRODUCTION CONFERENCES long before rehearsals begin. In addition to

these problems, it gradually becomes apparent that projected scenery cannot completely replace built scenery; PRACTICAL portions of the sets must still be built: doors that open and close, windows to allow CROSSLIGHTING, fireplaces that work, etc. There is little doubt that projecting scenery can be a fascinating and rewarding endeavor, but there is also little doubt that it is not the easy, cheap solution to putting scenery on the stage that it may appear to be at first blush.

Moving projections

Abstracts. Projections of moving abstract images can be made by introducing a turntable or revolving disk at the focal point between the objective lens and the condensing lens of a simple projector. Metal cutouts placed on the disk and rotated in and out of focus provide interesting patterns on the screen. *Caution:* The focal point is the hottest part of the light, and therefore, anything placed in this area must be heat resistant.

Cloud drum. Cutouts of clouds fastened to a wire mesh or painted on a plastic drum about 4' in diameter that can be slowly rotated around a strong light source will give the effect of clouds moving across the cyc. The clear lamp (not frosted) must have a concentrated filament and must be enclosed so the light is shielded from everything but the screen (see PROJECTOR LAMP). The moving drum must be geared down to something less than 1 rpm and provided with speed control. White clouds are projected through cutouts made in a black, opaque material (such as roofing paper), and dark clouds are opaque cutouts fastened to the mesh. CYCLORAMA LIGHTS may be used with the effect to give color to the sky.

Sciopticon. An attachment for a spotlight that includes a rectangular box housing a transparent disk, chosen from a selection of mica disks on which clouds, rain, snow, waterfalls, flags, etc., are painted. An electric motor rotates the disk through a beam of light, and an objective lens focuses the image on a sky drop or screen. The sciopticon is available through most theatrical supply houses or stage lighting manufacturers and is sold as an attachment that fits in the color frame slots of many large spotlights. Be certain to check fit before rental or purchase.

PROJECTION BOOTH. See BOOTH, PROJECTION.

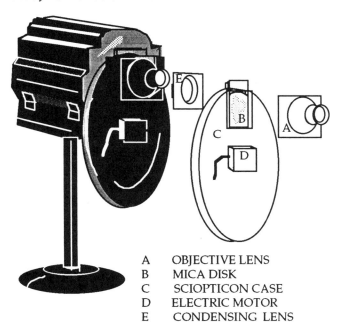

A   OBJECTIVE LENS
B   MICA DISK
C   SCIOPTICON CASE
D   ELECTRIC MOTOR
E   CONDENSING LENS

SCIOPTICON MOUNTED ON SPOTLIGHT

PROJECTION SCREEN (sheet). A flat surface on which a projection may be shown. For many years the best front-projection screens have been made of a highly reflectorized material such as glass beads. Welded plastic translucent screens are much more versatile than glass bead screens in that they may be used as a sky CYC as well as a projection screen for either front or rear projections.

Front screen. An opaque screen used for front projections only. Front screens can range from the simple seamless muslin or SCRIM stretched on a wooden frame to the more elaborate reflectorized screens, light-colored plastic screens, or plaster cycs. The major problem with front projections is coping with distortions. To keep the projector from being seen or from casting actors' shadows on the screen, front projections must come from a relatively steep angle, well above the OPTICAL AXIS with the screen. This produces what is known as KEYSTONING. Because the THROW is shortest at the top of the screen, the spread of light is less; therefore the picture is narrower and brighter at the top than at the bottom. Another frustration is trying to focus a slide with a throw variation of perhaps 20'.

Rear screen. A translucent screen with the projector placed behind (upstage). Good rear screens are made of plastic and are not easily fabricated, because of density. The plastic must be thin enough to allow maximum light transmission and yet dense enough to keep the projector lens from showing a HOT SPOT. Screens are available from Rosco Labs in white, cream, light gray, dark gray, and black, and may be used for front, rear, or dual projections. Obviously, a fair amount of space must be available behind the screen for rear-screen projection. (The rule of thumb is every 18" of picture width requires 12" of THROW.) The obvious advantage of rear screens is the lack of keystoning because the projector may be placed in the center of the optical axis with the screen.

Novelty screens. Various materials have been successfully used as screens for front projections, including vertically hung plastic strips that can be penetrated by actors; scrims that can be seen through when light is dimmed in front and brought up from behind; lengths of ribbons or rope hung on battens; balloons suspended overhead; even costumes on actors. Screens for front projectors may be virtually any kind of material, but unfortunately, materials able to be used for rear-screen projections are very limited.

PROJECTOR LAMP. Proper light sources have always been a leading problem in the development of projectors. Ideally the source should be a pinpoint of high-intensity light in the 3,200 Kelvin area and dimmable. Early incandescent lamps fell far short of these requirements. The older 2,100-watt 60-volt airport runway lamp of 40 years ago served the needs of DIRECT BEAM projectors at that time. Later, TUNGSTEN-HALOGEN LAMPS offered a partial solution for some projectors. Now, with the ENCAPSULATED ARC LAMP, HMI, and XENON, intensities and source size are certainly close to requirements; however, these lamps are not fully dimmable. LASER light sources are certainly in the future but are not yet a fully developed light source.

PROJECTORS. Thomas Wilford (1889–1968) spent his life designing and working with projectors in West Nyack, N.Y. Described in his book *Projected Scenery: A Technical Manual* are several projectors that could be built in the average theatre workshop. Among the more useful are a "uniplate," a single-slide projector; a "multiplate," a remote-controlled projector holding several slides; a "di-

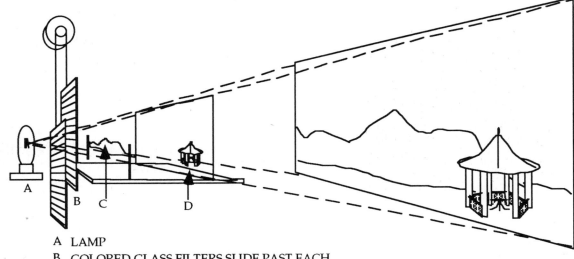

A LAMP
B COLORED GLASS FILTERS SLIDE PAST EACH
   OTHER TO GIVE SUBTLE COLOR CHANGES
C MOUNTAIN CUTOUT CLOSEST TO LIGHT SOURCE
   GIVES FUZZY DETAIL FOR DISTANCE EFFECT
D GAZEBO, FARTHER FROM LIGHT SOURCE,
   GIVES SHARPER DETAIL TO NEAR OBJECT

DIRECT BEAM PROJECTION

rect beam," a shadow Linnebach-type projector; and a "clavilux," a projector of moving abstract images.

Direct beam projector. A strong, clear light source, glass strips in graduated daylight to night colors mounted in a motorized frame, and a means

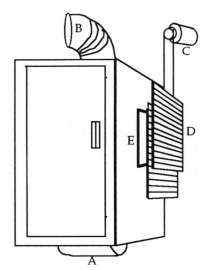

A COOLING FAN
B AIR VENT
C COLOR CONTROL MOTOR
D COLORED GLASS STRIPS
E OPENING MADE TO FILL SCREEN

DIRECT BEAM

of holding paper scenic cutouts from 3' to 5' away from the light source are the necessary parts for a direct beam projector. The cutouts and/or paintings on transparencies are inserted in the frame or placed between the frame and light source for projection on the screen. This type of projector lacks the clarity obtainable with lens projectors, but objects placed the farthest from the light will be in clearest focus, thus providing depth to the picture. The best lamp for direct beam projection is a clear, high-intensity, tight-filament lamp. A SPHERICAL REFLECTOR may be used.

Ellipsoidal spotlight gobos. Although the ellipsoidal spot was not designed as a projector, the popularity of GOBOS and the resulting multitude of designs now available have increased the demand for these spots as projectors. The lighting designer is advised to check new gobo designs on a regular basis.

Linnebach projector. The Linnebach projector was first introduced in this country by Kliegl Bros. in 1922. A direct beam–type projector looking a little like an old-fashioned FLOODLIGHT and designed for a single slide located 18"–24" from the lamp. Little detail shows in shadows cast from this projector due to the close proximity of slide to light. Projections like leaf patterns, tree silhouettes, and

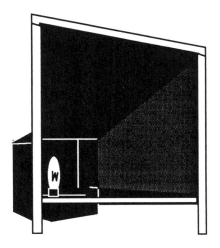

LINNEBACH PROJECTOR

distant skylines can only be suggested. Again, the light source should be a clear, high-intensity, tight-filament lamp.

Overhead projector. Designed largely for classroom use where the instructor writes on an acetate sheet with a felt-tip pen and the "slide" is projected by mirror to a screen behind the instructor. This overhead projector is adaptable to rear-screen projection. The slide used in this equipment is about 12" square, permitting the addition of much more detail than is possible with smaller slides. 1,000-watt tungsten-halogen lamps provide sufficient intensity for pictures up to about 15' square, depending on the opacity of the slide and the AMBIENT LIGHT onstage. As with the carousel projector, the fans of overhead projectors must be left on when the lamp is to be dimmed. Incidentally, this kind of projector is a great time saver in paint shops, where it may be used to project scenes,

cartoons, wallpaper, etc., on drops and flats for quick transfer. The electrician may be called on to set this up, and it will be found that interdepartmental cooperation will reap many dividends.

Rear-screen projector. Projector located behind a translucent screen. Such projectors generally have wide-angle lenses that project larger pictures in shorter throws to minimize the distance between screen and projector. When considering the necessary throw for projectors, it is well to remember the rule of thumb that establishes a 1' to 1 1/2' ratio (12" of throw for every 18" of width) as being near maximum for lensed projectors. Depending on the density of the screen (usually ranging between 30% and 80% light transmission) it may be necessary to keep the projector either below or above the direct line of vision of the audience. See **Rear screen** under PROJECTION SCREENS.

Slide projector (carousel, tray type). For multiple-screen or small-screen projections (up to about 10' square), the slide projector can be a very useful instrument. If the projector is to be dimmed or turned off during the show, the fan must be rewired to a HOT LINE. Most projectors of this type have many plastic parts, which will melt or distort beyond repair if the lamp is left on without the fan or if, after extended use, the lamp and fan are turned off simultaneously. Tungsten-halogen lamps and xenon light sources are preferred depending upon throw and size of image desired. The ZOOM LENS available for carousel projectors has the distinct advantage of offering greater latitude in placing the projector and still filling the screen.

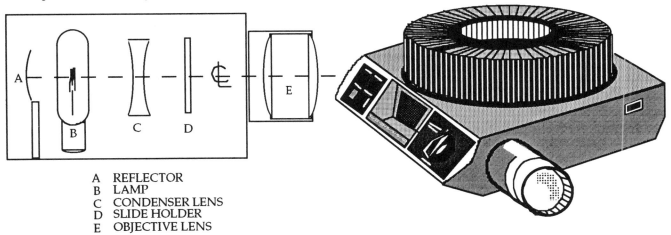

A   REFLECTOR
B   LAMP
C   CONDENSER LENS
D   SLIDE HOLDER
E   OBJECTIVE LENS
SIMPLE PROJECTOR

CAROUSEL SLIDE PROJECTOR

Uniplate projector. The simple uniplate projector consists of a high-intensity light source, a condensing lens for concentrating light, a slide holder, and an objective lens for focusing. To determine the focal length of the lens needed to fill a given screen, measure the size of the screen, the distance the projector will be from the screen, the size of the slide to be used, and use the following equation:

$S/f = I/D$, where S = slide size (height or width), f = focal length, I = image size (height or width), D = distance between screen and projector.

Example: What focal length is needed for an image 30' wide at a distance of 20' with a slide 5" wide?

$5/f = 30/20$, $f = 100/30$, $f = 3.33"$.

PROJECTOR, SLIDES. See SLIDES, PROJECTION.

PROJECTOR SPOT. See BEAM PROJECTOR.

PROMPT BOOK (book, script). Acting copy of a play used by the prompter or stage manager to record business and cues and help actors with lines.

PROMPT SIDE (PS). A professional stage direction in America, meaning the side of the stage on which the prompter is seated, generally stage right. See also AREAS; OP; STAGE DIRECTIONS.

PROPORTIONAL DIMMING. Mastering dimmers either electrically or electronically so all dimmers begin the dimming cycle simultaneously regardless of their reading during the scene. This differs from mechanical mastering, in which each dimmer engages the mastering device as it reaches that dimmer setting. See **Electrical master** under DIMMERS.

PROSCENIUM (proscenium arch). The frame separating the stage from the auditorium.

False proscenium (inner proscenium). An inner frame set upstage of the curtain to narrow the proscenium width or to set the action further upstage where, because of limited FOH lighting positions, it may be easier to light the scene.

PROSCENIUM LIGHTS. See PORTAL LIGHTS.

PROSCENIUM LINE (plasterline). A dashed line drawn on floor plans extending across the stage on the upstage side of the proscenium. This line is used as a reference point for accurate placement of the FOCUSING CLOTH. The upstage side of the proscenium wall in some drawings is referred to as the plasterline. Often marked on the stage floor so actors and props will not be left downstage of the curtain when it closes.

PROSCENIUM STAGE LIGHTING. This is a continuation of the discussion in the entry LIGHTING PRACTICE as related to the specific problems presented by a proscenium stage. After reading the script and consulting LIGHTING PRACTICE and DESIGN FOR LIGHTING, decide which approach to area lighting will best serve the needs of the script, equipment available, and predetermined ideas of the scene designer and director. The chosen formula is then applied to the designer's floor plan and repeated as many times as necessary to cover all acting AREAS. With a SCALE RULE and the floor plan, determine the approximate light THROW. At the same time, note the diameter of the area to be covered and with the help of the PHOTOMETRIC CHARTS, determine the spotlight and lamp wattage that will most closely fit the requirements for each area. Match as closely as possible with lights in the current inventory. Keep a written record of each spotlight to be used, the make, the wattage, plot number assigned, area to be covered, and color to be used. The list thus prepared makes it easier to gather necessary equipment before the time crunch of the SET-IN. This list also provides a guide for the crew's work during limited set-in hours. While choosing spotlights, remember that lights from the same manufacturer will provide greater uniformity in performance than will a mixed variety. Before hanging and preferably before set-in time, clean lenses and reflectors, and check each lamp to make certain it is the right size and not burned out. Check lead wires for frayed insulation or exposed wires. Open all shutters on ellipsoidals to avoid overheating (shortening lamp life) when turned on for the circuit check.

Lighting formulas or methods. One of the first books to deal exclusively with how to light a stage was written by Stanley McCandless of Yale University in 1932. It was simply titled *A Method of Lighting the Stage.* Possibly because theatre budget restrictions were a foregone conclusion in those depression days, McCandless was concerned with using a minimum number of spotlights and dimmers to provide modeling for the actor and to suggest mood and motivation for the setting. Because of wide acceptance of the McCandless method, many people regarded his book as "the method" and they never developed beyond those simple concepts. Although many more variations in lighting techniques have evolved over the years, the basic theories of McCandless are just as valid today as they were in the early thirties. As a matter of fact, it may still be recommended that theatres with very limited lighting equipment use the basic McCandless method to achieve some modeling of the figure, some motivational light source, and some color to help enhance the mood of the play. In any formula, it is assumed that the blending of light from one area to the other will depend on overlapping FIELD ANGLES of the spotlights striking those areas, as indicated in the illustration.

McCandless formula. Each area is lighted by two spotlights, placed at about a 45° angle from the floor and a 90° angle from each other. One light should be equipped with a warm color media, and the other with a cool color, with a single dimmer controlling both. *Advantages:* Requires minimum equipment, provides some modeling of the figure, some motivational light source, some use of color to enhance the mood of the play, and area color control. *Disadvantages:* Inability to handle complex moods and variations within the play; unnatural visual effect of always seeing one side of the actor's face warm and the other side cool; similarly, unpleasant visual effect of seeing the stage left scenic wall a different color from the stage right wall; and perhaps the most grating of all to the experienced lighting designer, seeing a play suffer lighting distractions at the hands of a designer restricted to "the method." (The illustration shows both field

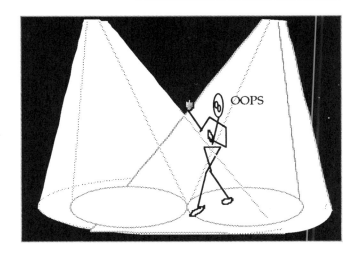

CHECKING BLENDING

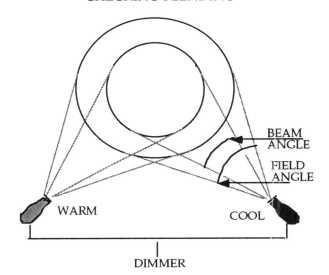

McCANDLESS FORMULA

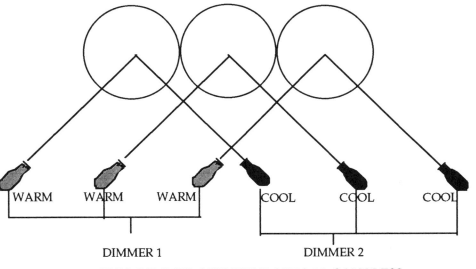

TWO-DIMMER, MULTIPLE-AREA McCANDLESS

angle and beam angle to further illustrate the necessity for blending. Successive illustrations will show only the beam angle area covered, assuming the field coverage for blend.)

Two-dimmer McCandless. Color control. Two spotlights using a warm color from one side and a cool color from the other. Control: two dimmers, one for each color.

Multiple-area McCandless. Color control of all downstage areas. Ganging all downstage area cools on one dimmer and all downstage warms on another dimmer. See **Color Combinations** under COLOR SCHEMES.

Wash formula. The wash formula probably evolved as a logical solution to some of the problems presented by the McCandless method. This is basically the **Wash and key** but with better ANGLES. The wash formula must not be confused with COLOR WASH. This formula consists of three spotlights: warm color from one side and cool color from the other; the third spotlight (wash light) of neutral color (usually lighter) focused straight into the area from a center position. In simplest form, the formula calls for one dimmer; two dimmers give better control; three dimmers (instrument and DIMMER PER CIRCUIT), the ultimate goal for all lighting control. *Advantages:* Tends to eliminate (or modify) exaggerated warm and cool sides of the face as well as different-colored walls; helps to blend areas to give smoother coverage; with separate dimmer, gives greater color control for subtle mood changes. *Disadvantages:* In very limited budget theatres the extra instrument over the McCandless formula is a problem.

Double-reverse McCandless formula. The double-reverse method is a logical extension of the original McCandless formula and was inevitable as more equipment became available. Four spotlights: first pair warm on right and cool on left; second pair reversed, with warm on left and cool on right. Four spotlights controlled by two dimmers, one to each color. Maximum control would be achieved with a dimmer to each light. *Advantages:* Potentially good control over each area; capable of overcoming the McCandless disadvantages and capable of changing warm and cool sides in response to demands of multiple-set plays or

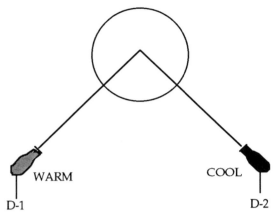

WARM   COOL

D-1   D-2

TWO-DIMMER McCANDLESS

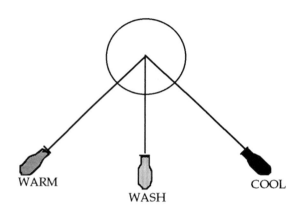

WARM   COOL

WASH

WASH FORMULA

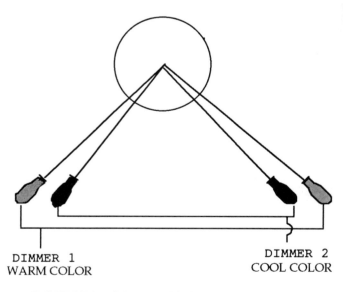

DIMMER 1   DIMMER 2
WARM COLOR   COOL COLOR

DOUBLE McCANDLESS COLOR CONTROL

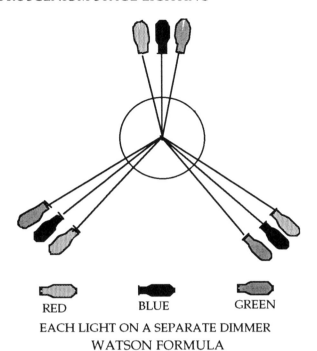

RED   BLUE   GREEN

EACH LIGHT ON A SEPARATE DIMMER
WATSON FORMULA

MAGENTA   BLUE-GREEN

COMBINATION FORMULA

day and night scenes in the same setting. *Disadvantages:* Requires twice the equipment of original McCandless.

Watson formula. The Watson formula was originally presented in the early 1950s as an experiment rather than a recommended method of stage lighting. Under near-laboratory conditions, Lee Watson, former professor of stage lighting at Purdue, conducted a lighting experiment in which he used nine spotlights arranged in 120° formula with primaries in the three locations. With this method it is possible to achieve virtually any color, including white. The light primaries (red, green, and blue) are used in each group of lights, and each light is assigned a dimmer. Absolute linear voltage control to each light is necessary. This is the ultimate in area color control and, as Watson complained, presented horrendous challenges and hours of rehearsal to light a simple dance recital that was over in a few minutes. *Advantages:* Absolute color control over each area. *Disadvantages:* Requires large numbers of lighting instruments and dimmers. Even with the precision of microprocessor control, the work necessary on the part of the designer to achieve a subtle flow of light is staggering.

Combination formula. A formula developed in the mid-1950s combining advantages of the double-reverse McCandless formula with a simplified version of the Watson formula. It uses blue-green and magenta and works well for exterior scenes but is not as good for interiors. Six spotlights arranged in two pairs, 90° apart from the front, and two backlights are used. The complementary color of medium magenta is used for the warm and blue-green for the cool. Two dimmers are used, with all cool lights on one and all warm lights on the other. *Advantages:* Formula works exceptionally well for moody exterior scenes. Reasonable color control. Will work with a minimum of control equipment but is more versatile with each instrument on its own dimmer. *Disadvantages:* Colors used do not adapt well to interior or bright, sunny scenes, but other complementary colors may be substituted that would be satisfactory.

Wash and key formula (crosslight and wash). For years, the wash and key formula and the double-reverse McCandless formula were the two standard methods of lighting both Broadway and ROAD SHOWS. Professional designers are now much more imaginative, and by experimention will find combinations that prove exciting. Basically, the formula consists of a low VERTICAL ANGLE WASH LIGHT from the FRONT OF THE HOUSE with KEY LIGHT and FILL LIGHT from the BOX BOOMS or from the wings. This method is similar to the wash formula in color use and effect, but because of the low vertical angle and extreme horizontal angle from the box booms, the overall result is more dramatic. Control may be all on one dimmer if equipment is limited but effectiveness improves with use of two or three dimmers. *Advantages:* Tends to modify the warm and cool face problem. Offers better blending of areas and, with separate dimmers, offers more subtle color control. *Disadvantages:* The same as with the wash formula.

Practice. Match locations for hanging instruments to optimum angles for lighting. If LIGHT BRIDGES or PIPE BATTENS are used, it is easier to lower the pipe to shoulder height to hang the instruments. At first, hang all spots loosely so that slight adjustments may be made as needed before tightening with a wrench. If the ELECTRIC includes a PLUGGING STRIP, circuiting may require only short cables, which should be noted on the hookup sheet. The numbers and lengths of long cables needed should also be listed on the hookup sheet so they may be gathered with the rest of the lighting equipment. In placing cables on the light batten, start with the longest and work toward the shortest, bundling and tying together during the procedure. Mark the circuit number on the male plug of each cable to avoid tedious tracing later. Always leave extra cable near the spotlight so adjustments may be made as required. Plug in the lights, check the circuitry, make certain all equipment is tightened with a wrench, and raise the electric or bridge to WORKING HEIGHT.

While hanging equipment in other locations, aim each instrument as closely as possible at its intended area to minimize hanging adjustments while focusing. Attach safety chain and plug in. If possible, have someone turn on the light to check the circuitry before installing the next light.

While the hanging and cabling of instruments is being done, another member of the lighting crew

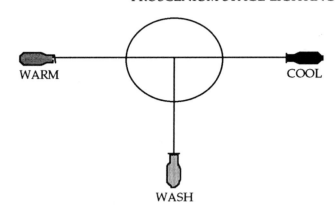

WASH AND KEY FORMULA

should be assigned the job of PATCHING the board. This will involve working from the light plot to make certain each instrument is cabled to the right circuit number and each circuit is assigned to its proper dimmer. This is a very exacting job and should be started far enough in advance to be finished well before focusing begins.

Most focusing requires ladder work. Use wooden ladders to guard against possible electrical shocks resulting from grounding through metal. Do not take chances. Find help to steady the ladder. If two spots are to cover the same area, leave the first one turned on while setting the second so a match may be made; otherwise, try to focus individually; more precise, cleaner focusing will result if it is done in relative darkness. When using spotlights with adjustable focus, such as fresnel lights, remember, the tighter the focus, the brighter the spot, so in the interest of obtaining maximum intensity, set the focus as tight as possible while still covering the intended area and allowing for blending. If gelatine frames do not reduce the size of the spotlight beam, focus all lights first and then add the color. It is easier to see and focus clear light. Wave a hand in front of the light while focusing to see exactly where the beam falls and, at the same time, to check for stray light that may be coming from a chipped lens, a reflecting surface, or a poorly designed ventilating hole. A visible light leak will surely divert audience attention during a dark scene. Find someone at least as tall as the tallest actor in the cast to walk through the areas during focusing, making sure that lights blend from area to area and no "holes" will leave faces of tall actors in the dark. After focusing is completed, bring all lights to full and check for "holes" again by walking through the areas, checking your extended hand for intensity variations (illustrated with **Light beams and areas** under BLENDING). Gel all spotlights according to light plot specifications.

PSYCHOLOGICAL LIGHTING. See under COLOR SYMBOLISM; SUBLIMINAL LIGHTING.

PYROTECHNICS. Use of flash powders and other chemicals and explosives to make flashes, smoke, and special effects. The electrician is often called upon to rig an electrical detonator for this type of effect. The terminals should be mounted on Bakelite or other noncombustible surface. One or two single strands of ZIP CORD or a piece of SOLDER fastened to the two terminals will serve as a detonator. The chemicals are placed on the detonator, the FLASH BOX is plugged into a HOT LINE controlled by a **toggle switch** (see under SWITCHES) and the effect is ready for its cue. *Caution:* Working with chemicals and flash powders can be very dangerous and special care must be taken. Make sure that the power in the hot line is *OFF* and that it cannot be activated; allow no open flame close to the set-up; use plastic spoons to avoid potential sparks; and *NEVER* put your face over the explosives.

Q

Q FILE. Obsolete. Trade name of a Century Lighting Company memory system light control.

QI. See QUARTZ-IODINE LAMP.

Q MASTER. Obsolete. Trade name for a single-package dimming system by Century Lighting Company.

QUALITIES OF LIGHT. Intensity, color, distribution, and movement are the four qualities of light that provide visibility, plausibility, composition, and mood.

QUARTZ-IODINE LAMP (quartz lamps, QI). Introduced in 1959, this small, compact, long-life lamp consisted of a tungsten filament enclosed in a transparent quartz envelope partially filled with iodine. When ordinary lamps burn, tiny particles of tungsten are released from the filament and deposited on the glass envelope as a black film, gradually reducing the intensity of the light. During the burning process of the quartz-iodine lamp, released particles of tungsten reacted chemically with the vaporized iodine and returned to the filament. Not only was the life of the lamp im-proved by this, but the black deposits on the inside of the envelope were eliminated. The ideal lamp had been created except for one small detail: As iodine sublimes, it turns a purple-violet color in both the warming (dim-up) and cooling (dim-down) cycles. Clearly, an untenable situation for theatre lighting. Further experiments substituted a related element, halogen, for iodine and heat-resistant quartz glass for the quartz envelope, producing a lamp that retained the favorable characteristics of the quartz-iodine lamp and eliminated the purple discoloration. The new lamp was rechristened and introduced to the market as a TUNGSTEN-HALOGEN (TH) LAMP.

QUICK CONNECT. Obsolete. A slider-type PATCH PANEL manufactured by the now defunct Ariel Davis Company. Similar patches are manufactured by several major companies.

QUIET PLEASE (command verb). Order for silence backstage usually given just before the curtain rises. Often understood as an unspoken part of the order "PLACES."

RACEWAY (gutter, wireway). A sheet-metal or extruded aluminum gutter or trough designed to carry electrical wires or cables in a protected channel.

RACK

A framework used for mounting dimmers or other lighting equipment.

A term used to denote mounting positions for INSTRUMENTS. "Top rack" means the instrument is above the mounting pipe. "Front rack" means the instrument is in front of the pipe.

FRONT RACKED
LEKO ON SHORT BOOM
TYPICAL OF SHINBANGERS

RACK AND PINION. A bar with teeth on one side (the rack), designed to engage in the teeth of a gear (the pinion) to convert horizontal motion to rotary motion. Most older dimmers with mechanical interlocking banks used the rack and pinion to transfer lever movement of the handle to rotary move-

ment of the dimmer arm; a chain and sprocket mechanism was used less often. See also **Mechanical master** under DIMMERS, MASTER.

RADIASTAT. Obsolete. An AUTOTRANSFORMER manufactured by Ward Leonard and successfully adapted to reasonably compact racking and mechanical interlocking, characteristic of midcentury installations.

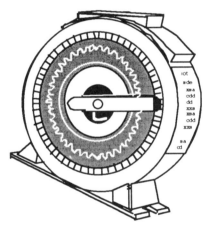

RADIASTAT

RAIL. The mounting position on the front of the lower balcony railing. This is a favorite position for low-angle COLOR WASH. See also BALCONY LIGHTS.

RAINBOW. An arc or bow of prismatic colors caused by the refraction and reflection of sun rays passing through drops of water. In the primary rainbow, colors appear in the following order beginning at the top: red, orange, yellow, green-blue, indigo, violet. In a double rainbow, the colors of the secondary rainbow, which appears above the primary, are reversed, with violet at the top and red at the bottom. Sometimes the prismatic effect of defective lenses can be utilized to form a kind of rainbow on the cyc, but mostly a **Linnebach** or

Direct beam projector (see under PROJECTORS) is used with an arc cut in the slide and colored gelatine glued in strips over the cutout. Obviously, colors should be in the proper order.

RANDOM LIGHT (gimmick light). Light for lighting's sake. Lighting added for effect only, nonmotivated, although it may be added to MOTIVATED LIGHT to enhance an effect. Many episodic plays and many nonrealistic plays do not need motivated light. In such plays lights are placed and used according to the lighting designer's judgment to provide dramatic value, emphasis, or mood.

RATTAIL. Colloquial for ADAPTOR.

REACTANCE DIMMER. Obsolete. A rather confusing term since it encompasses reactance dimmer, saturable reactor dimmer, magnetic amplifier dimmer, and thyratron-controlled reactor dimmer. Generally speaking the differences between the dimmers were in the control circuitry. A number of patents have been issued since the "Adjustable Inductive Resistance" (the first reactance dimmer) in 1887 filed by Westinghouse Electric Company.

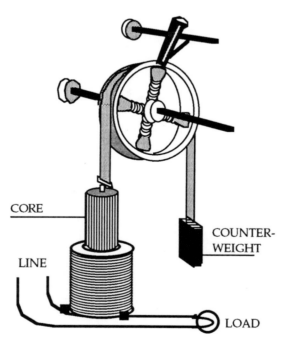

CORE

LINE

COUNTER-
WEIGHT

LOAD

REMOVABLE CORE REACTANCE DIMMER
INSTALLED IN THE EARL'S COURT
EXHIBITION THEATRE, LONDON 1890s

READING. The data indicated by the setting on a dimmer, sound equipment control, or other equipment on a scale usually calibrated from 0 to 10. On computer boards, the scale may well be 0 to 100 using digital readouts that provide more accurate data.

REAR SCREEN. See PROJECTION SCREEN.

REAR-SCREEN PROJECTOR. See **Rear-screen projector** under PROJECTORS.

RECEPTACLE. A wall outlet or line outlet equipped with a female receptacle (JACK). The male plug is the complement and plugs into the receptacle. See PLUGS.

RECORD. See under COMPUTER LIGHT BOARD TERMINOLOGY.

REFLECTANCE. The intensity of reflected light divided by the intensity of incident light, expressed in percentages.

REFLECTOR DROP. A plain or light-colored drop used to reflect a diffused light behind transparencies or SCRIMS. The reflector drop prevents the uneven coverage of direct light on the back of a transparent drop and is also commonly used behind scrims for CYC lighting.

REFLECTOR LAMP (R lamp). A self-contained lamp with built-in reflector and light source. See also LAMPS; PAR.

REFLECTORS. Concave surfaces of metal or glass used to increase efficiency of lighting instruments. Because light from FLOODLIGHTS and BORDER LIGHTS is best diffused, their reflectors are most often dull metal, either spun or stamped to shape. Efficiency of reflectors ranges from about 10% for a white surface to about 90% for mirrored glass and ALZAK REFLECTORS found in SPOTLIGHTS, PROJECTORS, BEAM PROJECTORS, and SCOOPS. Reflectors not only capture more light from the source, but by reflecting this light back through the filament, filament heat is increased, thereby causing the lamp to burn brighter. Besides the white surfaces used for reflecting in older floodlights, there are four basic kinds of reflectors used in lighting equipment, each designed for a specific purpose. See also DICHROIC FILTERS.

Ellipsoidal. A reflector with two FOCAL POINTS. Ellipsoidal reflectors surround a large portion of the lamp, thus capturing about 75% of the light rays and directing them to a second, or conjugate, focal point. Ellipsoidal reflectors are used in spotlights (ERSs) and scoops (ERFs).

Parabolic. Designed to reflect light from a focal point to parallel rays. Such reflectors are found in certain floodlights, beam projectors, scoops, and PAR lamps.

Spherical. Designed as a section of a sphere with the reflected focal point passing back through the filament, increasing efficiency by approximately 40% (depending on the ANGLE OF ACCEPTANCE). Most PLANO-CONVEX and FRESNEL SPOTLIGHTS use spherical reflectors, as do some beam projectors in front of the lamp.

Spherical-parabolic. This combination of spherical and parabolic reflectors is generally made of spun aluminum and is found in older types of border lights and FOOTLIGHTS designed for household lamps. The use of R 40 lamps in this kind of equipment eliminates the need for reflectors of any kind.

REFRACTION. The bending of light rays when they pass from one medium to another. The curvature of a lens refracts light to a FOCAL POINT. Water refracts light in a similar manner and sometimes becomes a problem when lighting water shows.

REHEARSAL, LIGHTING. Rehearsals intended for setting lighting levels and practicing and coordinating difficult CUES. Rehearsing many light cues can be a bore to actors and personnel not directly involved in the process, and as a result, time desperately needed for lighting rehearsal may be hurried or denied. It is therefore often advisable to call special lighting rehearsals, during which light intensities, cues, and sequences may be decided, practiced, and readied for scheduled dress rehearsals. These special rehearsals should involve the director, stage manager, lighting designer, board operator, a gofer or two from the lighting crew, and a volunteer actor or two (preferably in costume), walking through scenes for timing and intensity settings. The success of the lighting design and smoothness of the run of a show may well depend on the degree of competency reached at these rehearsals.

RELATED-TINT SYSTEM. A type of lighting using the **McCandless formula** (see under PROSCENIUM STAGE LIGHTING) where lights of similar colors to the colors found in the show are used to

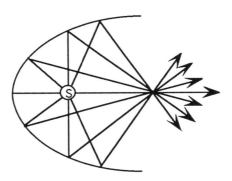

ELLIPSOIDAL REFLECTOR

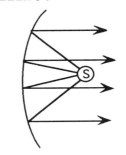

PARABOLIC REFLECTOR

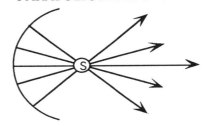

SPHERICAL REFLECTOR

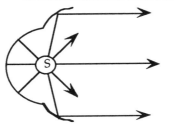

SPHERICAL-PARABOLIC

complement costumes and makeup and to otherwise reinforce the mood.

RELAY. An electromagnetic switch, usually located far from the control to eliminate noise. Larger units, called CONTACTORS, are particularly noisy.

RELOAD CONTROLS. An older system of relays and/or switches that allowed double patching to change lighting in the middle of a production or in a REPERTORY THEATRE situation.

REMOTE CONTROL. Remote control boards are sometimes compact portables that may be used in the auditorium to adjust light levels during rehearsals. See also **Console** under LIGHTING CONTROL.

RENTAL COMPANY. These companies are used by road shows to lease or rent lighting equipment for productions. Many stationary productions also rent equipment, and even fully equipped groups rent speciality equipment. Many companies are unable to afford large capital expenditures for equipment, and the idea of a rental company being responsible for the repair of equipment, particularly dimmers and computer boards, is appealing.

REPATCH. Assigning lighting instruments to a different set of controls for a different scene or a different show. See RELOAD CONTROLS.

REPERTORY THEATRE. Theatrical presentations in which different productions are scheduled to play in a random manner in the same theatre. Repertory often requires a single, elaborate lighting setup that can be used for all productions. Each show will then use the same basic light plot plus a few specials, with variations occurring in the individual CUE SHEETS.

RESET BUTTON. A button switch that resets a **Circuit breaker** (see under SWITCHES).

RESISTANCE. All electrical conductors offer a certain friction, or resistance, to the passage of electricity. The extent of resistance depends on the material, diameter, length, and temperature of the conductor. Resistance creates heat, which varies from the extreme of tungsten, which becomes so hot it incandesces, to the scarcely measurable heat of a silver conductor. The ohm is the unit of measurement of resistance. See ELECTRICITY.

RESISTANCE DIMMER (plate dimmer). Obsolete lighting control board. A device that controlled light intensity by adding a variable resistance in series with the light. Resistance dimmers are usually rated according to minimum-maximum load, and for maximum efficiency, loads cannot be less than minimum rating. Thus, a dimmer rated 900-watt minimum and 1,200-watt maximum will not dim a 500-watt light all the way out unless a GHOST LOAD is introduced somewhere in series with the dimmer (in parallel with the light). Overloading a resistance dimmer for a sustained period will overheat wires and cause a break in circuit.

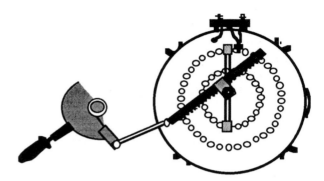

RESISTANCE DIMMER WITH
RACK AND PINION DRIVE

Sometimes a break in the resistance wire can be repaired temporarily by locating the dead contact button on the dimmer plate with a continuity tester and bridging or shorting it to the adjacent button with a piece of copper wire. This will cause a slight jump in intensity when the brush passes over the repaired point but may serve temporarily until replacement can be made. Clean contact buttons with tuner cleaner or rouge paper. Do not oil or grease contacts on any brush-contact-type dimmer.

RESPONSE TIME. The time it takes an equipment operator to execute a CUE from the word "GO."

RETROFIT LAMP. The more efficient tungsten-halogen lamps are available for older lighting instruments in what are known as retrofit lamps. These are specially designed tungsten-halogen lamps with bases made to fit the older sockets and conform to the LCL dimensions specified for these instruments. Available in a wide variety of wattages ranging from 300 to 5,000 watts.

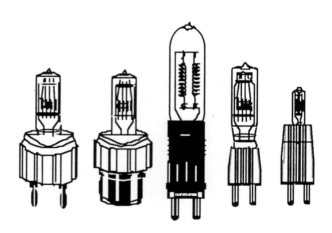

RETROFIT LAMPS

REVERSE VIDEO (highlighted). A shaded area used to show a particular piece of information on the display screen. See COMPUTER LIGHT BOARD TERMINOLOGY.

RF NOISE IN LAMPS (radio frequency noise). Audible vibration of lamp filaments caused by certain electronic dimmers. Most dimmers that might offend have built-in chokes to control filament RF. If not, manufacturers should be consulted to determine the correct choke.

RGB. An abbreviation for red, green, and blue. The term is used most often to refer to color monitors. See also COMPUTER LIGHT BOARD TERMINOLOGY.

RHEOSTAT. A variable resistor that regulates the current in a circuit by varying resistance in series with the load. See RESISTANCE DIMMER.

R LAMP. See REFLECTOR LAMP.

ROAD SHOW LIGHTING (touring show). Professional productions planning to open in New York City often schedule extended tryout performances on the road. Although these productions may have runs of variable lengths in different cities, technically, they are previews, not road shows. This type of production is designed as a "shakedown" to determine what will be retained, reworked, or thrown out. The treatment applies to script, songs, scenes, settings, costuming, lighting, the entire production. During this period, the lighting designer may have to redesign several scenes or possibly even light new scenes that may be added.

The road show lighting discussed here is for a show that has been presented in its "home" theatre and, therefore, has already been designed and lighted. The problem is one of adjusting the design to the limitations imposed by trucking. The first thing to be understood about the touring theatre concept is that the entire show must be self-contained. The lighting designer must plan to fit all equipment in trucks and assume that the theatres to be visited will provide nothing. The list of equipment needed will include all INSTRUMENTS, CABLES, CONNECTORS, CLAMPS, LAMPS, COLOR MEDIA, DIMMERS, LIGHT BOARDS (usually COMPUTER BOARDS), specialized units such as cable boxes, crossover pipes, CRADLES, dimmer RACKS, and TRUSSES, if required. In professional tours, producers often rent equipment to reduce initial expenses. However, it

should be noted that in the case of a long tour, it probably would be cheaper to buy. To further curb expenses, the designer will be called on to reduce the volume and weight of all material to be carried, which translates into redesigning the entire production, trying to achieve the original effect with half the equipment. The new design also must reflect the need to minimize set-in time, so costs will be reasonable enough to make the tour financially feasible. One last consideration for the professional, unless otherwise decided: The lighting designer's name will appear on the programs, and a poor lighting job on a good show can jeopardize a designer's reputation from coast to coast.

Cutting down the show. When faced with the need to truck scenery and lights, most shows are cut considerably. For example, the Broadway show *Cats* was cut from an original 17 truckloads of scenery and lights to 4 when it was taken on the road. Some methods of cutting lighting equipment and costs include reducing the number of spotlights per area; using multiconnector cables; ganging circuits on dimmers to reduce the size of the control board requirement; limiting numbers of followspots (if any); using box trusses, which will protect the prewired, prefocused lights inside the trusses during transportation; using BATTEN TAPES if no trusses are used, to save HANG time. If feasible, a lighting designer faced with redesigning lights for the road should talk with experienced road electricians, who will probably provide many suggestions for saving time, energy, and money.

Design and hang. With help from the local crew, the road electrician is in charge of hanging the show, including hookup and testing of instruments and dimmers. The stage manager usually supervises the focusing using the FOCUS CHART and the FOCUSING CLOTH. The final INSTRUMENT CHECK is often a joint effort of the stage manager and electrician. Normally a show in constant performance does not need lighting REHEARSALs at each theatre unless there are a number of complex cues involving a house crew.

Drag out. The STRIKE of the electrical equipment is done by the JUICER with the help of the local crew.

ROMEX WIRE. See under CABLE.

RONDEL. See ROUNDEL.

ROSCODYE. Trade name for a dye with a binder manufactured by Rosco Laboratories and used for painting slides on glass, acetate, or polyester film. Roscodye is heat resistant.

ROSCOGEL, ROSCOLENE, ROSCOLUX. Trade names for different types of COLOR MEDIA manufactured and sold by Rosco Laboratories.

ROSETTE. A serrated disk used to lock a mounting device such as a YOKE to a lighting INSTRUMENT.

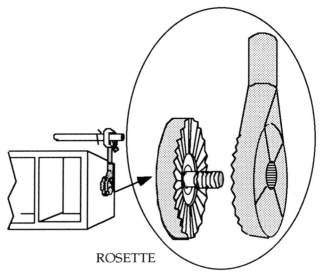

ROSETTE

ROTARY SWITCH. A special switch used to interconnect dimmers and circuits in PATCH PANELS.

ROTOLECTOR. Trade name for an older form of rotary switch used to interconnect dimmers and circuits. See **Rotary switch** under PATCH PANEL.

ROTOR. The part of an electric motor that revolves within the stationary body (stator). See also INDUCTANCE DIMMER.

ROUGE CLOTH. A very fine abrasive cloth, made with jeweller's rouge, which works well for shining and cleaning electrical contacts and armatures. Wet rouge cloth may also be used to remove scratches from clear plastic or to smooth clear plastic without scratching.

ROUGH FOCUS. Aiming the light in its prescribed direction, making the beam a given size, and giving the beam a HARD or SOFT focus. While hanging spotlights for a show it is advisable to give them a rough focus to minimize ladder work during the following, final focus. See also DEAD FOCUS.

ROUNDEL (rondel). A round, heat-resistant, glass color filter available for certain types of border lights and footlights. Color selection in roundels is greatly limited in comparison with other types of color media, but colors will not fade or burn out. See also COLOR MEDIA.

RULE, SCALE. An architect's triangular scale rule is used for making and reading scale drawings. Triangular rules have 10 scales ranging from 3/32" = 1' to 3" = 1', plus a standard 1" rule on one face. When the rule is flat on the table, two scales are exposed on the top side, one reading from left to right, the other from right to left. Calibrations appearing before the zeros on each end represent inches or, in larger scales, fractions of inches. When measuring feet only, start from zero; when measuring fractions of a foot, start with number of inches desired before zero and proceed to additional feet desired.

RUN

(command verb). To lay a CABLE or to operate a LIGHT BOARD or FOLLOWSPOT.

The term also refers to the total time a play will be shown in a city. The term "running time" refers to the hours and minutes the show takes at each performance.

RUNNING CREW. The working crew for a show in production.

RUNNING TIME. The length of time of an individual performance. In many theatres the stage manager keeps a daily log of the time of every performance as a check on the performance record. Significant time variations may call for special rehearsals to get the cast back on schedule. Such variations can affect automatically timed light cues.

RUN-THROUGH. An uninterrupted rehearsal of an entire play usually without scenery or lights. However, with the director's permission, the lighting designer may watch a run-through to get a sense of timing for long cues that involve fading or building as well as other clues for cues that may need to be noted.

RUNWAY (Jolson strip). A narrow extension of the stage into the audience; common in Japanese Kabuki theatre (*hanamichi*), used in some burlesque houses and fashion shows, and made very popular by Al Jolson in the United States in the first third of the twentieth century. Runways are difficult to light without spilling into the audience on either side. Fortunately, the kind of shows using runways rely on followspots for action on the runway. One of the easiest solutions is to try to provide TONING with a DOWNLIGHT from the BEAM position and pick up the actors with FOLLOWSPOTS from the projection booth.

S

SAFETY. Theatre technicians are always searching for new materials and new ideas and one major problem that confronts them is the difficulty of learning about potential hazards of new products. Often unknown health hazards exist with new materials, particularly chemicals used in plastics, solvents, or cleaning agents. Never work with chemicals or cleansers of any kind in unventilated areas and avoid breathing chemical fumes. Other safety measures the technician should take include checking for hot instruments next to materials that could be combustible, including draperies; checking for frayed wires, arcing connectors, overloaded circuits; checking fire extinguishers on a regular basis. In short, protect yourself, fellow workers, and patrons. There are special safety precautions to be taken with various procedures and pieces of equipment. Note the *Caution* messages in this book, which concern a few of the hazards found backstage. Read and heed warnings on products to be used. OSHA has many regulations that usually help prevent dangerous situations. See also SHOCK.

SAFETY FACTOR. The ratio of a tested stress limit to the rated stress limit expressed in percentages. Electricians are concerned with the AMPERE load limit of fuses, dimmers, conductors, plugs, and circuits, as well as the weight limit of LIGHT BATTENS and the wire ropes that hold the lighting equipment they want to fly. Rated safety factors are usually about 20% below tested maximums, but it is unwise to take advantage of safety factors over a period of time. Abide by specified safety limits

SALTWATER DIMMER. A crude, makeshift, unsafe dimmer, predating commercial light control. The saltwater dimmer is basically a RESISTANCE DIMMER that provides an interesting classroom demonstration but should not be given any practical value. It consists of a 5- or 10-gallon crock, one stationary electrode (metal plate) in the bottom of the crock, and an adjustable electrode attached to an arm to allow calibrated control of distance between electrodes. Saltwater is used as the electrolyte. Insulated wires connect the two electrodes in series with the line (power supply) and the load (lamp), as illustrated. Sufficient water is placed in the crock to almost touch the top electrode in its highest position. The circuit is turned on and the top electrode is lowered to barely touch the water. Common salt is added to the water until the lamp starts to glow. The amount of salt used will vary with the load, so the total wattage to be controlled

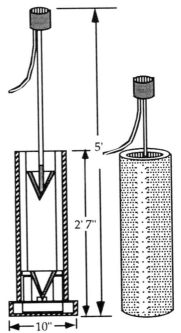

FROM A MID-CENTURY **VENRECO** CATALOGUE, ENGLAND

COMMERCIAL SALTWATER DIMMER

should be used in the initial preparation. As electrodes are brought closer together, the light intensity increases until full brightness is reached when the electrodes touch. *Caution:* The demonstrator of this experiment must keep insulated from all electrical lines, copper plates, and saltwater.

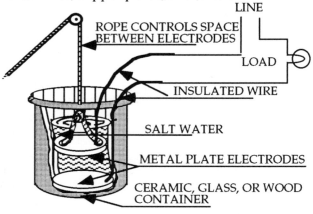

IMPROVISED
SALTWATER DIMMER

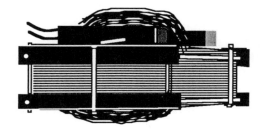

REACTANCE DIMMER

SATURABLE CORE DIMMER. Primary and secondary coils are wrapped around opposite ends of a laminated core and a control coil is wrapped in the center. A variable low-voltage DC current applied to the control coil changes the flow of current in the secondary coil, thereby varying the voltage supplied to the load. Although this principle sounds simple and straightforward, there is a direct relationship between the load current and the control current, restricting the use of the dimmer to a relatively small range of operation close to its rated capacity. In other words, basically, this is the same problem the resistance dimmer has, plus additional bulk and weight and an annoying time lag in operation. See REACTANCE DIMMER.

SATURATED COLOR. An undiluted hue, or a pure color. See COLOR.

SCALE DRAWING. See DESIGN FOR LIGHTING; DRAWINGS.

SCALE RULE. See RULE, SCALE.

SCALE STICK. Colloquial for architect's scale rule. See RULE, SCALE.

SCANNER

A type of AUTOPAN lighting instrument.

A design tool for computer drafting and drawing programs that scans printed information and translates it into digitals, which are then used in the computer program.

SCENE. A BANK of controllers on a PRESET BOARD. The preset board has its size designated by the number of scenes it has: a 2-scene board is the smallest and a 10-scene board is a large one.

SCENE DESIGNER. A creative person who integrates the concepts of playwright, director, lighting designer, and costume designer into designs for scenery. Ideally, scenery is visually exciting, practical to build, and under budget. A big order.

SCHEMATIC. A diagram, plan, or drawing. Electrical schematics include SYMBOLS (switches, fuses, transformers, rectifiers, etc.) showing all component parts of the circuit.

SCIOPTICON. See under PROJECTED SCENERY.

SCOOP. An improved design for a FLOODLIGHT. Scoops are spun aluminum, using parabolic or ellipsoidal reflectors that function as both reflectors and outside housings. The resulting lightweight instruments are particularly useful as hanging floodlights for lighting cycloramas or as single-source light units for windows or wing positions. Scoops are designed to use 250- to 400-watt lamps for the 10" units (WIZARDS), 300- to 500-watt lamps for the 14" units, and 750- to 1,500-watt lamps for the 18" units. Equipped with either C-CLAMPS for pipe mounting or swivel attachments for a telescoping floor stand, scoops offer a much greater concentration of light than the old-style floodlight.

INCANDESCENT   TUNGSTEN-HALOGEN
SCOOPS

Focusing scoop. Focusing scoops usually use a TUNGSTEN-HALOGEN LAMP in an AXIAL MOUNT. The socket and lamp mounted on a slide mechanism move into or out of the FOCAL POINT of the matte-finished reflector, changing the beam spread from narrow to wide angle (approximate range between 70° and 110°). The wide-focus position is commonly used to light CYCS and for onstage COLOR WASHES.

FOCUSING SCOOP

SCR. Acronym for SILICON CONTROLLED RECTIFIER.

SCREEN

Projection screen. Any surface on which an image may be projected. See PROJECTION SCREENS.

Scenery. Gray fiberglass insect screening often used on stage windows to simulate glass. The transparency of this surface depends on how it is lighted. Angled lighting on the screen renders it partially translucent; lighted objects behind with no light on the screen can be seen. Bold GOBO patterns may be projected on the screen.

SCREW BASE. The lamp base for all standard household bulbs. For many years sockets in all theatre lighting instruments were designed for the screw base. The development of more sophisticated instruments requiring positive filament positioning led to the introduction of the bipost, prefocus, and recessed single contact bases. At present, there are only a few older model instruments left that still use the screw base lamp. See LAMPS.

SCRIM. A loosely woven material somewhat resembling cheesecloth, used for special effects drops. Successful use of scrim depends on careful focusing, choice of instruments, and positioning of lights. Scenes dye-painted on scrim can appear as either solid walls or as transparencies, depending on the lighting. Lights shining on the scrim from the front make it opaque. When the wall is to be opaque, avoid lights behind the scrim, which will

allow objects to show through. Also, a flat light on the scrim from in front may shine through to reveal objects placed too close to the scrim. Front lighting should therefore be at a fairly steep angle but may be kept at low intensity as long as all lights are out behind. Objects lighted behind the scrim are visible when all light is kept off the front of the scrim.

Fog effect. A scrim hung just upstage of the ACT CURTAIN and lighted from the front will produce a hazy, foggy effect in upstage areas, particularly if those lights are kept at a low intensity. FOH lights should be focused to provide uniform coverage of the scrim and may be positioned from a reasonably flat angle; shining through will supplement lights on objects behind the scrim. Intensity balance between acting area lights and scrim lights will determine the degree of visibility. REFLECTOR DROPS may also be used to ensure opacity. Scrim is available in widths up to 30' at theatrical supply houses.

SCRIPT. The acting edition of a play used in a production.

SCROLL COLOR CHANGER (scroller). A device that attaches to the front of a lighting instrument and changes the light color by rolling a series of 10 or 12 different colors in front of the light. A special tape is used to join the individual colors. The unit is controlled remotely and can usually change from one color to another in about 2 seconds. A new development is a type of scroller with three PRIMARY COLORS, each on separate tracks, perforated with 1/4" holes allowing more or less WHITE light through, in effect making tints through saturates. This unit, with high-speed mo-

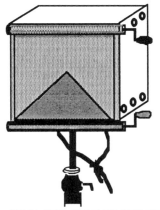

SILK COLOR SCROLLER
MADE BY LOUIS HARTMANN FOR
THE 1900 PRODUCTION OF *MADAME BUTTERFLY*. ANGLED JOINT BLENDS COLORS.

tor drives on each track, is coupled with a lap-top computer and is programmed to replicate any color made by the major media manufacturers. It is very expensive. The use of color scrollers on stage equipment dates back to the nineteenth-century gaslight era, when silk was used as the color medium and rolled from one roller to another in front of the gas flames. The idea was updated to an electric flood by Louis Hartmann for David Belasco's production of *Madame Butterfly* in 1900.

SEALED BEAM LIGHTS. See **Parabolic reflector** under LAMPS.

SECONDARY COIL. Output coil of a TRANS-FORMER.

SECONDARY COLORS

   Light. Magenta, blue-green, amber.

   Pigment. Purple, green, orange. See COLOR.

SECONDARY SOURCE OF LIGHT. Usually in reference to bounce light from floor, walls, ceiling, and assorted objects. If carefully considered as a source light, some very interesting and subtle lighting effects can be realized.

SECTION DRAWING. A drawing of a cutaway view through a three-dimensional object.

SELECTIVE VISIBILITY. A term used to describe a comfortable intensity of light in the selected areas where action is taking place and implying the control mobility necessary to follow that stage action with the same intensity through other areas. See **Aesthetics** under LIGHTING PRACTICE.

SELECTOR SWITCH. See under SWITCHES.

SERIES CIRCUIT. See under CIRCUITS.

SET-IN (in, hang). Moving the scenery, lights, and props of a production into a theatre and setting it in place.

SET LIGHTS. To focus the lighting equipment for a play. See LIGHTING PRACTICE; ARENA STAGE LIGHTING; BALLET LIGHTING; DANCE THE-ATRE LIGHTING; MUSICAL LIGHTING; OPERA LIGHTING; OUTDOOR THEATRE LIGHTING; PROSCENIUM STAGE LIGHTING; ROAD SHOW LIGHTING; THRUST STAGE LIGHT-ING.

SET UP

   To facilitate a complicated cue on a manual or preset board.

To make or check the procedures and/or controller settings on a computer board for any given cue.

SHADE. A variation in pigment color made by adding black to a color. Distinguished from TINT, a variation in pigment color made by adding white.

SHADOWS

   Good shadows. The only way detail becomes really visible is through the use of shadows. A flat light from the front will wash out detail, leaving two-dimensional objects, with no apparent depth. General, diffused light covering everything with equal intensity produces a similar flatness. Add to that general light a special light of brighter intensity from another angle, and a third dimension becomes apparent. A controlled shadow has been introduced, a shadow that may be sharpened or softened by changing the ratio of intensities. In its simplest form, the general light (BASE LIGHT and FILL LIGHT) and the special light (KEY LIGHT) have been used here to create the beginning of good lighting. Shadows used to introduce atmosphere, to suggest time and place, and to further enhance the play are good shadows. Leaf patterns, venetian blind patterns, jail bar shadows, stained glass windows, or whatever may be suggested by the action or setting of the play can be good shadows. Simple facts to remember: Grouped light sources cast multiple shadows; a high-intensity, concentrated filament light source casts a single, clear shadow; light too close to an object casts an exaggerated, fuzzy shadow; the greater the distance between the light source and the object, the sharper the shadow and the closer to actual size it will appear; light from below will exaggerate the height of an object, and light from above will shorten the object.

   Bad shadows. If the shadow of one actor obliterates another actor, either the light casting that

LONG THROW   SHORT THROW

SHADOWS

154

shadow is in the wrong position or the stage blocking is wrong. If the director is unwilling to change the business of the actors, try to hang the light from a different angle. The shadow of an actor on a pastoral backdrop will obviously destroy any illusion of distance. Place the offending light at a steeper angle or use CROSSLIGHTS. Multiple shadows of footlights on the backwall of a set are far more interesting than the actor casting them. Reduce intensity of the footlights until shadows no longer offend.

SHAKESPEAREAN STAGE. Any stage resembling the shape of the stage of the Globe Theatre, which is generally considered to have been a thrust stage extending into the auditorium with the audience on three sides and a two-storied backwall containing an INNER BELOW and an INNER ABOVE. Sometimes a third story for orchestra is included. See also STAGES.

SHARP FOCUS (hard-edge). A beam of light focused to provide a sharp, well-defined edge as opposed to a SOFT-EDGE, diffused light such as produced by a FRESNEL LIGHT or light with a FROST gel.

SHIELD, LIGHT. See LIGHT SPILL CONTROL; WRAP.

SHIN BUSTER (shin kicker, shin banger). Shin busters are lights mounted on low booms in the wings

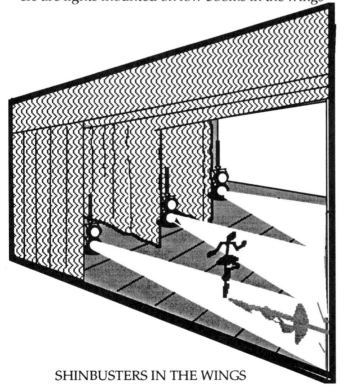

SHINBUSTERS IN THE WINGS

and used primarily for lighting dance productions. For the safety of the dancers, fluorescent tape or low-wattage lamps should be placed near or on the base of shin busters to make them visible during blackouts. See BALLET LIGHTING; DANCE THEATRE LIGHTING.

SHOCK. The result of contacting an energized electrical line with the body. *Caution:* Electrical shock may be fatal. It can just cause a tingling or it can throw the victim off the energized wire. It can maim or kill by causing falls from ladders. Many safety inspectors consider anything over 25 or 30 volts to be a possible hazard. Regular household current of 120 volts has serious implications and the 220 volts found in electric stoves, hot water heaters, and some other appliances is extremely dangerous. Always protect yourself and treat any line as HOT; it could save your life. Body tolerance to shock varies considerably among people. Do not try to determine your threshold for pain or shock.

SHOE. See BRUSH.

SHOP ORDER. Professionally, an order (or contract) for rental equipment needed for lighting a production. Most educational and community theatres own their equipment and have only occasional need for special rental units. However, professional theatre lighting usually calls for complete rental: lighting instruments, cable, control boards, accessories, color media, lamps, and everything. The shop order, assembled from the instrument schedule and hookup sheets described in DESIGN FOR LIGHTING, is often let out for bid and must include everything the designer plans to use, from C-clamps and lamps for the instruments to feeder cables and work lights for the switchboard. Rental agencies do not take anything for granted and neither should the designer. The shop order is a binding contract.

SHORT CIRCUIT (short). A circuit completed by a SHUNT of low resistance. Short circuiting results in blowing a FUSE or tripping a BREAKER. Before replacing fuses or resetting breakers, try to determine the cause of the short, and repair or correct it. Replace fuses with correct sizes.

SHORT FOCUS. A wide-angle lensed instrument which is also considered a SHORT THROW unit. A 4 1/2" x 6" ELLIPSOIDAL REFLECTOR SPOTLIGHT is in this category.

SHORT THROW. A lens system designed for a throw of less than 25'.

SHOW CURTAIN. An ACT CURTAIN designed for a specific show.

SHOW LIGHTING. See under individual classifications or under TYPES OF SHOWS AND THEATRES.

SHUNT. A conducting element bridged across a circuit or part of a circuit, providing an auxiliary path for the current to follow.

SHUTTER. The framing device on an ELLIPSOIDAL REFLECTOR SPOTLIGHT. In the United Kingdom some ERFs (see PROFILE SPOTS) use two sets of framing shutters (8 in all): one set in HARD FOCUS, one set in SOFT FOCUS. See also **Barndoor** under LIGHT SPILL CONTROL.

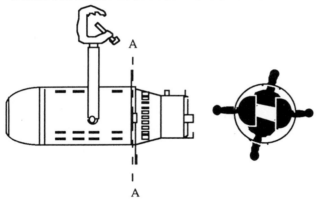

SECTION THROUGH A-A SHOWING POSSIBLE SHUTTER CONFIGURATION.
SHUTTERS FOR ELLIPSOIDAL SPOTLIGHT

SIDE ARM. See ARM.

SIDELIGHT. The instrument used for CROSSLIGHTING.

SIDELIGHTING. Lighting from the left and right sides of a stage coming from high, medium, or low angles for either special effect or dimensionality. See CROSSLIGHTING; SLIT.

SIGHTLINE. The line of vision from a seat in the auditorium to the stage. Sightlines are laid out on the floor plan to determine visibility of actors and settings from seats at the sides of the auditorium and also to determine the number of masking flats necessary for all openings. Elevation sightlines are also plotted to determine masking for the flies from the first row and visibility of the backwall from the balcony (if any). The lighting designer and electrician are concerned with sightlines and the restrictions they impose on positioning lighting equipment. In the staging of many modern shows, lights are visible to the audience and are either ignored or considered part of the scenery. In many other productions lights are best concealed. When these questions are decided in advance at PRODUCTION CONFERENCES, the lighting designer uses the sightlines to determine where CROSSLIGHTS may be placed in the wings, the TRIM of the LIGHT BATTENS, how high floor CYC LIGHTS may be without being seen from the balcony, etc. Vertical sightlines must be considered too, particularly if platforms and elevations are being used. If the GRAND VALANCE or masking BORDERS are trimmed too low for FOH lights, other locations must be found for these lights. Dress rehearsals are too late to determine these solutions.

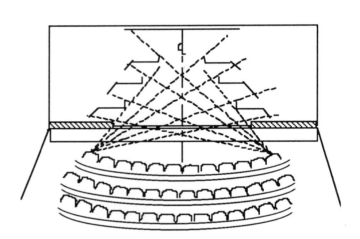

FLOOR PLAN SIGHTLINES

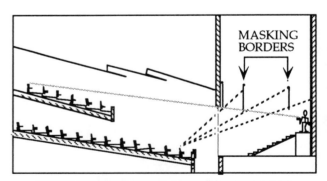

FROM THE BALCONY, MASKING BORDERS DECAPITATE THE ACTOR AND PREVENT LIGHTING HIM FROM OVERHEAD ELEVATION SIGHTLINES

SIGNAL LIGHT. A system of signaling CUES from stage manager to electrician, sound technician, or orchestra. See CUE LIGHTS.

SILICON CONTROLLED RECTIFIER (SCR). An

SCR is composed of two rectifiers and two "gates" used to control the flow of electricity through the rectifiers. The function of an SCR can be explained with the aid of a few standard symbols. The symbol for alternating current in one complete cycle is shown by this pattern, in which the top half-cycle represents forward flow of current and the lower half-cycle represents reverse, or return, flow of current. A rectifier, placed in the circuit permits flow of current in one direction only, either forward or return. This symbol, represents one half-cycle of alternating current. If two rectifiers are placed in a parallel-inverse connection (commonly called back to back), rectifier A blocks forward movement of current, and rectifier B

blocks reversed movement of current. A gate (controlled by an electrical impulse) used in conjunction with a rectifier, ←GATE, allows intermittent passage of current, through the rectifier. If a gate is used in each rectifier, a control is established over the length of time during each cycle when current is permitted to pass through the rectifiers. Actual time control is determined by a low-voltage signal imposed upon the gates. If there is no signal, gates remain closed and a lamp connected with the SCR output is off. If the signal is varied with a small voltage control device such as a POTENTIOMETER, intensity of the lamp load varies correspondingly. Low-voltage signal control such as this makes possible a wide variety of mastering, presetting, and cross-

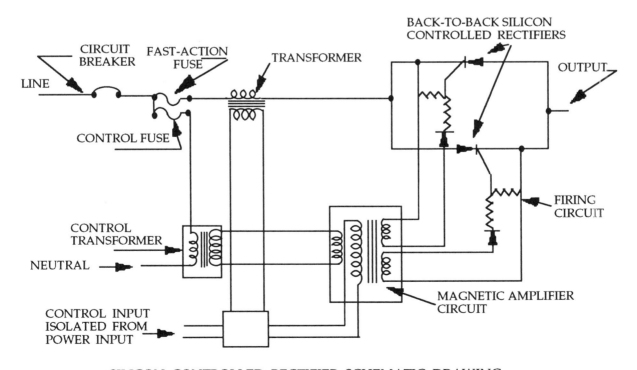

SILICON CONTROLLED RECTIFIER SCHEMATIC DRAWING

fading. Although basic circuits and explanations are relatively simple, the inherent peculiarities and sensitivities of the SCR require numerous protective devices, including AMP TRAPS, heat sinks, and radio frequency (RF) chokes, which tend to complicate circuits. Some brands of SCRs require a GHOST LOAD because they cannot detect a load if it is under a certain wattage (e.g., 50 watts or less), such as a flame or candle flicker lamp. Certain designs of SCRs use plug-in printed circuit boards (PCBs) for quick exchange in case of a defective part. Of interest to some lighting designers is the ability to shape different dimmer curves to meet certain requirements; see LIGHTING CONTROL.

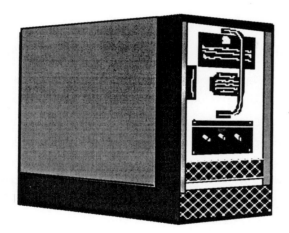

SILICON CONTROLLED RECTIFIER

SINGLE-COLOR FORMULA. Probably the simplest of all lighting schemes, in which the major area lighting is all one color. This is commonly used in ARENA STAGE LIGHTING and in OUTDOOR THEATRE LIGHTING, where daylight intrudes on the lighting.

SINGLE POLE SWITCH. See **Toggle switch** under SWITCHES.

SINGLE THROW SWITCH. See **Toggle switch** under SWITCHES.

SIXTY-CYCLE HUM. Noise in a sound system caused by audio cables running parallel with 120-volt electrical lines. It may be necessary for the electrician to re-route cables that offend in this manner.

SKETCHES. Lighting designer's rough drawings, not necessarily finished "works of art" but sufficiently detailed to define intentions. Sketches are required by United Scenic Artists Locals 829 and 350 for their entrance examinations. The student aiming to be a professional lighting designer should be encouraged to become reasonably proficient at sketching and rendering. See also DESIGN FOR LIGHTING.

SKIRPAN LIGHTING. A lighting control manufacturer in the 1970s and 1980s.

SKY. See **Cyclorama colors** under COLOR SCHEMES; CYC LIGHTS.

SKY CYC. See under CYC.

SLAM OUT. An abrupt BLACKOUT often preceded by a partial slow dim.

SLASHLIGHT. A high-angle diagonal beam of light across a curtain or other scenic piece.

SLIDE PLANE APERTURE. The slot in the side of a projector designed to receive the slides.

SLIDE PROJECTOR. See PROJECTORS.

SLIDES, PROJECTION

Direct beam slides. Slides for direct beam projectors are usually such large scale (3'–4' x 5'–7') that they may be simple cutout shadow projections or painted on sheets of acetate. Use rigid acetate rather than film because large sheets of film are likely to ripple with air movement.

Gobos. Simple gobos for ELLIPSOIDAL REFLECTOR SPOTLIGHTS may be cut from lightweight aluminum flashing or aluminum pie pans. However, the lighting designer should become familiar with the great variety of designs available commercially at reasonable prices.

Linnebach slides. Because the slide of a Linnebach projector is so close to the light source, projections are fuzzy and lacking in detail. Mylar may be used to make colored cutouts for distant horizons or it may be painted as a slide to suggested filtered sunlight, skylines, etc.

Moving projections. See under PROJECTED SCENERY.

Painted slides. Materials most commonly used for making slides are glass, Mylar, and acetate. Pyrex glass withstands the most heat, with Mylar next and acetate following; acetate distorts at 130° F and melts by 250° F. ROSCODYE and alcohol-based felt-tip pens work well for most slides, although it is advisable to test the medium used in the projector. Be aware that a small mistake or scratch on a small slide becomes a major distraction when blown up to full size. Designers painting their own slides will have to check the heat level within the projector and choose materials and dyes accordingly.

Photographic slides. Many professional photographers and photoengravers have had experience making slides from photographs and may well go out of their way to make reasonably priced theatre slides for program credit. The experienced photographer should also be able to assist in correcting distortions caused by KEYSTONING. Check photographers, photoengraving, laser beam, and acid etching companies in the yellow pages for assistance in turning photos into slides.

Distortion correction. Some distortion caused by keystoning may be corrected through drawing or photography. If the slide is to be painted or drawn, determine the amount of distortion needed to compensate for keystoning by drawing a grid on the slide and projecting it on the screen from the projector in its proper location. The grid will appear distorted on the screen. Measure this projected distortion and scale it back to the size of the slide. Draw the distorted grid on a new slide. This corrected grid may then be superimposed on all slides to be painted in the future and all drawing will conform to the distorted grid. If slides are to be photographed, keystoning can also be corrected by taking the picture in counterdistortion by focusing the camera on the picture from opposite the angle of projection.

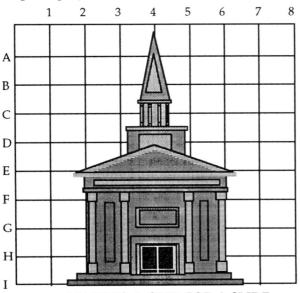

MAKING A GRID FOR A SLIDE

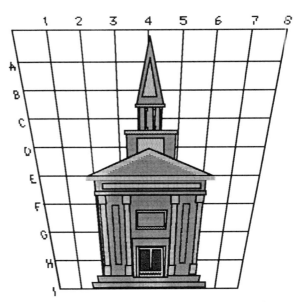

GRID CORRECTED FOR KEYSTONING

Slide sizes. Standard sizes for slides in the United States: 35 mm, 8 mm, 16 mm, 70 mm, 3 1/2" x 4", 5" x 7". European standards (including PANI PROJECTORS) include the aforementioned millimeter sizes plus 7" x 7" and 9 1/2" x 9 1/2" slides.

SLIP CONNECTOR. See **Pin connector** under PLUGS.

SLIT. A term given to CROSSLIGHTING that is SHUTTERED to a narrow beam of light crossing the stage without touching the wings or floor and illuminating the performers in a space such as IN one. This effect is often used from the TORMENTOR position although it can be used from any BAY.

SLOW-MOTION EFFECT. See LOBSTERSCOPE; STROBE LIGHT.

SLOW-MOTION WHEEL. Obsolete. Older SWITCHBOARDS with mechanical interlocking handles and masters that locked 40 or 50 DIMMERS together created a frictional load too heavy for many electricians to handle. A large wheel mounted on the board and geared by RACK AND PINION to the dimmer shafts was often installed to provide a mechanical advantage that made smooth dimming possible for even the lightweight electrician.

SMOKE EFFECTS. Can be produced in a variety of ways, many of which involve the electrician or sometimes the lighting designer.

Ammonium chloride. Will give smoke when sprinkled on a hot plate or any hot surface. Sometimes used in conjunction with FLASH POWDER, where the powder provides the heat to make the smoke. *Caution:* Avoid breathing this smoke.

CO_2 fire extinguisher. Can be used for blasts of smoke if sound can be covered or justified. This effect works very well for the sound and look of a steam locomotive leaving a station.

Dry ice. Dry ice in hot water produces a heavy, white, foglike smoke that will stay close to the ground unless agitated. Keep the hot water near boiling with a heating element (usually 220 volts). *Caution:* Use gloves and paper to handle dry ice; it gives nasty "burns" to flesh.

Dry ice machine. Great quantities of heavy white smoke that will fill the stage and hover near the floor can be made with dry ice and hot water, using a machine on each side of the stage. The dry ice machine consists of a 55-gallon metal drum mounted on casters and equipped with a clamp-down top; a 4" dryer hose coming from the upper side of the drum, with 110-volt squirrel cage fan to force the smoke out; 220-volt hot water elements in the bottom of the drum to heat the water; a wire-mesh basket to hold a quantity of dry ice broken into small pieces; and a means of lowering the basket into the water on cue. In operation, the water is heated to boiling, the basket is filled with up to 25 pounds of dry ice, just ahead of the cue the basket is lowered into the hot water, and on cue the fan is turned on. Smoke billows from the 4" tube concealed behind the wings at the side of the stage.

Flash box and chemicals. A bright flash with a puff of white smoke can be made with a FLASH BOX and powdered potassium nitrate mixed with powdered magnesium. The flash box consists of a heat-resistant, fireproof base (Bakelite), two terminals with the LINE attached, a 10-amp or less FUSE in the circuit, and one or two strands of wire from a ZIP CORD or a short length of fine solder joining the terminals. One-half teaspoon each of powdered potassium nitrate and powdered magnesium mixed and thoroughly ground with mortar and pestle is placed in the flash box and ignited electrically when the circuit is closed. More potassium nitrate produces more smoke; more magnesium produces more flash. Chemicals will not ignite unless ground to a fine powder. Keep flash box away from costumes, draperies, etc. A smaller variation of this effect uses a celluloid-covered 5- or 10-amp PLUG FUSE with the celluloid cut out and flash powder put in over the fuse wire inside. *Caution:* When handling flash powder, make sure all circuits are dead and that no tools and containers can make a spark. Use plastic spoons and always load powder from the side. Use of commercially made explosives and smoke tends to make the work safer; however, by the very nature of the chemicals, it is hazardous. Flash powders of several types are available from full-service theatrical supply houses.

Smoke machine (fog machine). Several varieties of compact smoke machines are available through theatrical manufacturers. "Fog juice" (basically a silicone-based liquid), available from the manufacturers, is vaporized into a nontoxic, white smoke by an electric element in the machine. Many of these machines are equipped with attachments to hold dry ice, which increases the smoke and makes it hug the ground; otherwise this smoke rises. This smoke is relatively nontoxic and does not interfere with the speaking or singing voice; however, it can make dancing surfaces very slippery if used extensively.

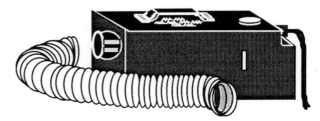

GREAT AMERICAN MARKET FOG MACHINE

Lighting smoke. A heavy layer of smoke becomes quite opaque no matter how it is lighted. However, if scenery or people are lighted from behind a fairly light screen of smoke, the effect is similar to that of lighting objects behind SCRIM. If the lighting position is then shifted to above and in front of the smoke, the smoke again becomes nearly opaque and difficult to see through. This is one reason why it is often advantageous to combine smoke with dry ice so it will hug the ground and hide only the lower half of the actors. If fog is the desired overall effect, the degree of haze is much easier to control with lights on scrim than with lights on smoke.

SNEAK A CUE. To slowly dim up or dim down at an imperceptible speed. It is sometimes necessary to set a mood at the beginning of a scene with low-intensity light and to sneak the lights up above the point of eyestrain as the scene progresses. Because of COMPUTER BOARDS, this can be easily accomplished with a very long count even when other lights are dimming up or down.

SOCKET. A receptacle for a LAMP.

SOFT-EDGED. See SOFT FOCUS.

SOFT FOCUS. Soft-edged light as opposed to the SHARP FOCUS, hard-edged light of the ELLIPSOIDAL REFLECTOR SPOTLIGHT. FOLLOWSPOTS should be capable of producing both a hard-edged and a soft-edged light so they may be framed precisely or follow the actor with subtlety.

SOFT LIGHT. A diffused light from a source with a frosted medium or a FRESNEL lens.

SOFT PATCH. An electronic computer patch system that allows any circuit or dimmer to be patched into any control channel.

SOLDER. A metal alloy that can be melted around electrical wires to join them in a positive contact. To solder two wires, twist them together and heat with a soldering iron, dip the solder in FLUX, and touch it to both the iron and the wire. The joint should fuse with solder flowing freely. If solder stays in a round drop without fusing, use more flux and heat. Solder is available as a solid wire or with an acid or rosin core. Core solders require no additional flux. Because acid cores corrode electronic joints, use only rosin core solder.

SOLDERLESS CONNECTORS. See CONNECTOR, SOLDERLESS.

SOLID STATE. In electronics, solid state refers to crystals or transistors such as the SILICON CONTROLLED RECTIFIER, in which electrons are passed or blocked by other electrons of a like charge in a DC circuit. Many solid state devices are extremely efficient, take up very little space, and are as reliable as any previous device used for switching and dimming.

SOURCE LIGHT. See **Motivational light** under LIGHTING PRACTICE.

SPECIAL. A spotlight set for a specific purpose for a specific play, as distinguished from standard AREA or wash spotlights.

SPECIAL EFFECTS. Many of the following listings are available for either rental or purchase from full-service theatrical supply houses.

Autopan. A spotlight or PARcan motorized to tilt, pan, and even change color. These units may be preset for automatic control or may be JOY STICK operated from a control board. Popular in rock, heavy metal, and rap shows, the autopan has relatively little place in play production. Used mostly as a gimmick to add movement, excitement, and anticipation for splashy production numbers. Some of these lights pan left and right, tilt up and down, open and close the iris, and change color all by remote control.

Bubble machine. Blows bubbles in volume, filling the air

Chaser. Turns lights on and off in a sequence that causes them to appear to be chasing each other.

DIRECT MOVEMENT
AUTO PAN

BUBBLE MACHINE

Color changer. Remotely controlled devices that change color media. See SCROLL COLOR CHANGER.

Flicker light. A tiny lamp that blinks on and off rapidly.

Fog machine. See under SMOKE EFFECTS.

Helicopters. A rotating head with 4 to 12 colored sealed beam lights spinning.

REMOTE CONTROL
COLOR CHANGER

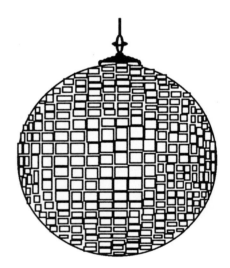

MIRROR BALL

Mirror ball. A motor-driven globe covered with mirror squares that reflect light from spotlights focused on it.

Multiheaded lights. Many lights shining in circular patterns on the floor. These lights usually spin, blink, or chase.

Rope lights. Strips of tiny lights or LEDs. Often used to light aisles in movie theaters.

Scanner. A type of **autopan** light. See above.

Scroller. See SCROLL COLOR CHANGER.

Sound light. Light which is pulsed by sound to go "on and off" or "bright to dim."

Spinner. A light that spins its beams in a circle on the floor.

Starlight. Many small hollow tubes in a sphere with an internal lamp. The tubes may be multicolored and have fan- or laser-shaped beams and they rotate.

Strobe. A bright light from a gaseous-discharge tube that has a quick recovery time and can flash repeatedly. Often the rate of flash can be adjusted. At certain speeds it will give a slow-motion or stop-action effect, reminiscent of the action in early motion pictures. The strobe supersedes the LOBSTERSCOPE.

Sweeper. A light that pans back and forth across the area on which it is focused.

SPECIFIC LIGHT. A light assigned to an area or location.

SPECTROPHOTOMETER (spectrometer). A scientific instrument that breaks light into its wavelengths and records the results in a spectrogram.

SPECTRUM. See COLOR SPECTRUM.

SPECULAR REFLECTION. Reflection from a flat, highly polished metal mirror or a front-surfaced glass mirror as opposed to diffused reflection from a matte surface.

SPEED-THROUGH. A rehearsal of a play in which the actors say their lines as fast as possible without emotion or pauses. Used to help set lines with performers and absolutely worthless as far as the technician is concerned.

SPHERICAL REFLECTOR. See under REFLECTORS.

SPIDER. See **Multiple pin connector** under PLUGS.

SPIDERING. The use of temporary CABLE hookups from INSTRUMENTS to DIMMERS on road shows.

SPIKE MARKS. Marks either taped or painted on the floor to mark positions of sets, furniture, props, or floor lights for each scene. In multiple-scene shows spike marks are often color-coded by scene to minimize mistakes.

SPILL. Stray beams of light, uncontrolled light, or poorly focused lights striking the stage or auditorium in unwanted places. Spill may be caused by imperfect lenses, which should be replaced; by dusty lenses, which should be washed; by improper focusing, which should be corrected; or by lights inadvertently knocked out of focus. Sloppy lighting detracts from a production and should not be tolerated. See also ABERRATIONS; LIGHT SPILL CONTROL.

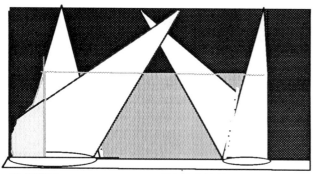

SLOPPY   FRAMED TO PROSCENIUM

SPILLS

SPILL RING. See **Louvre** under LIGHT SPILL CONTROL.

SPLICE (verb). To fasten electrical wires together by twisting and/or soldering and then taping. Solderless connectors are legally used for easy splicing. See CONNECTOR, SOLDERLESS.

SPLIT FADER. A FADER involving two handles operating opposite each other so when moved together, one is dimming down as the other is dimming up, CROSS-FADING from one scene to another. The split fader has the advantage of allowing time delays in a cross-fade, which cannot be accomplished with a single fader.

SPLIT STAGING. See under STAGING.

SPOT

(noun). SPOTLIGHT.

(verb). To focus a spotlight or a followspot on an actor or given object.

SPOT BAR. British term for the pipe (LIGHT BATTEN) on which instruments are hung.

SPOTLIGHT (spot). Instrument equipped with a lens, a reflector, and a lamp with some means of controlling the beam size, either through varying the distance between lamp and lens (fresnel spot) or framing the beam with shutters (ellipsoidal spot). See under individual names: ARC LIGHT; BABY SPOT; ELLIPSOIDAL REFLECTOR SPOTLIGHT; FOLLOWSPOT; FRESNEL LIGHT;

PARcan; PLANO-CONVEX SPOTLIGHT; ZOOM ELLIPSE.

SPOT LINE. See under LINE.

SPOT MARKS. Marks placed on walls in a BOOTH or on sheets of paper on the walls of the booth and used to help difficult PICKUPS with FOLLOWSPOTS. A special light leak in the followspot allows a ray of light to be used for this marking system. It is the only way to HIT a performer coming out of the wings in the dark.

SPOTTING LIGHT. A low-wattage light, often in color, usually located on the backwall of the auditorium or the front of the balcony and used to help dancers face front during turns and to help find their places onstage during a BLACKOUT.

SPREAD OF SPOTLIGHT. Area covered by the light from a spotlight, determined by the size and FOCAL LENGTH of the lens and the distance of THROW. The spread may be expressed in degrees (as a 20° BEAM ANGLE) or in feet (as a 20' spread in a 40' THROW). See also FIELD ANGLE; FIELD DIAMETER.

SQUARE LAW. See LAW OF SQUARES.

STAGE CREW. Arranged in order of responsibility.

Stage manager. In complete charge of all performances after final dress rehearsals and responsible for calling special rehearsals for understudies or for disciplinary reasons. The stage manager also calls all light, sound, carpenter, fly, and crew CUES, checks entrances, often holds the prompt book, and keeps the show moving. In professional theatre and most other productions, the stage manager has attended all rehearsals and has recorded blocking, business, and changes in the master prompt script.

Master carpenter. Responsible for handling and repairing scenery onstage, in charge of set-in, scene changes, and strike. Responsible for overseeing the cleanliness of offstage areas.

Flyman. The person responsible for the rigging and operation of that rigging during a show. Reports to the master carpenter.

Flymen. Part of the carpentry department and responsible to the flyman for rigging and its operation.

Second hand. The main assistant carpenter. If there is only one, the second hand is often in charge of the stage left area during the run of the show. It is not unusual to have more than one assistant carpenter, who with a group of grips are assigned specific tasks. In the hierarchy of the carpentry department there can be a second hand (stage left carpenter), stage right carpenter, and the winch operator, each person with a group of grips.

     Grips. Work as carpenters and are responsible to the master carpenter and assistant carpenters. During scene changes they move all scenery except that allocated to the flymen.

     Master electrician (juicer). In charge of electrical set-in, running lights during the show, and striking lughts after the show.

     Assistant electricians. Help the electrician with set-in and strike and run auxiliary boards.

     Sound master. Responsible for all sound reinforcement and sound effects. Sometimes under the direction of the master electrician.

     Sound crew. Sound technicians or assistant electricians will sometimes be included under the sound master.

     Property master (prop master). In charge of all properties: hand, set, furniture, and dressing. Also responsible for overseeing the cleanliness of the onstage areas.

     Property crew. Works with and under the supervision of prop master.

STAGE DIRECTIONS. See also AREAS. Directions according to actors' right or left as they face the audience, and upstage or downstage in accordance with the sloped construction of early stages. Abbreviations by letter are common practice: DL, downleft; DCL, downcenter left; DR, downright, etc. Directions found in acting editions of old plays were based on entrances according to wings. These are used mostly in professional theatre and are sometimes confusing to the nonprofessional wishing to stage plays from original acting editions.

     R.1 - Stage right, first entrance upstage of proscenium.

     R.2 - Stage right, second entrance upstage of proscenium.

     R.C. - Right center.

     R.U. - Right upstage entrance.

     O.P. - Opposite prompter (stage left).

     P.S. - Prompt side (stage right, or side with curtain control).

     (E) - Enter.

     (X) - Crosses.

STAGE PLUG (floor plug). Obsolete. See under PLUGS.

STAGES. Acting areas designed in many configurations, some of which are identified below. There is some debate as to what constitutes a 3/4 arena versus a thrust stage. Here we assume the arena stage floor to be the same level with or slightly lower than the first row of seats, with successive seats tiered, and the thrust stage to be a platform, with the first row of seats beginning slightly below the level of the stage. The authors make this presumption based on the fact that Glenn Hughes, the father of the modern arena stage, was inspired by the Paris one-ring circus.

    Arena stages

     Full arena. Acting area completely surrounded by audience. Successfully introduced by

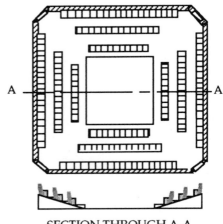

SECTION THROUGH A-A
ARENA STAGE

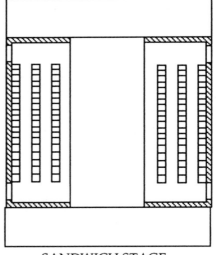

SANDWICH STAGE

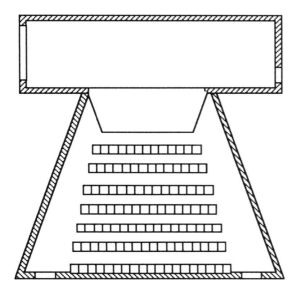

EXTENDED-APRON STAGE

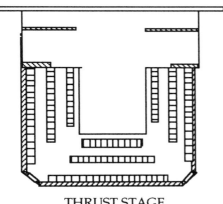

THRUST STAGE

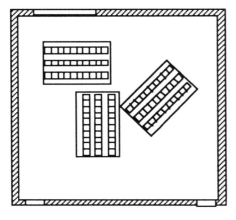

FLEXIBLE STAGE

Professor Glenn Hughes. His first full arena stage was the Penthouse Theatre built at the University of Washington in 1940. Usually the floor level of the arena stage is either the same as or lower than the first row of seats. The lower acting area is preferred because it is easier to keep the lights out of the audience. See also ARENA STAGE LIGHTING.

Three-sided arena. Audience on three sides of the main acting area, which can be backed with a scenic wall. Sometimes this configuration is called the T- or U-shaped stage. It is similar to a thrust stage, except the first row of audience is usually on or slightly above the acting floor level.

Two-sided arena (sandwich arena, football field shape). A long, narrow acting area with audience on two sides. The audience seats are at stage level or slightly above, with successive rows tiered.

Apron stages

Extended-apron stage. Basically a proscenium stage with a large APRON supplementing the stage acting area. The apron often extends between 9' and 12' in front of the proscenium, with no provision made for seating on the sides. The extended apron is not as large as the thrust stage.

Thrust stage. Follows the principles of the Shakespearean stage, with the acting area thrust into the auditorium and seating on three sides of the stage. The stage is elevated above the first row of the audience, and successive rows usually rise above stage level. The configuration can be confused with the three-sided arena.

Flexible stage (black box, open stage). Enclosed space equipped with seats on movable risers, permitting a variety of seating possibilities around an acting area. Larger flexible stages often have winch grids overhead. In some spaces the auditorium and stage are integrated into a single unit, with architectural tormentors defining lateral extremities of the stage and serving as screens for entrances and exits.

Proscenium stage. Conventional stage separated from the auditorium by a PROSCENIUM, or "picture window." Usually the first row of the audience is seated below stage level, with successive rows tiered.

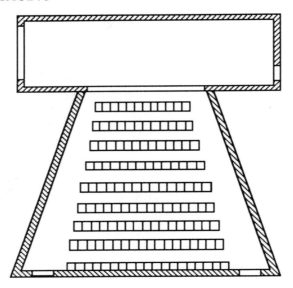

PROSCENIUM STAGE

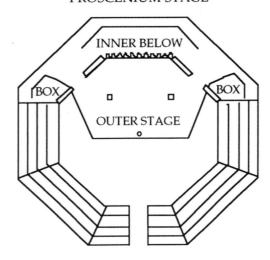

SHAKESPEAREAN STAGE

Shakespearean stage. The SHAKESPEAREAN STAGE is a two-story thrust stage within an octagonal building. It has a curtained INNER BELOW, INNER ABOVE, and boxes in conventional locations on the sides of the stage. The original apparently included an orchestra space on a third level.

STAGING. Directing a play onstage; planning settings, lights, props, platforms, etc.

STAGING STYLES

Formal (space staging). Platforms, steps, ramps, etc., give varied and interesting levels for stage business and direction.

Naturalistic. Realistic box sets behind a proscenium.

Simultaneous. Action takes place on two or more separate parts of the stage, but not necessarily simultaneously. Simultaneous staging requires careful setting and focusing of lighting equipment to avoid spills or overlaps between any two areas.

Split. Simultaneous staging in which two unrelated scenes can be performed at the same time.

Symbolic. Backgrounds suggesting or enhancing plots or offering character interpretations.

STANDARD (boom, light standard, stand, boomerang). A pipe in a metal base used to support a spotlight or floodlight. See also LIGHT MOUNTING EQUIPMENT.

STAND BY (command verb). Warning to be ready for a CUE.

STAND-OFF. A device using two COLOR FRAMES spaced apart by 4" bolts. Used to create a space between the color media and the very hot INSTRUMENTS so the color will not fade as rapidly. This is a necessity for some blue colors in particular, which tend to burn out quickly. If there is a light leak, mask with WRAP.

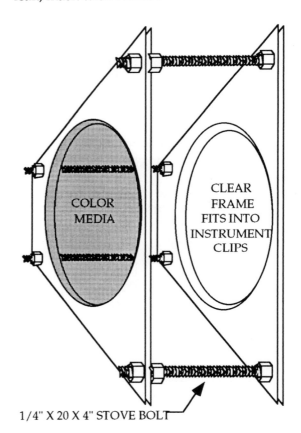

1/4" X 20 X 4" STOVE BOLT

COLOR FRAME STAND-OFF

166

STAR. Professionally made, laser-cut GOBOs make the best stars. Simply insert in the pattern holder in an ELLIPSOIDAL REFLECTOR SPOTLIGHT and focus. Tiny pin scratches on a Pyrex glass slide painted with heat-resistant black paint and used in a projector or in any spotlight to which a second (objective) lens can be attached may also work.

STAR FROST. See under FROST.

STEAK KNIFE. Hard-edged light such as is usually found in a FOLLOWSPOT or an ELLIPSOIDAL REFLECTOR SPOTLIGHT. Derivation is from "as sharp as a steak knife."

STEAL. See SNEAK A CUE.

STEP

The rise or drop in intensity from one contact to another on a DIMMER.

A segment of a chase program in a COMPUTER BOARD. See under COMPUTER LIGHT BOARD TERMINOLOGY.

STEPDOWN TRANSFORMER. Transformer designed to reduce voltage from a higher input to a lower output level. Commonly used in BELL circuits, where 120 volts is stepped down to 12 or 16 volts. LOW-VOLTAGE LAMPS will either be wired in series or plugged into a stepdown transformer. Transformers cannot be dimmed with SILICON CONTROLLED RECTIFIER DIMMERS.

STEPLADDER. See LADDERS.

STEP LENS. See under LENSES.

STEPUP TRANSFORMER. Increases voltage to a higher output level from a lower input voltage. The Variac dimmer ranges from 0 to 135 volts, thereby becoming a stepup transformer from 120 to 135 volts. This is useful when extra intensity is needed for special spotlights or projectors. See VARIAC. *Warning*: The Variac cannot be controlled by electronic dimmers.

STEREOPTICON. A dual projector arranged so that one picture seems to dissolve as the other materializes. Adaptations of stereopticons have been used for projecting scenery of various kinds.

STICK. The center vertical extension of an A-LADDER. *Caution:* It is most important that at least two crew members hold the base of the A-ladder when someone is on the stick. These ladders can extend to 36' high.

STOP COLLAR. A cast-iron ring with bolt for tightening. The device is used on a telescoping light

STANDARD to hold the inner pipe at a given height while still allowing rotation.

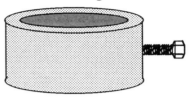

STOP COLLAR

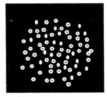

STRAINER

STRAINER. A lightweight sheet metal square, perforated with small holes and cut to fit the COLOR FRAME clips in a spotlight. Strainers reduce the amount of light but maintain the brilliance. See also MOONLIGHT.

STRAND CENTURY. Obsolete. British-American manufacturer of lighting control and instruments. Also appears as Century Strand. Now known as Strand Lighting.

STRAND CORPORATION. British-based manufacturer of lighting equipment sold throughout the world.

STRANDED WIRE. Stranded wire is used in electrical conductors to provide flexibility. The smaller the wire size of each strand, the greater the flexibility. See also CABLE.

STRAY LIGHT. Uncontrolled spills of light. See ABERRATIONS; LIGHT SPILL CONTROL.

STRIKE

Set. To remove all scenery and props from the stage. The strike may occur at the end of a scene (in preparation for the set-in of the next scene), the end of a performance (in preparation for rehearsals or other shows the following day), or the end of the production (the final closing of the show).

Lights (derig [British usage]). To dismount or take down lighting equipment.

STRIP GLASS. Color media made of narrow widths (about 1") of colored glass to withstand heat expansion. The strips are placed in a special color frame and used in high-intensity instruments. Occasionally two different colors are alternated in the same frame to blend into a third color. Colored strips may also be placed in a sequence, graduated from light to dark, and mounted in a motorized frame to allow a gradual change from a day to a night scene. Such installations have been used successfully in conjunction with projected scenery, for example, with the **Direct beam** (see under PROJECTORS).

STRIPLIGHTS (strips). Early striplights were aptly named, consisting of a strip of three or more 40- to 60-watt lamps mounted in a black trough painted white on the inside. The small strips were used as BACKING LIGHTS, hung on toggles, and provided a general flooding of the area behind the door or window to which they were assigned. On occasion, the lamps were dipped in pink, red, or blue dye to provide a little color, but that was a trade-off of color for intensity and usually at least some of the lamps remained white. Longer striplights from this period were laid on the floor behind GROUNDROWS, providing a mild horizon glow to the lower section of CYC. As the concept developed in the 1920s, striplights became larger; 200- to 300-watt lamps were placed in compartments with gelatine frame holders. Striplights suddenly became multipurpose general-coverage lights that could double as top or bottom CYC LIGHTS, be used on occasion as BORDER LIGHTS in small theatres, and could even pinch-

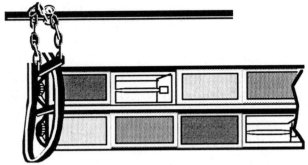

TUNGSTEN-HALOGEN STRIPLIGHTS
USED AS BORDERS, STRIPS, OR CYC LIGHTS CA 1970s

hit as FOOTLIGHTS, although their height obstructed vision from the first few rows. By the early 1950s, PAR light strips, in which either the clear PAR 38 or the R 40 (see **Reflector** under LAMP) colored lamps could be used, became available. The dichroic PAR 38s, with their pure primary color, can also be used in striplights although their expense is something of a deterrent. TUNGSTEN-HALOGEN LAMPS in striplights provide an intense, hot light that can be used to light either the top or bottom of the cyc in a three-color system that ensures maximum color control from sunset through sunrise. These 300- to 500-watt border light and striplight combinations also double well as border lights from the first pipe where needed; but as mentioned elsewhere, color washes from spotlights offer better control of toning lights and greater efficiency because their light may be specifically directed to cover exact areas. See BORDER LIGHTS; CYC STRIPS; FOOTLIGHTS.

STRIP OUT (strip) (command verb). To make a low but wide band of light across the stage from a FOLLOWSPOT. Stripping out is accomplished by widening the focus (beam size) with the TROMBONE and narrowing the top and bottom aperture with the DOUSER. True to the LAW OF SQUARES, the intensity of the stripped-out light is only a fraction of the intensity of the tight spot.

STRIPPING THE STAGE. To cover the stage with a beam of light from a followspot that is wider than it is high, as opposed to the general practice of following a performer with a narrow cone of light.

STROBE LIGHT. A bright light from a gaseous-discharge tube that has a quick recovery time and can flash repeatedly. See also **Strobe** under SPECIAL EFFECTS.

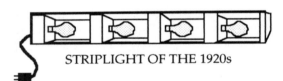

STRIPLIGHT OF THE 1920s

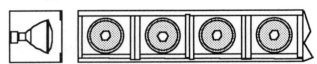

PAR STRIPLIGHTS
FOUR-CIRCUIT STRIPLIGHTS DESIGNED FOR EITHER PAR 38, SEALED-BEAM, 150-WATT LAMPS OR R 40, 150-WATT FLOODLIGHTS AND USED AS BORDER LIGHTS, FOOTLIGHTS, OR CYC LIGHTS

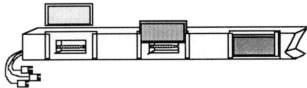

TUNGSTEN-HALOGEN STRIPLIGHTS
GLASS COLOR MEDIA

STRIPPING AND SPOTTING

THE LEFT FOLLOWSPOT STRIPS THE CHORUS
AS THE RIGHT FOLLOWSPOT SPOTS THE SOLOIST

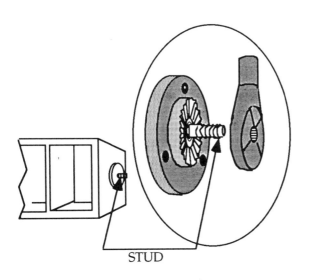

STUD

STUD. A 1/2" threaded shank extending from an INSTRUMENT (usually STRIPLIGHTS) on which a threaded hand wheel tightens to hold the instrument in place.

SUBLIMINAL LIGHTING. The concept of identifying characters of a play by assigning them different colors of light was successfully tried for *John Brown's Body* by one of the authors. Not only did color identification seem to register subliminally with the audience, but in a show in which each actor plays several roles, the actors themselves found it helpful in keeping characters straight. Obviously, such a concept has a limited number of applications.

SUBMASTER. A dimming device controlling a given number of dimmers but being controlled itself by a master dimmer (see DIMMERS, MASTER).

SUBTRACTIVE METHOD OF COLOR MIXTURE. See under COLOR MIXING.

SUNLIGHT EFFECT. Best obtained from a single-source, high-intensity light, such as a 1,000-watt or 1,500-watt ELLIPSOIDAL REFLECTOR SPOTLIGHT or narrow BEAM PROJECTOR. Color should contrast with basic colors used for area; for example, if amber is predominant onstage, sunlight through windows or doors should be clear; if blues or pinks are predominant, light amber may be used for the sun. See also LIGHTING COLORS.

SUPER TROUPER. A brand name for a large and very intense FOLLOWSPOT from Strong International. For years, it and the TROUPER were the standards for the professional theatre.

SURE CLAMP. A trade name for J. R. Clancy's light-mounting device used in place of a C-CLAMP.

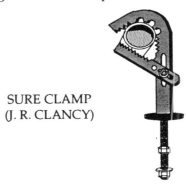

SURE CLAMP
(J. R. CLANCY)

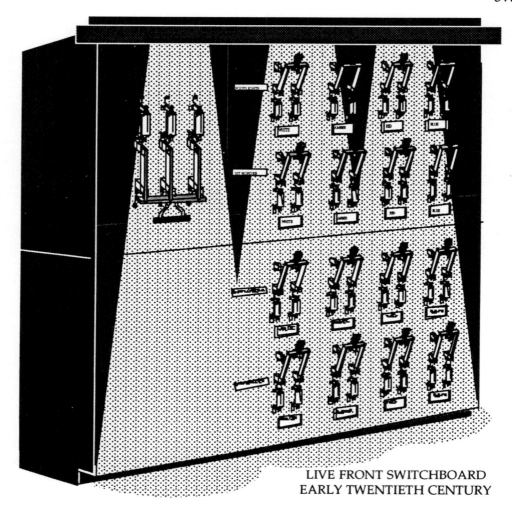

LIVE FRONT SWITCHBOARD
EARLY TWENTIETH CENTURY

SURGE (glitch). Aberrant voltage pulses that can cause malfunctions in COMPUTER BOARDS. Reacting to the irregularities, the microprocessor may think the pulses are commands and jump a cue or BLOW an entire show. Surges can be harmful to silicon controlled rectifier circuits as well as sound equipment and computers. Electronic surge protectors should be used for sensitive equipment. See also **Glitch** under COMPUTER LIGHT BOARD TERMINOLOGY.

SURGE PROTECTOR. A most necessary unit, usually built into a plugging strip to protect COMPUTER BOARDS and other electronic equipment from aberrant voltage pulses.

SWATCH BOOK. A color media sample book with all the colors in a particular product line from a manufacturer. Often the light transmission factors, the wavelengths, the names, and code numbers are included information.

SWING JOINT. A mounting device with two circular ROSETTES, one with a STUD and the other with a hole. The stud is tightened against the second rosette with a hand wheel, nut, or wing nut.

SWITCHBOARD. Board consisting of the switches, fuses, and dimmers necessary to control stage lights. Ideally, switchboards have sufficient dimmers to control lights for each area of the stage, plus special effects lights, general toning lights (washes), cyclorama lights, and house lights. For small theatres, between 30 and 40 dimmers are minimal for light control. A system of mastering individual dimmers to one or two controls should be included by either mechanical interlocking or, preferably, electrical interlocking (see DIMMERS, MASTER). Dimmer controls should be compactly arranged for rapid manipulation and clearly marked to avoid errors. For dimmer protection, fuses or breakers should be placed in readily accessible positions between dimmers and circuits. Switchboards for small theatres should be capable of handling a minimum of 50,000 watts. Patch panels should be provided close to switchboards, enabling the operator to plug any light or set of lights into any dimmer or any dimmer into any control. Switchboards equipped with SCR dimmers, FADERS, SUBMASTERS, and PRESETS are highly recommended. See also DIMMERS; PATCH PANEL; LIGHTING CONTROL.

SWITCHBOARD HOOKUP. A detail of the light plot showing instruments, locations, accessories, instrument numbers, area of focus, color media, dimmer control, and all pertinent details. See **Hookup sheets** under DESIGN FOR LIGHTING.

SWITCHBOARD, LOCATIONS. See LIGHTING CONTROL LOCATIONS.

SWITCHES. Make-and-break devices for electrical circuits placed in series with a load.

Circuit breaker (breaker switch). A switchlike fuse placed in series with a load and designed to open automatically if the circuit is shorted or overloaded. The circuit can be closed again by pushing

a **Reset button** or by turning the breaker to the "off" and then to the "on" position. Breakers have superseded fuse plugs for several reasons: The tripped breaker is easily spotted, easily reset, and because it is wired into the circuit, it cannot be exchanged for a fuse of higher capacity, threatening safety.

Knife switch. Obsolete. An electrical switch consisting of a copper blade hinged on one end to engage in a spring receptacle on the other. Simple knife switches were not enclosed and were therefore dangerous to use on anything but low-voltage, low-amperage circuits. See illustration under KNIFE SWITCH.

Master switch. Obsolete. Generally a knife switch enclosed in a metal box and equipped with a handle outside the box. Master switches were rated for maximum load of combined branch circuits and were fused accordingly. Many master switches provided for fusing within their boxes.

Main breaker. A high-amp breaker placed before any branch circuit (see under CIRCUITS). The main breaker is today's equivalent of the master switch.

Mercury switch. A silent toggle switch in which mercury makes the contact between terminals in the "on" position. Because they are noiseless, either mercury switches or other varieties of silent toggles are favored where switches have to be used close to the audience. Most mercury switches are designed to operate in vertical or near-vertical position only and will not function when mounted flat.

Reset button. Usually a button switch designed to reactivate a fuse or breaker after being blown by an overload or short.

Rotary switch. Switch with two or more contacts activated by rotating a handle or knob.

Selector switch. A multiconnector rotary switch designed to connect lighting equipment and dimmers.

An "in line" type switch that pivots to and fro with several positions is also used as a selector switch. Primarily used for preset boards, they are placed with the controllers and show the controller to be independent, off, or on master. See also PATCH PANEL.

Toggle switch. Standard household "on-off" switch, also standard for PRESET BOARDS.

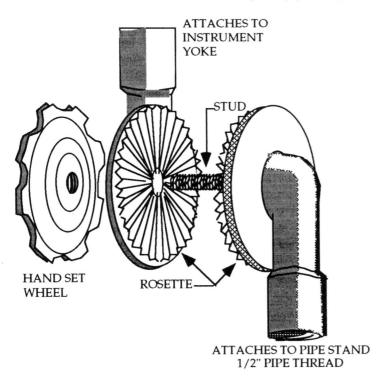

ATTACHES TO INSTRUMENT YOKE

STUD

HAND SET WHEEL

ROSETTE

ATTACHES TO PIPE STAND 1/2" PIPE THREAD

SWING JOINT

Single pole-single throw toggle. Designed for one side of the line, with one "on" position and one "off" position.

Single pole-double throw toggle (three-way switch). Designed for one side of the line, with two "on" positions. Used in circuits where two switches in different locations control the same light.

Double pole-single throw toggle. Designed for both sides of the line, with one "off" and one "on" position.

Double pole-double throw toggle. Designed for both sides of the line with two "on" positions for multiple controls on the same light. Known also as a double-pole three-way.

Double throw toggle. These switches often have a center "off" position.

SWITCH NUMBER. Obsolete. On PIANO BOARDS, a knife switch controlled the electricity to a RESISTANCE DIMMER and its number became the dimmer number as well (e.g., switch 12 really referred to dimmer 12).

SWIVEL (verb). To move a spotlight in the horizontal plane. Usually this is accomplished by swinging the YOKE at the C-CLAMP connection.

SYMBOLS. The following symbols are used extensively for lighting in the theatre:

SYSTEM LOCK. A locking device, usually key operated, that protects the control board from use by unauthorized personnel.

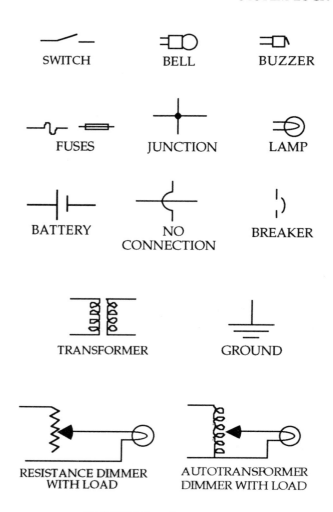

SWITCH   BELL   BUZZER

FUSES   JUNCTION   LAMP

BATTERY   NO CONNECTION   BREAKER

TRANSFORMER   GROUND

RESISTANCE DIMMER WITH LOAD   AUTOTRANSFORMER DIMMER WITH LOAD

ELECTRICAL SYMBOLS

T

TAP AND DIE SET. Tools for threading pipes or rods. The electrician is primarily concerned with threading pipe and will therefore need only a die set that will accommodate pipe of the following IDs (inside diameters): 1/2", 3/4", 1 1/4", and, possibly, 1 1/2" for larger stages. Pipes of these sizes are used to make hanger extensions for instruments, additional LIGHT BATTENS, BOOMERANGS, TREES, and LADDERS.

TAPE. The electrician will find the following kinds of tape useful:

    Dielectric tape. Scotch brand electrical tape used as an insulating and self-sticking tape for splicing wires. A single layer of this tape can protect against several thousand volts.

    Friction tape. Obsolete. Now replaced by dielectric tape.

    Gaffers tape. Black, gray, or silver cloth rug tape is used backstage for almost everything.

    Tape measure. A flexible steel, fiberglass, or cloth measuring tape, calibrated in feet and inches or in metric measure. The fiberglass or cloth tape equipped with a paper snap clip is invaluable in measuring the TRIM height of borders and ELECTRICS. Clip the snap clip onto the pipe, take the PIPE out to the measured height, and pull the snap clip off. Among the many uses the electrician has for measuring tapes is the accurate positioning of instruments on the electrics during the HANG.

TEASER. Name used today for the older term GRAND VALENCE. The first of the overhead cloth borders.

TEASER BATTEN (first pipe, first border, first electric). The electric pipe batten hung immediately upstage of the teaser and act curtain; used for hanging lighting equipment. One of the reasons the term "first border" fell from use is that it was confused with the first (cloth) border.

TECHNICAL DIRECTOR (TD). In non-Broadway theatre the technical director is responsible for the construction, lighting (either designing, executing, or both), setting the show, organizing scene shifts, troubleshooting the production run, the strike, and disposing of the scenery. In many theatres, the technical director is also responsible for designing and painting. As regional and educational theatres become more affluent, scenic and lighting designers will be added to the staff or contracted to work by the show.

TECHNICAL REHEARSAL (tech, tech rehearsal). A rehearsal scheduled for the technical crew to establish scene changes, lighting cues and intensity levels, sound cues and volume levels; everything concerning the technical personnel. Occasionally an actor or two will be asked to assist with visual and word cues as they walk through parts of scenes to help timing and coordination. It is critical that all lights be set and gelled for the tech rehearsal and that all patching be done with the right dimmers assigned to the right lights. Intensities will be recorded during this rehearsal. It should be understood that the tech rehearsal is for the benefit of the entire technical personnel, and no one department should be allowed to usurp attention at the expense of another. If a particular production is a HEAVY LIGHT SHOW, a special light rehearsal should be called to establish levels and rehearse cues. The success of a show may partially depend on the level of proficiencies established in tech and lighting rehearsals.

TECHNICIAN (techie). Anyone working on one of the technical aspects of a production.

TED LEWIS. See **Top hat** under LIGHT SPILL CONTROL.

TEE. See under PIPE FITTINGS.

TEE JOINT HANGER. A special TEE pipe fitting for the HANGER of an INSTRUMENT that permits it to slide along a SIDE ARM and lock to the pipe with a thumbscrew.

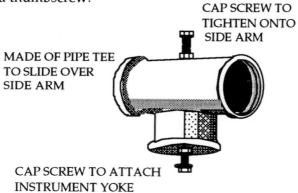

CAP SCREW TO TIGHTEN ONTO SIDE ARM

MADE OF PIPE TEE TO SLIDE OVER SIDE ARM

CAP SCREW TO ATTACH INSTRUMENT YOKE

TEE JOINT HANGER

TELEPHONE PATCH. See **Telephone type** under PATCH PANEL.

TELESCOPTER (tallescope [British usage]). A telescoping metal framework and platform or a telescoping boom with bucket, which is raised or lowered by a cable and pulley mechanism and is designed to replace a ladder for high work. In the low position the framework-type unit can be moved about on large wheels. When in place, outriggers are swung out and set to the floor, the railing around the platform is raised into position, and the unit is elevated by crank or motor, depending on its size. These devices can reach 80' in height with a 4' x 6' working area on top. See also GENIE LIFT.

TEMPERATURE, COLOR. See COLOR TEMPERATURE.

TEMPLATE. A design pattern used in building or drafting. The lighting template is a plastic card with easily traced cutout symbols for ELLIPSOIDAL REFLECTOR SPOTLIGHTS, FRESNEL LIGHTS, SCOOPS, STRIPLIGHTS, PROJECTORS, FOLLOWSPOTS, BEAM PROJECTORS, and SPECIALS. Lighting templates are available in either floor plan or elevation symbols. The floor plan templates are probably more widely used. Lighting equipment manufacturers or full-service suppliers usually stock three different scales of templates: 1/8" = 1', 1/4" = 1', and 1/2" = 1' for both floor plans and elevations. The size of the stage and the scale most often used by the scene designer will

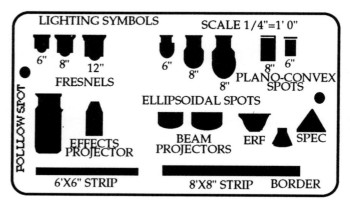

LIGHTING TEMPLATE

help the lighting designer choose the most appropriate template scale.

TEMPORARY WIRING. A term describing the type of wiring brought into a theatre by a road show. All runs of cable are made for the duration of the production within the particular theatre.

TERMINAL. One end of an electrical circuit, usually providing a lug or threaded post for attaching a conductor.

TEST LAMP. A low-wattage lamp or neon lamp with short leads used to test circuits. Two low-wattage lamps in series are used for testing 220-volt and 110-volt circuits. If the lamps glow at normal brightness, the voltage is 220; at half brightness, the voltage is 110.

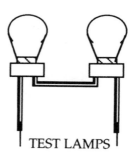

TEST LAMPS

TEXTURE. The plasticity or dimensional quality (as opposed to flat, smooth, and dull) that lighting can give a production. GOBO projections are often used to achieve a texture.

TH. See TUNGSTEN-HALOGEN LAMP.

THERMOGARD. A trade name for a heat-resisting medium used between the LAMP and the COLOR MEDIA. It generally requires a STAND-OFF to provide a couple of inches of spacing between the two media to be effective.

THREE-FER. See **Two-fer and three-fer** under PLUGS.

THREE-WIRE SYSTEM OF WIRING. See **Three-wire, single-phase circuit** under CIRCUITS.

THROW

The distance between a lighting instrument and the area to be illuminated. A light intensity of 50 footcandles is considered minimum for most stage lights. Therefore, the practical throw of a given instrument is the distance between the instrument and the place where an intensity reading of 50 footcandles on a photometer is obtained. These figures are usually given in the PHOTOMETRIC CHARTS. When choosing instruments for a show, the throw is easily calculated by imagining the spotlight and its beam as forming a right triangle with the floor. The altitude is the distance off the floor; the base is the distance between the area to be covered and the perpendicular to the spotlight; the hypotenuse is the throw. Measure the base of the triangle from the floor plan and the altitude of the

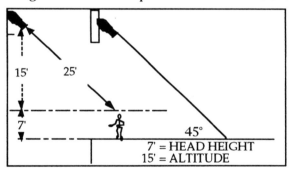

ELEVATION

ALTITUDE (15') SQUARED   = 225
+BASE (20') SQUARED (FLOOR PLAN) = 400
                                                      ‾‾‾‾‾
                                                       625
SQUARE ROOT OF 625 = 25' (HYPOTENUSE)
THROW OF INSTRUMENT = 25'

CALCULATING THROW

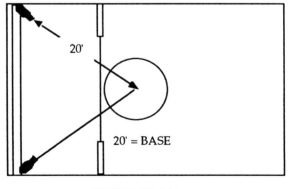

FLOOR PLAN

triangle from the elevation. In a right triangle, the hypotenuse (throw) is the square root of the sum of the square of the base and the square of the altitude. It should be remembered that the throw must take into consideration the height of the actor, and calculations should be made from a 6' or 7' height. A line drawn at this height on the elevation then becomes a measurement point for determining throw. It should be understood that throw cannot be a critical measurement because the distance will vary somewhat within the area to be covered. However, reasonable approximations ensure better blending and better lighting.

The term "throw" may also apply to turning a switch on or off.

An INSTRUMENT is said to "throw" light in a given direction.

THRUST STAGE LIGHTING. The thrust is a three-sided stage, usually with a scenic wall behind or in some cases a full proscenium stage behind, the thrust being in essence a large apron surrounded by an audience. If a similar set-up exists level with the first row of audience seats, it is usually considered a three-sided **Arena stage** (see under STAGES). Principles outlined under LIGHTING PRACTICE and DESIGN FOR LIGHTING provide the basics for most forms of stage lighting. Following further procedures suggested for PROSCENIUM STAGE LIGHTING, the thrust stage is divided into essential acting areas as determined by the play and director. The size of each area (usually between 8' and 12' in diameter) will be determined by the instruments used and their distance from the stage. The number of areas to be lighted will be determined by the play and the size and shape of the stage. Because, with the thrust stage, most of the actors are viewed from three sides, it is necessary to focus a minimum of three lights on each area. As with arena lighting, instruments are usually located on a pipe grid above the thrust stage. A rectangular stage can be minimally lighted from a grid of four pipes, a little longer than the width of the stage. Try to keep the lighting angle about 45° as long as light does not spill into the audience. Increase the angle to 60° when lighting the edge of the stage from the inside position.

Practice. Use three spotlights for each area, 90° between lights, one from the front and one on each side. As with arena lighting, some steep-angle

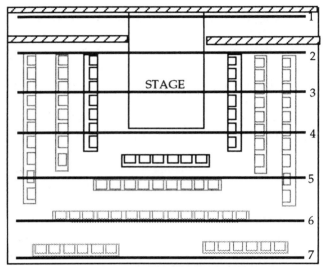

1 THROUGH 7 - LIGHT PIPES FOR MOUNTING
LIGHTING INSTRUMENTS
THRUST STAGE

lighting will be necessary. Lighting angles over the thrust should be duplicated upstage to maintain uniformity. Again as with arena lighting, it is common practice to use either no color or one color of light for areas and to provide overall toning with special COLOR WASHES. Some color washes may be mounted on the inner pipes, crossing at a fairly steep angle to the outer areas of the stage, but most washes will be mounted in front of the stage and placed at a fairly low angle. As with arena lighting, preventing light from spilling into the eyes of the audience becomes a major factor in determining the kind of equipment to be chosen. Since the THROW on most thrust stages is short to medium and ambient light from a soft-edged fresnel will spill into the auditorium, the hard-edged, variable-focus (ZOOM ELLIPSE) ellipsoidal is the obvious choice of instrument for area lighting. If color washes come from the front of the house, FRESNEL LIGHTS with BARNDOORS may well prove to be the most easily blended instrument for that purpose.

Color. Colors are handled in the same manner as for ARENA STAGE LIGHTING. The lighting of the scenic wall or upstage area will be much the same as for the proscenium stage. Color considerations should be conceived and based on the type of presentation being shown.

Control. The control of lights necessary for thrust stages is similar to that needed for proscenium stages. Individual area controls, entrance controls, special effects and special area controls, and color wash control in preferably two or three different colors will be necessary. As with the arena stage, either the slow dim-out or fast blackout is the substitute for a curtain, so these capabilities must be provided.

THUMBSCREW. A screw with a flat head designed to be turned by the thumb and forefinger. This kind of setscrew is often found on lighting equipment.

THUMBSCREW

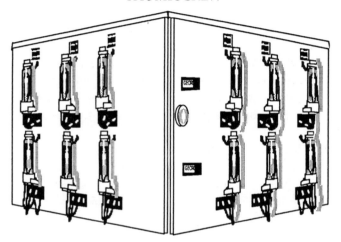

THYRATRON TUBE DIMMER

THYRATRON TUBE DIMMER (tube dimmer, tube board). Obsolete. Superseded by SILICON CONTROLLED RECTIFIER DIMMERS (SCRs). The tube dimmer used two thyratrons (gas-filled electron tubes with control grids) to carry the load current. Since the thyratron tube is always a rectifier (a direct current device), two tubes must be connected back-to-back to permit the use of alternating current circuitry. The thyratron, like the SCR, acts as an electronic switch. Dimming is accomplished by varying the time in the half-cycle when conduction occurs, or, in other words, altering the length of "firing periods." Research and development of thyratron tube dimmers was done by George Izenour of Yale University in the late 1940s, although the use of the vacuum tube as a dimming device was known long before that. Early installations of vacuum tube dimmers included the Chicago Civic Opera Theatre in 1929,

Radio City Music Hall in New York in 1930, and Severance Hall in Cleveland in 1931. Among the several factors contributing to the demise of the thyratron tube dimmer were the following: the relatively short life and great expense of the thyratron tube; the sheer bulk of the dimmer; the loss of dimmers when tubes burned out; expense of power to operate; and finally, the advent of transistors in the late 1940s, which led to development of the SCR. The SCR could duplicate the GATING action of the thyratron tube at a fraction of the cost, needed no warm-up period, wasted little power, and offered long life. See REACTANCE DIMMER.

THYRISTOR. European name for the SILICON CONTROLLED RECTIFIER DIMMER.

TILT (verb). To move an INSTRUMENT or FOLLOWSPOT up or down on its vertical axis.

TIMED FADE. A fade up or down according to a predetermined speed as set by the lighting designer or director and counted out or checked on the board timer or clock. See also COMPUTER LIGHT BOARD TERMINOLOGY.

TIME LAG. Time lapse between activation and action; for example, the lag between the time a switch is closed and the filament of a large lamp reaches incandescence. Some SILICON CONTROLLED RECTIFIER controllers have time lag, requiring compensation by anticipation of cues. See HEAT UP.

TINNING WIRE. Precoating an electrical wire with SOLDER to make a faster, better bonding when soldering two wires together. Heat the wire with a soldering iron until the solder and FLUX melt into the strands of wire or cover the entire surface to be tinned. When soldering electronic parts or wires for electronics, use rosin core solder. Acid core solder or flux tends to corrode.

TINT. A lighter, or DILUTE, color. A variation in pigment color created by adding white to the color, as distinguished from SHADE, a variation in pigment color created by adding black to the color.

T LAMP. Tubular-shaped bulb. See **Bulb shapes** under LAMPS.

TOGGLE SWITCH. See under SWITCHES.

TONE. A color of middle value, a grayed HUE.

TONING LIGHTS. Lights used for general color and mood to set the tone of the play and to enhance the colors of costumes and settings on the stage. A white light made from the primary, secondary, or dilute primary colors from the toning lights will make all colors on the stage much more vibrant. Toning may be done with the colors in BORDER LIGHTS or with COLOR WASHES. See also **Color washes** under LIGHTING PRACTICE.

TOP HAT. See under LIGHT SPILL CONTROL.

TORCH (prop). Made of sticks built up with papiermâché to any desired shape and holding two flashlight batteries, a switch, and a flashlight lamp, or an entire flashlight embedded in the body of the torch as illustrated. Cover the top with scraps of COLOR MEDIA to resemble a flame. Colors should include frost, amber, straw, red, and blue. GELATINE will adhere to itself if moistened; plastic color media require glue or acetone to bind.

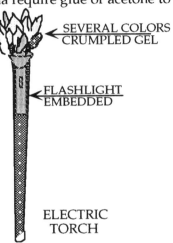

SEVERAL COLORS
CRUMPLED GEL

FLASHLIGHT
EMBEDDED

ELECTRIC
TORCH

TORMENTOR (torm). A masking piece used to terminate the downstage wall of a set on each side of the stage or to form an inner frame (inner PROSCENIUM) so that action can be set further upstage and in a better position for lighting. In the latter case, walls of the set are terminated by returns. Tormentors are usually flats with a 6" or 12" thickness.

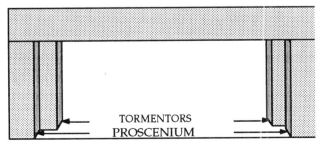

TORMENTORS
PROSCENIUM

TORMENTORS

TORMENTOR LIGHTS (torm lights, light tower, torm towers, teaser tower). Spotlights mounted upstage of tormentors on each side of the stage. The tormentor position is ideal for sidelighting. Spotlights may be hung from BOOMS, LADDERS, TOWERS, or TREES. If there is no danger of light spill on a return or drapery, tormentor lights may be FRESNEL LIGHTS, which offer good blending characteristics. If spill occurs, use BARNDOORS or change to ELLIPSOIDAL REFLECTOR SPOTLIGHTS. In either case, follow the procedure outlined in CROSSLIGHTING, using short-throw spots for lower positions, medium-throw spots for center positions, and long-throw lights for upper positions.

TOURING THEATRE LIGHTING. See ROAD SHOW LIGHTING.

TOWER (light tower, torm towers, teaser tower). A mounting device designed for the 1st wing position and originally built in the early 1900s to resemble a tower on casters. Largely supplanted by the less bulky BOOM, LADDER, and TREE (usually suspended or flying). See also LIGHT MOUNTING DEVICES.

TRACING PAPER. A lightweight, translucent paper used for making drawings, especially drawings to be blueprinted. Available in sheets and tablets in various sizes at art and drafting stores.

TRANSFER BOX. Professional term for a COMPANY PATCH.

TRANSFORMER. A core of laminated iron on which two coils of wire are wound. The primary coil, carrying an ALTERNATING CURRENT, induces an alternating current in the secondary coil. Voltage in the secondary coil is determined by the

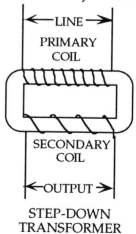

STEP-DOWN
TRANSFORMER

ratio of windings on the primary to windings on the secondary. The less windings on the secondary, the lower the voltage output. Bell transformers, available in hardware stores, are of this type and are useful for making "bell boards." See BELL; also AUTOTRANSFORMER; STEPDOWN TRANSFORMER; STEPUP TRANSFORMER.

TRANSLUCENT DROP. See SCRIM.

TRANSMISSION FACTOR. The percentage of light passing through COLOR MEDIA. This percentage will vary between less than 5% for primary blue to more than 90% for the TINT no-color straw.

TRANSPARENCIES. See SCRIM.

TREE, LIGHT. See LIGHT-MOUNTING DEVICES.

TRIM

(noun). A set of carbon electrodes in an ARC LIGHT.

(command verb). To replace carbon electrodes in an arc light. The pencil-sized carbons used in the ARC LIGHTS of the 1950s, 1960s, and 1970s will burn about 1 hour and 20 minutes between trims.

TRIM HEIGHT. The distance from the floor to the bottoms of borders and other overhead maskings. Lighting instruments are usually just above the border trim height. SIGHTLINES are the predetermining factors for setting trim heights, and since the trim will help determine the THROW required of the instruments, it should be determined before making the light plot. See DESIGN FOR LIGHTING; see also WORKING HEIGHT.

TRIP (verb). To break a circuit through a CIRCUIT BREAKER. If a SHORT CIRCUIT occurs, it "trips" the breaker. See also KICK.

TRIPE (bundle). A British term for a group of cables bound into a single bundle and tied or taped together.

TRIPLING. Multiplying by 3 the number of instruments from the same position to shine on the same area. If two units normally light an area, when tripled it means six instruments would do the same work. Tripling is used to do color shifts and to enrich the color in a given space.

TROMBONE. A hand-operated sliding device in a FOLLOWSPOT that varies the positions of the objective lenses, thus changing the size of the beam of light.

TROUGH. Obsolete. Formerly used to refer to toning lights in metal trough REFLECTORS.

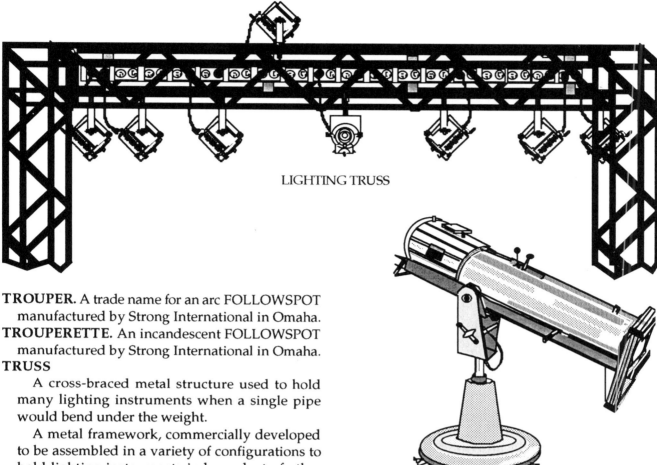

LIGHTING TRUSS

TROUPER. A trade name for an arc FOLLOWSPOT manufactured by Strong International in Omaha.

TROUPERETTE. An incandescent FOLLOWSPOT manufactured by Strong International in Omaha.

TRUSS

A cross-braced metal structure used to hold many lighting instruments when a single pipe would bend under the weight.

A metal framework, commercially developed to be assembled in a variety of configurations to hold lighting instruments independent of other supports. Many touring shows save HANG time by using these freestanding trusses to support prewired and prefocused lighting instruments for the show. These so-called box trusses are partially enclosed structures in which the spotlights can be mounted and protected during transportation.

TUBE BOARD. Colloquial for the THYRATRON TUBE DIMMER boards of the late 1940s and early 1950s.

TUNER CLEANER. A special cleaner made for TV tuners but also used to clean many other electronic parts, for example, potentiometers.

TUNGSTEN-HALOGEN LAMP (TH, quartz, QI). The tungsten-halogen lamp is made with a heat-resistant synthetic quartz ENVELOPE, filled with halogen gas. Under the intense heat of the burning process, bits of tungsten released from the filament react chemically with the halogen to return to the filament. This process not only improves the life of the lamp but eliminates black deposits on the inside of the envelope that are commonly found

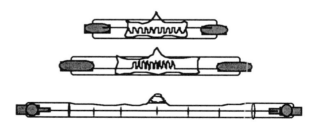

STRONG TROUPER
CA. 1950s

with standard tungsten lamps filled with inert gases. Another favorable feature of TH lamps is that they burn equally well in any position and therefore have made possible improvements in the design of instruments, including the AXIAL MOUNT ELLIPSOIDAL REFLECTOR SPOT-LIGHT. Because TH lamps offer higher intensity, longer life, and soot-free envelopes, they are obvi-

RECESSED SINGLE-CONTACT (RSC)

DOUBLE-ENDED TUNGSTEN-HALOGEN LAMPS

ously the favored lamps for stage-lighting instruments. Common wattages include 300, 400, 500, 750, 1,000, 1,500, 2,000, and 5,000 watts. *Warning:* Do not touch the synthetic quartz envelope of the lamp with bare fingers; skin oil deposited on the envelope will cause hot spots to develop when the light is turned on, shortening the life of the lamp. Use the paper wrap packed with the lamp as a shield when handling. See under LAMPS.

TV (television, monitor). Commonly used in many productions, a TV camera in the auditorium relays the picture to the stage, where the monitor provides visual cues and a view of the action. Lighting COMPUTER BOARDS use monitors for readouts.

TWINKY LIGHTS. Colloquial expression for a set of small blinking lights or Christmas tree lights sometimes used on stage for special effects.

TWISTLOCK. Electrical male and female plugs that lock together with a twist. See under PLUGS.

TWO-FER. See **Two-fer and three-fer** under PLUGS.

TYPES OF SHOWS AND THEATRES. The following is a list of productions and spaces for those productions that the lighting designer may be called upon to light.

Amphitheatre	Aqua theatre	Architectural
ARENA	BALLET	Carnival
Childrens'	Circus	CONCERT
DANCE	Dance halls	Disco
Experimental	Fair	ICE SHOW
Industrial	Landscape	Light show
Mime	MUSICAL	Night club
OPERA	Operetta	OUTDOOR
PROSCENIUM	Puppetry	REPERTORY
Revue	ROAD SHOW	Television
THRUST		

U

ULTRAVIOLET LIGHT (UV, black light). Light rays with wavelengths shorter than 4,000 ANGSTROMS, invisible to the human eye but causing certain colors and materials to glow or fluoresce in the dark. If the source of light can be placed close to the object to be fluoresced, tubular UV lamps may be used. Available in 15- and 40-watt sizes, the tubular lamp has the advantage of having no warm-up period. Mercury arc lamps with UV filters require a 4- to 10-minute warm-up period before they will operate, and when turned off, they require a 15-minute cooling-off period before reigniting. Despite the unfortunate lack of instant control, the mercury arc lamp remains the most efficient UV source for high-intensity concentration of light. Maximum throws recommended for effective use of mercury arc lamps are 15'–20' for 100-watt flood lamp; 25'–30' for 100-watt spot lamp; 30'–35' for 150-watt flood lamp. Effective coverage or spread is about equal to the throw (a 25' throw will give about a 25' spread). Some of the many available fluorescent products are ribbons, fringes, paper, paints, dyes, crayons, various cloth materials, stage makeup, and artist's chalks and pencils in a wide variety of colors. Most of these are available through full-service theatrical supply houses.

UNDERLIGHTING. Low lighting intensity. If long dark scenes are appropriate to the action, they should open with low intensity, establishing the proper mood, and then gradually build in intensity to a point beyond eyestrain.

UNDERWRITERS KNOT. See KNOTS.

UNDERWRITERS' LABORATORY (UL). An independent laboratory that tests equipment to make certain it meets safety standards under proper usage. All electrical equipment used in the theatre should bear the UL label.

UNION, PIPE. See under PIPE FITTINGS.

UNIONS

    ABTT (UK). Association of British Theatre Technicians.

    AEA. Actors Equity Association.

    ADC. Associated Designers of Canada.

    AFM. American Federation of Musicians.

    AFTRA. American Federation of Theatre and Radio Artists.

    AGMA. American Guild of Musical Artists.

    AGVA. American Guild of Variety Artists.

    ATPAM. Association of Theatrical Press Agents and Managers.

    BSTLD. (UK) British Society of Theatre Lighting Designers.

    IAIW. International Alliance of Iron Workers.

    IATSE. International Alliance of Theatrical Stage Employees.

    IBEW. International Brotherhood of Electrical Workers.

    IBT. International Brotherhood of Teamsters.

    NABET. National Association of Broadcasters, Employees and Technicians.

    SAG. Screen Actors Guild.

    SBTD (UK). Society of British Theatre Designers.

    SSDC. Society of Stage Directors and Choreographers.

    USA. United Scenic Artists.

UNISTRUT. Trade name of slotted steel angle iron. A great variety of useful structural units may be assembled by simply bolting Unistruts together.

UNIPLUG. A single-pole connector used with FEEDERS. Available in both male and female configurations.

UNITED SCENIC ARTISTS. USA is the union for LIGHTING DESIGNERS in the United States. This union is divided into four regions.

Eastern Region - Local No. 829, 575 8th Ave., 3d floor, New York, NY 10018.

Midwest Region - Local No. 350, 343 S. Dearborn St., Chicago, IL 60604.

West Coast Region - Local No. 829, 5410 Wilshire Blvd., Suite 407, Los Angeles, CA 90036.

Southern Region - Local No. 829, Holiday Inn, Golden Glades, 148 NW 167th   St. North, Miami Beach, FL 33169

The separate classification of lighting designer was allowed by USA Local No. 829 in 1963 largely through the efforts of lighting designers Tharon Musser and Jean Rosenthal.

UNIT NUMBER

Refers to the lighting INSTRUMENT number in a **Lighting schedule** or **Hookup sheet** (see under DESIGN FOR LIGHTING).

Unit numbers referring to PIANO BOARD numbers on hookup sheets are obviously obsolete.

UNIVERSAL JOINT. Available for PAR mountings that use a ball-and-socket device. They usually have two separate joints, one for the vertical plane and the other for the horizontal.

UPSTAGE. That part of the stage closest to the backwall and furthest from the audience. See STAGE DIRECTIONS.

UPSTAGING. Intentionally stealing audience attention when it belongs to something or someone else. It is very easy for the lighting designer or the control board operator to upstage actors or action by focusing lights or light intensity on the wrong part of the stage. This practice destroys the mutual effort of all theatre personnel to present the best possible performance to their paying customers.

USITT GRAPHIC STANDARDS. The United States Institute of Theatre Technology sets standards, often where there have been none in the past.

Lettering should be easy to read and rapidly penned. Usually uppercase, Gothic style will meet these demands.

Title block is a sheet identification and should show the following data: name of production, sheet number (if more than one), scale, designer, date. Professionally, the date recorded is the date of completion, when the entire package is turned in. Revisions, if any, must be approved and noted in or around the title block

THEATRE OR PRODUCING ORGANIZATION	
NAME OF PRODUCTION	
KIND OF DRAWING OR TITLE	
DWG NUMBER/ OF TOTAL	SCALE
DESIGNER	DRAWING BY
APPROVAL/DIRECTOR	DATE OF DRAFTING

TITLE BLOCK USING SINGLE
STROKE LETTERING AS PER
USITT GRAPHIC STANDARDS

Symbols. If all pertinent information necessary were to be recorded within each instrument's icon on a light plot, the light plot would become much too cluttered. Therefore, sets of standard symbols are available in 1/4" or 1/2" TEMPLATES. Although these are a great help, no single template seems to offer all the symbols the electrician needs. When more information is needed for the plot, USITT suggests the use of the following symbols:

USITT RECOMMENDED LIGHTING SYMBOLS

PARCANS	FRESNELS
PAR 38	3 "
PAR 56	6"
PAR 64	8"
SPECIAL OR PRACTICAL	12"

SCOOPS / ERFS	BEAM PROJECTORS
10" WIZARD	12"
14"	16"

FLOOR X-RAY
BATTEN X-RAY
EFFECTS PROJECTOR
FOLLOWSPOT
16"
2 WAY BARN DOOR
4 WAY BARN DOOR
CAROUSEL PROJECTOR

LEKOS / ERSS

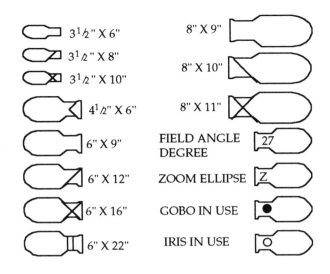

3½" X 6"	8" X 9"
3½" X 8"	8" X 10"
3½" X 10"	8" X 11"
4½" X 6"	FIELD ANGLE DEGREE — 27
6" X 9"	ZOOM ELLIPSE — Z
6" X 12"	GOBO IN USE — ●
6" X 16"	IRIS IN USE — O
6" X 22"	

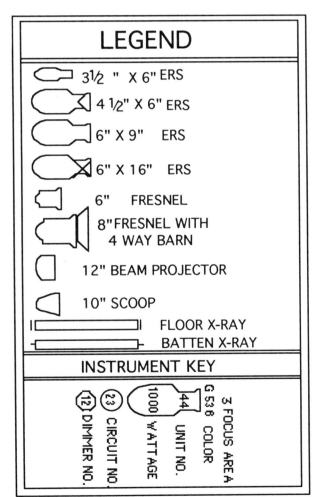

LEGEND

	3½ " X 6" ERS
	4 ½" X 6" ERS
	6" X 9" ERS
	6" X 16" ERS
	6" FRESNEL
	8" FRESNEL WITH 4 WAY BARN
	12" BEAM PROJECTOR
	10" SCOOP
	FLOOR X-RAY
	BATTEN X-RAY

INSTRUMENT KEY

3 FOCUS AREA
G 536 COLOR
44 UNIT NO.
1000 WATTAGE
23 CIRCUIT NO.
12 DIMMER NO.

LEGEND FOR LIGHT PLOT

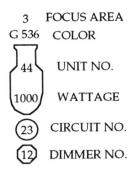

3 FOCUS AREA
G 536 COLOR
44 UNIT NO.
1000 WATTAGE
23 CIRCUIT NO.
12 DIMMER NO.

INSTRUMENT NOTATION
USITT STANDARD LABELING

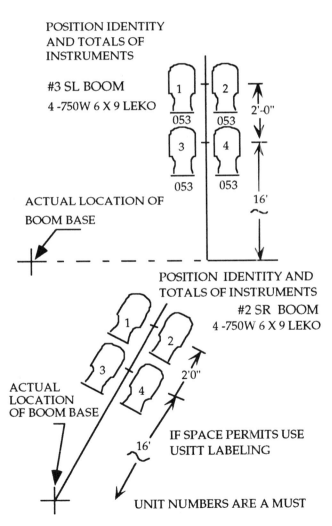

POSITION IDENTITY AND TOTALS OF INSTRUMENTS

#3 SL BOOM
4 -750W 6 X 9 LEKO

ACTUAL LOCATION OF BOOM BASE

POSITION IDENTITY AND TOTALS OF INSTRUMENTS
#2 SR BOOM
4 -750W 6 X 9 LEKO

ACTUAL LOCATION OF BOOM BASE

IF SPACE PERMITS USE USITT LABELING

UNIT NUMBERS ARE A MUST

TWO METHODS OF POSITIONING
BOOM LIGHTS DEPENDING UPON
SPACE AVAILABLE

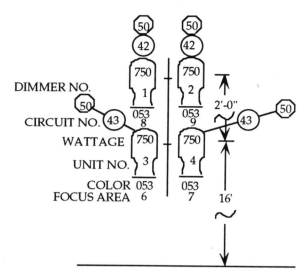

DIMMER NO.

CIRCUIT NO.

WATTAGE

UNIT NO.

COLOR

FOCUS AREA

BOOM INSTRUMENT NOTATION STYLES
(INLINE AND ANGLED)
USITT STANDARD LABELING

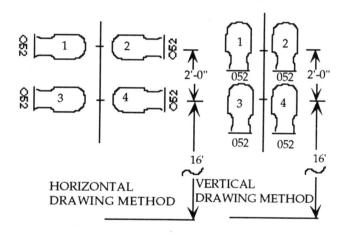

HORIZONTAL
DRAWING METHOD

VERTICAL
DRAWING METHOD

TWO BOOM MOUNTING CONVENTIONS
USITT LABELING

Legend is a key to the instrument icons and a guide to the lights used in a production.

Instrument notes provide information for individual lighting instruments. Included in order from front to rear of the instrument will be area of focus, color, instrument number, lamp wattage, circuit number, and dimmer or controller number.

Labeling is usually a matter of space and the label is often shortened.

Templates are a means of quickly drawing standard symbols for each unit and are usually available in 1/8", 1/4", 3/8", and 1/2" scales, in both plan and elevation symbols. Usually only the 1/4" and the 1/2" are used for professional drawings.

Line weights for pens: (thin) 0.010"–0.0125"; (thick) 0.020"–0.025". For pencils: (thin) 0.3 mm; (thick) 0.5 mm. In both cases an extrathick line (pen, 0.035"–0.040"; pencil, 0.9 mm) is used for borders, cutting plane lines, etc.

Drafting protocols are shown in the drawings.

ALIGNED METHOD IS A SPACE SAVING STYLE

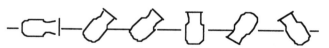

AIMED METHOD ALIGNS THE UNIT WITH
THE OPTICAL AXIS OF THE AREA

ALIGNMENT IN DRAWING INSTRUMENTS
ON OVERHEAD BATTENS OR BARS
(THE STYLE USED IS A MATTER OF CHOICE)

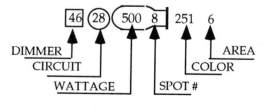

DIMMER

CIRCUIT

WATTAGE

SPOT #

COLOR

AREA

USITT LABELING

184

VALANCE. A short drape used as an overhead masking piece hung downstage of the main curtain and used to change the height of the proscenium opening.

VALUE. The relationship of light and dark in a given HUE. A TINT is considered high value and a SHADE low value.

VARIABLE-FOCUS SPOTLIGHT. See ZOOM ELLIPSE.

VARIAC. Trade name for an AUTOTRANSFORMER. Built primarily as a voltage regulator for laboratories, the Variac is a very reliable dimmer that many amateur theatre electricians designed into control boards in the late 1940s and 1950s. Little effort was made by the manufacturer to cater to theatre needs for compactness, grouping, and interlocking—characteristics that many other companies were able to supply. One of the advan-

VARIAC

tages of the Variac dimmer is that the output voltage ranges from 0 to 135, stepping up maximum voltage by about 12%. This added voltage will decrease the life of a standard lamp but will increase the intensity to 150% of normal. This trade-off is sometimes worth it if an intense light is needed, possibly for a projection.

VARIEGATED GEL (composite gel [British usage]). Pieces of various colored media glued on a light-colored base to give a multihued effect. These work well in fireplace effects and when there are too few

instruments to have enough color for costumes. A typical variegate would have light straw as the base with irregular shaped bits of pink, blue, and amber attached. The now-defunct Brigham Gelatine Company manufactured several variegated gels until the 1980s.

VELCRO. A nylon material used for fastening. Consisting of two dissimilar pieces of tape, one with tiny nylon hooks and the other with a bushy pile. When pressed together, the two tapes interlock. Velcro is particularly useful for costumes and temporary fastenings of many kinds, but electricians find it especially useful for tying coils of stage cable. See CORD LOCK.

VERTICAL ANGLE. The angle in lighting from the floor (0°) to directly overhead (90°). Good facial lighting is obtained with a 39° angle. Remember that arena and thrust lighting is much steeper, usually 50%–60%, though smaller angles may be used if the audience's eyes are not at risk. See **Determining angles** under LIGHTING PRACTICE.

VOLT. A unit of electromotive force; a difference of electrical potential that will cause a current of 1 amp to flow through a conductor against a resistance of 1 ohm. Most stage circuits in the United States carry a potential of 110–120 volts, and most equipment available for stage lighting is rated within this range. See also ALTERNATING CURRENT; ELECTRICITY.

VOLTAGE-CONTROLLED EQUIPMENT. Many electronic dimmers have their output voltage controlled by a variable, low-voltage input signal. Some SPECIAL EFFECTS instruments also use this method of control.

VOLTMETER. See MULTIMETER; VOM; WIGGY.

VOM (multimeter, wiggy). A volt-ohm-millimeter. A portable meter for testing voltage, resistance, continuity, and electrical circuits, both AC and DC. An indispensable tool for the electrician.

W

WALL BRACKET.

An older lighting position in which a bracket was mounted on a backstage wall and an INSTRUMENT was mounted from that. The wall bracket is still used in some European theatres.

Various kinds of ornamental light fixtures designed to hang on walls. Over the past hundred years wall brackets have undergone extensive design changes and may be helpful in establishing period, decor, and set location. They also provide the lighting designer with a MOTIVATED LIGHT source, but one must be careful to shield against glare and keep intensity under control. Low-wattage (7 1/2 or 15 watt) lamps are recommended. If light cues involving the wall brackets are part of the action, auxiliary spotlights supplementing the light from the brackets should be put on the same dimmer so the control board operator will be able to synchronize cue action.

WALL POCKET. The sidewall version of a FLOOR POCKET. In newer theatres PIN CONNECTORS or TWISTLOCK receptacles are wired into the proscenium arch areas, on the sidewalls, and from DROP BOXES.

WARD LEONARD COMPANY. Obsolete. A manufacturing company that made dimmers and control equipment in Mount Vernon, N.Y.

WARM COLORS. Derivatives of reds and yellows are considered warm colors. See under COLOR.

WARNING, CUE

Written notation on a cue sheet anticipating a cue.

Verbal notice or signal to get ready for a cue. Warnings are given by the stage manager by means of an intercom system, signal light, or visual contact l5–30 seconds before the actual cue. After the warning, the word "go" is given as the command cue. For a cue example, see CUE.

WASH AND KEY. A formula of lighting based on low-angle front wash as a BASE LIGHT from the RAIL and with strong KEY LIGHT and FILL lighting from the BOX BOOMS. It has been a standard of professional touring shows and even Broadway. See also **Double reverse McCandless** under PROSCENIUM STAGE LIGHTING.

WASH LIGHT. Lighting instruments used in wide focus to provide general coverage (BASE LIGHT), as contrasted with sharply focused instruments used to highlight or illuminate a specific area (KEY LIGHT). Wash lights are often used with strong colors to provide mood (COLOR WASH). See also LIGHTING PRACTICE; ARENA STAGE LIGHTING; BALLET LIGHTING; DANCE THEATRE LIGHTING; PROSCENIUM STAGE LIGHTING; THRUST STAGE LIGHTING.

WASHTUB (BP, tub). Older slang used for a BEAM PROJECTOR.

WATER RIPPLE EFFECT. Use a broken mirror or aluminum foil on the bottom of a shallow, flat pan filled with water. A spotlight or PARcan aimed at the pan from a flat angle reflects off the water as it is agitated by hand or with an electric fan.

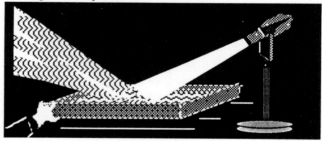

WATER RIPPLE EFFECT

WATT. Unit of measurement of electrical power.

WAVELENGTH OF VISIBLE LIGHT. See ANGSTROMS; NANOMETER. See also COLOR SPECTRUM.

WEST VIRGINIA FORMULA. W = VA. See under ELECTRICITY.

WHITE

When the three PRIMARY COLORS are mixed in the proper amounts, white light is the result.

Said to be the color of a light if no color medium is in the instrument.

WIDE-ANGLE LENS. Fast lens. Lens with a short focal point, producing wide-angle coverage.

WIGGY. A professional term for a Wiggins tester, used to check voltage and polarity. The wiggy's popularity comes from its hard shell and its ability to fit in a back pocket.

WING AND DROP (drop and wing). Two-dimensional scenery using an upstage scenic background (drop) and several flat scenic side maskings. If the same arrangement is made in stage drapes, the upstage is still called the drop or backdrop and the side maskings are the legs. An entire set of drapes will often be called by their color: blacks, reds, blues. They may also be called cyclorama drapes. The spaces between side maskings are known as IN one, IN two, etc. This terminology is also used for stage directions: left one, right one, etc. These spaces also provide primary locations for lighting instruments.

WIPE OUT. To destroy the image on a projection screen with AMBIENT light. Use steep-angle AREA LIGHTS or CROSSLIGHTS. FRESNEL LENSES and dusty, dirty lenses diffuse light and are more apt to cause spill on screens than clean plano-convex or step lenses. Reflected light off light-colored floors, furniture, costumes, or set dressings will also contribute to a wipe out. Sometimes a faint picture on the screen is the result of accumulated spill from several sources. The image will be improved by cleaning the lenses, reflectors, and color filters of the projector.

WIRE. Metal conductor. See CABLE.

WIRENUT. A solderless connector that uses a twisting motion to screw onto two or more wires to attach them to each other. The wires are screwed into a metal insert which has a nonconducting plastic covering.

WIREWAY (gutter, raceway). See RACEWAY.

WIRING. See CIRCUITS.

WIZARD. 10" SCOOP, often used as a BACKING LIGHT.

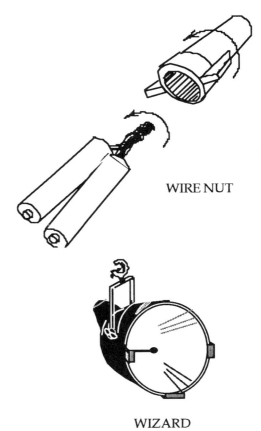

WIRE NUT

WIZARD

WORKING DRAWING. In lighting, a drawing to guide the hanging of a show. Also, any drawing from which scenery is built, trimmed, painted, and set-in. See DESIGN FOR LIGHTING; DRAWINGS.

WORKING HEIGHT. Predetermined height off the floor at which flown scenery or light pipes will be set during a production. Although the working height is the trim height for some objects, like borders, the trim height is not the working height on many things in the flies. It is up to the lighting designer to set the height of the light bridges or light battens and to work with the scene designer when these working heights are being established. See TRIM HEIGHT.

WORK LIGHT

A light or group of lights controlled from the stage as well as from the light control board. Work lights are used for rehearsals, work on the stage, and sometimes for intermissions in order to save lighting instruments with their more expensive lamps. Work lights should be provided with two-way switches so they may be controlled from the light control area as well as the stage. There is nothing more devastating to the lighting design than to have the curtain go up with the work lights still on.

Night light (ghost light). A single naked lamp in a wire cage mounted on a standard and placed center stage after rehearsals and performances as a safety light.

WRAP. The professional term for black aluminum foil. An extremely handy material to help prevent light leaks and a necessity for wrapping STAND-OFFS.

NIGHT LIGHT

XENON LAMP. A very intense, point source of light created by the spark between two tungsten electrodes enclosed in a xenon gas filled quartz envelope and used in projectors and large followspots. These lamps are designed for low-voltage, high-amperage direct current and must therefore be provided with their own power sources and igniters. They are available in a wide range of wattages, with a rated lamp life of about 1,500 hours. Since the xenon lamp is an arc light of the short-arc variety, it cannot be electrically dimmed. The lamp has had the misfortune of exploding on occasion, which has necessitated the imposition of safety regulations. The lamp also produces ozone and ultraviolet radiation, but it may be used in relative safety in projectors and followspots if proper safeguards are taken. See also LAMPS; PROJECTORS.

X-RAY. Professional theatre technicians use "X-ray" as a generic term for any BORDER LIGHT. The original X-ray was a particular type of border light with a highly efficient silvered-glass reflector invented by Everly Haines in 1896 and adapted to theatre use about a year later by August D. Curtis. At about this same time in Germany, Professor W. C. Roentgen discovered a powerful ray of light that he called "X-ray" because of its unknown nature. Perhaps it was to capitalize on the name, perhaps it was because Haine's silvered-glass reflector seemed equally important to him—for whatever reason, the Curtis border light became known as the X-ray. Mirrored-glass reflectors have long since disappeared from border lights but their name X-ray has persisted. See BORDER LIGHTS.

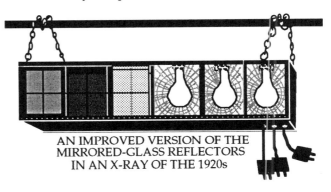

AN IMPROVED VERSION OF THE
MIRRORED-GLASS REFLECTORS
IN AN X-RAY OF THE 1920s

X-WASH. A shortened method of writing "crosswash." This is a common term used in the writing of focus sheets and instrument schedules (see under DESIGN FOR LIGHTING). See CROSSLIGHT.

YELLOW. The complementary color of blue. Usually referred to as "lemon" in lighting; AMBER is the lighting SECONDARY COLOR.

YOKE. A U-shaped hanger designed to bolt to each side of the housing of a lighting instrument and provide a balanced support for easy focusing and adjusting. Originally spotlights were mounted on floor stands and the first spots to be used on overhead pipes were equipped with rings on the back of the housing and either slid onto the pipe or hung by chain from the pipe. C-clamps and yoke CLAMPS were invented in the early 1920s and the first lighting instruments to use them were equipped with a single side-arm support which was then clamped to the ELECTRICS. Expansion and contraction from heat loosened the attaching nut and allowed the unbalanced light to slip. Improved yoke clamps that could be tightened on both sides of the instruments (at first with a wrench) made a more positive lock on the focus. The final improvement seems to be a wheel nut that locks on a disk attached to the housing, thus providing easy adjustment without wrenches—a simple evolution taking place over a half-century.

YOKE CLAMP. See under CLAMPS.

CHAIN   SIDE ARM   YOKE   DISK LOCK

EVOLUTION OF INSTRUMENT HANGERS

Z

ZETEX. A flameproof fiberglass fabric used as a heat shield between border lights and potential combustibles hanging in the flies. Zetex replaces asbestos borders, which are now illegal in the United States. See also FIRECHIEF.

ZIP CORD (ripcord). Lightweight electrical wire of the type used for household lamps usually in black, brown, white, and clear (showing the copper wire), available in both 18/2 (18 gauge with 2 conductors) and 16/2 (16 gauge with 2 conductors). Not approved for stage use except for PRACTICAL lamps and appliances onstage and for low-voltage signal or speaker systems. See also CABLE.

ZIP STRIP. Trade name for a CYC STRIP type unit made by Altman using 10 MR 16, 12-volt lamps in series, eliminating the need for a TRANSFORMER. These strips are excellent for lighting sky cycs from above or below at very close quarters; they have an effective THROW of about 24'.

ZOOM ELLIPSE (zoom spot, zoom ellipsoidal). Variable-focus ellipsoidal spotlight. Zoom ellipses are very efficient instruments because they can be used in a variety of locations. Where once several different sizes of spotlights were necessary for different throws, the FIELD ANGLE of the zoom ellipse may be varied from 20° to 45° by changing the lens configuration within the instrument. In some models this is accomplished with a slide mechanism that varies the distance between lenses, and in other models, the spotlights must be opened and lenses physically moved from one fixed slot to another, thereby changing the field angle by 10° increments. Within reason, FIELD INTENSITIES remain approximately the same.

ZOOM FOLLOWSPOT. Trade name for a Century Strand followspot using a 1,000-watt TUNGSTEN-HALOGEN LAMP. Designed for throws of up to 80'.

ZOOM LENS (variable focus). A system of lenses in which focal lengths can be changed either manually or electrically. Frequently used in moving pictures and television but also adaptable to the stage for projection equipment to make an object appear to grow larger or smaller on the screen (e.g., an approaching ship).

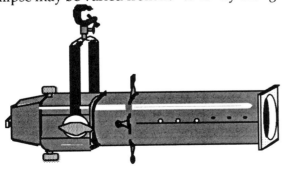

ZOOM ELLIPSE
LEE COLORTRAN

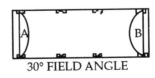

30° FIELD ANGLE

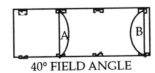

40° FIELD ANGLE

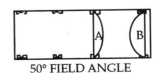

50° FIELD ANGLE

A   4.5"X 9"   LENS
B   4.5"X 6.5" LENS

ZOOM LENS CONFIGURATIONS
LEE COLORTRAN MINI-ELLIPSE

Selected List of Manufacturers and Distributors

For a more complete listing of manufacturers and distributors of all theatrical equipment, the reader is referred to:

Theatre Crafts, P. O. Box 630, Holmes, PA 19043-6030. The present policy of *Theatre Crafts* is to publish a new directory of manufacturers and distributors in the June-July issue each year.

Lighting Dimensions, 135 Fifth Ave., New York, NY 10010-7193. Publishes a directory issued in December each year.

Explanation of designations used in the following entries:

Full service. Suppliers of theatrical equipment and materials including rigging systems, draperies, curtain tracks, electrical connectors, wire, stage lighting equipment, color media, followspots, lighting control, projections, gobos, fabrics, tools, hardware, templates, and shop supplies.

Lighting control and instrument mfg. Suppliers of control boards, lighting instruments, and lighting accessories.

Specialty. As listed.

Aero-Tech Light Bulb Co.
514 Pratt Ave. N.
Schaumburg, IL 60193
Specialty: Long-life lamps

Altman Stage Lighting Co., Inc.
57 Alexander St.
Yonkers, NY 10701
Lighting instrument mfg.

American DJ Supply, Inc.
5051 E. Slauson Ave.
Los Angeles, CA 90040
Specialty: Effects machines

American Stage Lighting Co., Inc.
1331 North Ave.
New Rochelle, NY 10804
Full service

Avab Americal Inc.
967 Howard St.
San Francisco, CA 94103
Specialty: Control, instruments

Bash Theatrical Lighting, Inc.
3401 Dell Ave.
North Bergen, NJ 07047
Full service

Bulbman
P.O. Box 2918
Reno, NV 89505
Specialty: Lamps

Century Strand. *See* **Strand Lighting, Inc.**

Clay Paky S.R.L.
Celco/Elektralite
200 Sea Lane
Farmingdale, NY 11735
Specialty: Automated instruments

Clear-com Intercom Systems
945 Camelia St.
Berkeley, CA 94710
Specialty: Communications

Coemar Spa
2506 Freedom Broadway Trade Center
San Antonio, TX 78217
Specialty: Automated instruments

Colortran, Inc.
1015 Chestnut St.
Burbank, CA 91506
Specialty: Light control, instruments

Columbus McKinnon Corporation
140 John James Audubon Pkwy.
Amherst, NY 14228
Specialty: Lodestar hoists

Crosby Group, Inc.
2801 Dawson Rd.
Tulsa, OK 74110
Specialty: Rigging hardware

Duff-Norton
P.O. Box 7010
Charlotte, NC 28241
Specialty: Coffing hoists

Dyna-Might Sound & Lighting
3119-A S. Scenic
Springfield, MO 65807
Specialty: Special effects

Electro Controls. See Strand-Electro Controls

Electronics Diversified, Inc.
1675 NW 216th Ave.
Hillsboro, OR 97124
Lighting control mfg.

Entertainment Technology, Inc.
1771 N.W. Pettygrove
Portland, OR 97209
Lighting control mfg.

GE Lighting
Nela Park
Cleveland, OH 44112
Specialty: Lamps

Genie Industries
P.O. Box 69, 18340 NE 76th St.
Redmond, WA 98073
Specialty: Lifts

Gerriets International, Inc.
R.D. #1, 950 Hutchinson Rd.
Allentown, NJ 08501
Specialty: Cycs, projection screens

The Great American Market
826 N. Cole Ave.
Hollywood, CA 90038
Specialty: Gobos, special effects

GTE Electrical Products
Sylvania Lighting Div.
100 Endicott St.
Danvers, MA 01923
Specialty: Lamps

Harlequin
3111 West Burbank Boulevard
Burbank, CA 91505
Specialty: Dance floors

Claude Heintz
29621 Gimpl Hill Rd.
Eugene, OR 97402
Specialty: Lighting CAD (MacLux)

High End Systems, Inc.
2217 W. Braker Lane
Austin, TX 78758
Specialty: Dichroic filters

Hoffend & Sons, Inc.
34 E. Main St.
Honeoye, NY 14471
Specialty: Stage rigging, shells, lifts

Holzmueller Corp.
1275 Minnesota St.
San Francisco, CA   94107
Full service

J C N
P.O. Box 9986
Oakland, CA 94613-0986
Specialty: Lighting CAD (Argus)

Lee Filters
1015 Chestnut St.
Burbank, CA 91506
Specialty: Color filters

Leprecon/ Cae, Inc.
10087 Industrial Dr.
Hamburg, MI 48139
Specialty: Dimmers and control

Lycian Stage Lighting
PO Box D, Kings Hwy.
Sugar Loaf, NY 10981
Specialty: Followspots

Mole-Richardson
937 N. Sycamore Ave.
Hollywood, CA 90038-2384
Lighting control and instrument mfg.

Mutual Hardware Corp.
5-45 49th Ave.
Long Island City, NY 11101
Specialty: Stage rigging and hardware

Nady Systems
6701 Bay St.
Emeryville, CA 94608
Specialty: Communications

Norcostco, Inc.
3203 N. Highway 100
Minneapolis, MN 55422
Full service

Oasis Stage Werks
249 Rio Grande
Salt Lake City, UT 84101
Full-service specialty: D'Anser

Olympic Lighting, Inc.
2401 6th Ave.
Tacoma, WA 98406
Full service

Osram Corp.
110 Bracken Rd.
Montgomery, NY 12549
Specialty: Lamps

Packaged Lighting Systems, Inc.
PO Box 285
(29-41 Grant St.)
Walden, NY 12586
Lighting control and instrument mfg.

W. E. Palmer
134 Southampton
Boston, MA 02118
Specialty: Firechief (flameproof borders)

Pancommand Systems, Inc.
1271 Alma Court
San Jose, CA 95112
Specialty: Control, color changers

Peter Albrecht Corporation
325 E. Chicago St.
Milwaukee, WI 53202
Specialty: Motorized stage machinery,
air casters, rigging, shells

Peter Wolf Concepts
5535 Military Pkwy.
PO Box 270729
Dallas, TX 75227
Specialty: Design, mfg., rental scenic
backgrounds

Petes Lights, Inc.
2675 American Ln.
Elk Grove, IL 60007
Specialty: PARcans, trusses

Philips Lighting Co.
200 Franklin Square Dr.
Somerset, NJ 08875
Specialty: Lamps

Phoebus Manufacturing
2800 Third St.
San Francisco, CA 94107
Specialty: Instruments, followspots

PNTA
333 Westlake Ave. N.
Seattle, WA 98109-5282
Full service

Pulsar Light of Cambridge Ltd.
Henley Rd.
Cambridge CAB1 3EA
United Kingdom
Specialty: Control

Rosco Laboratories
36 Bush Ave.
Port Chester, NY 10573
Specialty: Color filters, plastic projection
screens

SFX Design, Inc. (Theatre Magic)
6099 Godown Rd.
Columbus, OH 43235
Specialty: Effects and special effects

Stagecraft Industries, Inc.
1330 N.W. Kearney St.
PO Box 4442
Portland, OR 97208
Full service

Strand-Electro Controls
2975 S. 300 West
Salt Lake City, UT 84115
Lighting control and instrument mfg.

Strand Lighting, Inc. (Formerly Century-Strand)
P.O. Box 9004
18111 S Santa Fe Ave.
Rancho Dominquez, CA 90224
Lighting control and instruments mfg.

Strong International
1712 Jackson
Omaha, NE 68102
Specialty: Motion picture projectors and
followspots

Summa Technologies, Inc.
2179 Stone Ave., Suite 23
San Jose, CA 95125
Specialty: Automated instruments

Teatronics, Inc.
3100 McMillan Rd.
San Luis Obispo, CA 93401
Lighting control mfg.

Theatre Magic
6099 Godown Rd.
Columbus, OH 43235
Specialty: Effects and special effects

Theatre Production Service, Inc.
3519 Chamblee-Dunwoody Rd.
Atlanta, GA 30341
Full service

Theatre Techniques, Inc.
60 Connolly Pkwy.
Hamden, CT 06514
Lighting control mfg.

Theatrical Services and Supplies, Inc.
170 Oval Drive,
Central Islip, NY 11722
Full service

Theatrix, Inc.
1630 West Evans, Unit C
Englewood, CO 80110
Full service

Thomas Engineering
201 Sherlake Lane
Knoxville, TN 37922
Specialty: Trussing, PARcans

Tobins Lake Studio
7030 Old US 23
Brighton, MI 48116
Full service

Valentino, Inc.
151 W. 46th St.
New York, NY 10036
Specialty: Recordings, tapes, sound
effects

Vari-Lite, Inc.
6207 Commercial Rd.
Crystal Lake, IL 60014
Specialty: Automated instruments

BIBLIOGRAPHY

Bellman, Willard F. *Lighting the Stage: Art and Practice.* 2d ed. New York: Chandler and Intex, 1974.

_____. *Scene Design, Stage Lighting, Sound, Costume & Makeup.* New York: Harper & Row, 1983.

Bowman, Ned A. *Handbook of Technical Practice for the Performing Arts.* Wilkinsburg, Pa.: Scenographic Medias, 1972.

Bowman, Wayne. *Modern Theatre Lighting.* New York: Harper and Bros., 1957.

Boyle, Walden. *Central and Flexible Staging.* Berkeley: University of California Press, 1956.

Bureau of Naval Personnel. *Basic Electricity.* 1969 ed. Washington D.C.: U.S. Government Printing Office, 1969.

Burris-Meyer, Harold, and Edward C. Cole. *Theatres and Auditoriums.* New York: Reinhold 1949.

Cimbalo, Guy. *A Guide to Stage Lighting Instruments.* Emmaus, Pa.: Theatre Crafts Magazine, 1968.

Dunlap, William. *A History of the American Theatre.* New York: J. and J. Harper, 1932.

Erhardt, Louis. *Radiation, Light, and Illumination.* Camarillo,Calif.: Camarillo Reproduction Center, 1977.

Fuchs, Theodore. *Stage Lighting.* 1929; reprint, New York: Benjamin Blom, 1963.

Gillette, A. S., and J. Michael Gillette. *Stage Scenery.* 3d ed. New York: Harper & Row, 1981.

Gillette, J. Michael. *Designing with Light.* 2d ed. Mountain View, Calif.: Mayfield Publishing Co., 1989.

Gruver, Bert. *The Stage Manager's Handbook.* Rev. by Frank Hamilton. New York: Drama Book Specialists/Publishers, 1972.

Hartmann, Louis. *Theatre Lighting.* New York: D. Appleton and Co., 1930.

Held, McDonald Watkins. *A History of Stage Lighting in the United States in the Nineteenth Century.* Ann Arbor: University Microfilms, 1965.

Hewitt, Bernard. *Theatre U.S.A., 1668 to 1957.* New York: McGraw-Hill Book Co., 1959.

Hood, W. Edmund. *Practical Handbook of Stage Lighting and Sound.* Blue Ridge Summit, Pa.: Tab Books, 1981.

Hughes, Glenn. *A History of the American Theatre, 1700-1950.* New York: S. French, 1951.

Lounsbury, Warren C., and Norman C. Boulanger. *Theatre Backstage from A to Z.* 3d ed. revised and expanded. Seattle: University of Washington Press, 1989.

McCandless, Stanley R. *A Method of Lighting the Stage.* 4th ed., amended and revised. New York: Theatre Arts Books, 1958.

_____. *A Syllabus of Stage Lighting.* New York: Drama Book Specialists/Publishers, 1964.

Nelms, Henning. *Lighting the Amateur Stage.* New York: Theatre Arts Books, 1931.

Parker, W. Oren, and Harvey K. Smith. *Scene Design and Stage Lighting.* Rev. ed. New York: Holt, Rinehart and Winston, 1968.

Parker, W. Oren, and R. Craig Wolf. *Scene Design and Stage Lighting.* 6th ed. New York: Holt, Rinehart and Winston, 1990.

Pecktal, Lynn. *Designing and Painting for the Theatre.* New York: Holt, Rinehart and Winston, 1975.

Penzel, Frederick. *Theatre Lighting before Electricity.* Middletown, Conn.: Wesleyan University Press, 1978.

Philippi, Herbert. *Stagecraft and Scene Design.* Boston: Houghton Mifflin Co., 1953.

Pilbrow, Richard. *Stage Lighting.* Rev. ed. New York: D. Van Nostrand, 1979.

Rosenthal, Jean, and Lael Wertenbaker. *The Magic of Light.* Boston: Little, Brown and Co., 1972.

Rubin, Joel E., and Leland H. Watson. *Theatrical Lighting Practice.* New York: Theatre Arts Books, 1954.

Rubin, Joel Edward. "The Technical Development of Stage Lighting Apparatus in the United States." Ph.D. dissertation, Stanford University, 1959.

_____."Stage Lighting—a Survey since 1906." *Illuminating Engineering* 51 (1956): 113-22.

Selden, Samuel, and Hunton D. Sellman. *Stage Scenery and Lighting.* Rev. ed. New York: Appleton-Century-Crofts, 1959.

Sellman, Hunton D., and Merrill Lessley. *Essentials of Stage Lighting.* 2d ed. Englewood Cliffs, N.J.: Prentice-Hall, 1982.

Smith, Howard M. *Principles of Holography.* Rochester: John Wiley & Sons, 1969.

Streader, Tim, and John A. Williams. *Create Your Own Stage Lighting.* London: Bell & Hyman, 1985.

Warfel, William B. *Handbook of Stage Lighting Graphics.* New York: Drama Book Specialists, 1974.

Warfel, William B., and Walter R. Klappert. *Color Science for Lighting the Stage.* New Haven: Yale University Press, 1981.

Watson, Lee. *Lighting Design Handbook.* New York: McGraw-Hill, 1990.

Wilfred, Thomas. *Projected Scenery: A Technical Manual.* New York: Drama Bookshop, 1965.

Williams, Rollo G. *The Technique of Stage Lighting.* London: Pitman & Sons, 1952.

Wolcot, John R. "Philadelphia's Chestnut Street Theatre: A Plan and Elevation." *Journal of the Society of Architectural Historians* 30, no. 3 (1971).

PERIODICALS

Lighting Dimensions. The magazine for the lighting professional. Published seven times a year. 135 Fifth Ave., New York, NY 10010-7193.

Theatre Crafts. A magazine for professionals in theatre, film, video, and the performing arts. Published ten times a year. PO Box 630, Holmes, PA 19043-6030.